Laboratory of Deficiency

REPRODUCTIVE JUSTICE:
A NEW VISION FOR THE TWENTY-FIRST CENTURY

Edited by Rickie Solinger, Khiara M. Bridges, Zakiya Luna, and Ruby Tapia

1. *Reproductive Justice: An Introduction*, by Loretta J. Ross and Rickie Solinger

2. *How All Politics Became Reproductive Politics: From Welfare Reform to Foreclosure to Trump*, by Laura Briggs

3. *Distributing Condoms and Hope: The Racialized Politics of Youth Sexual Health*, by Chris A. Barcelos

4. *Just Get on the Pill: The Uneven Burden of Reproductive Politics*, by Krystale E. Littlejohn

5. *Reproduction Reconceived: Family Making and the Limits of Choice after Roe v. Wade*, by Sara Matthiesen

6. *Laboratory of Deficiency: Sterilization and Confinement in California, 1900–1950s*, by Natalie Lira

Laboratory of Deficiency

STERILIZATION AND CONFINEMENT
IN CALIFORNIA, 1900–1950S

Natalie Lira

UNIVERSITY OF CALIFORNIA PRESS

University of California Press
Oakland, California

© 2022 by Natalie Lira

Library of Congress Cataloging-in-Publication Data
Names: Lira, Natalie, 1986– author.
Title: Laboratory of deficiency : sterilization and confinement in
    California, 1900–1950s / Natalie Lira. Other titles: Reproductive
    justice ; 6.
Identifiers: LCCN 2021016871 (print) | LCCN 2021016872 (ebook) |
    ISBN 9780520355675 (cloth) | ISBN 9780520355682 (paperback) |
    ISBN 9780520975965 (epub)
Subjects: LCSH: Involuntary sterilization—California—20th century.
    | Developmentally disabled—California—20th century. | Mentally ill—
    Commitment and detention—California—20th century. |
    Mexican Americans—California—20th century.
Classification: LCC RG138 .K58 2022 (print) | LCC RG138 (ebook) |
    DDC 363.9/7—dc23
LC record available at https://lccn.loc.gov/2021016871
LC ebook record available at https://lccn.loc.gov/2021016872

Contents

List of Illustrations   vii

Acknowledgments   ix

Note on Terminology   xiii

Introduction: Life, Labor, and Reproduction at the
Intersections of Race, Gender, and Disability   1

1. The Pacific Plan: Race, Mental Defect, and
   Population Control in California's Pacific Colony   25

2. The Mexican Sex Menace: Labor, Reproduction, and
   Feeblemindedness   72

3. The Laboratory of Deficiency: Race, Knowledge, and
   the Reproductive Politics of Juvenile Delinquency   109

4. Riots, Refusals, and Other Defiant Acts: Resisting
   Confinement and Sterilization at Pacific Colony   144

   Conclusion: "We Are Not Out of the Dark Ages Yet,"
   and Finding a Way Out   181

Appendix   193

Notes   197

Bibliography   239

Index   259

Illustrations

FIGURES

1.	Pacific Colony, ca. 1939	26
2.	Sterilization requests by Spanish surname per year, 1928–51	70
3.	Laundry Building at Pacific Colony, ca. 1921	73
4.	Pacific Colony nursery cribs jammed together due to overcrowding, 1950	105
5.	Pacific Colony, Cottage for Boys, ca. 1921	110
6.	Admissions to Pacific Colony: Mexican-origin by sex, 1927–47	113
7.	Pacific Colony nurse demonstrates an electroencephalograph on patient, 1950	139
8.	Interior corridor in Hospital at Pacific Colony, Spadra, 192?	145

TABLES

1.	Economic status of Pacific Colony residents, 1926–46	58
2.	Age of Pacific Colony residents, 1936–46	62

3. Residents "on escape" from Pacific Colony, 1939–49   160

4. Spanish-surnamed patient requests processed by Pacific Colony,
    1928–51   194

5. Admissions to Pacific Colony by Mexican-origin and sex, 1927–47   195

6. Racial descriptors used to label individuals admitted to Pacific
    Colony, 1927–47   196

Acknowledgments

I owe an enormous debt of gratitude to so many for making this book possible. I want to start by thanking my mother, Armida Lira, for the example, encouragement, and support she has given me my entire life. Thank you for never letting me off the hook and for reminding me that if you could raise four kids as a single immigrant mother who barely spoke English, then I could certainly write a book. Your support carried me through several moments of frustration and fatigue.

I have had the fortune, opportunity, and privilege of learning from and working with an incredible group of feminist scholars. Elena R. Gutiérrez sparked my interest in the politics of reproduction and my passion for Reproductive Justice with her scholarship many years ago. I was lucky enough to meet her at a conference (thank you, Ricky!), and she has been so generous with her time, advice, and mentorship ever since. This book would not be possible without her scholarship and mentorship. Maria E. Cotera quite literally helped me survive graduate school and has been invaluable throughout this entire book process. Thank you for teaching me all about Women of Color feminisms and for reminding me over and over again that what I was working on in this book is part and parcel of Chicana feminist discourse and activism. This book started when Alexandra M. Stern took me on one summer as a graduate student research assistant, and I can never thank her enough for her unsparing support and mentorship since then. Thank you for pushing me to expand my analysis of disability and for all of your encouragement and insight over the years.

As the place that started my intellectual career, the Department of Latina/Latino Studies (LLS) at the University of Illinois at Urbana–Champaign (UIUC) is very close to my heart. Current colleagues and longtime mentors Lisa M. Cacho, Edna Viruell-Fuentes, Johnathan X. Inda, Julie Dowling, Isabel Molina, Gilberto Rosas, Rolando Romero, and David Coyoca played important roles in my intellectual development and also offered their comments on this project at various stages. While no longer at UIUC, Richard T. Rodriguez is also part of this list—thank you for giving me my first copy of *Fertile Matters: The Politics of Mexican-origin Women's Reproduction* (by Elena R. Gutiérrez), for convincing me that I could be a scholar, and for mentoring me through many stages in my career. I extend my deepest gratitude to Sandra Ruiz, who has been the best colleague and friend along the way. Thank you for being so generous with your advice and for talking me through all of the ups and downs of not only writing a book but getting it published. Alicia P. Rodriguez and Laura M. Castañeda provided much need support—administrative and moral—while I researched and wrote this book, and I appreciate them very much.

Of course, so many other UIUC colleagues and students have offered their insights and support throughout the process, and I apologize in advance to anyone I have forgotten to mention here. Chapter 1 was written and revised with the support of a fellowship from the Illinois Program for Research in the Humanities (IPRH, now the Humanities Research Institute). Thank you to Antoinette Burton and Nancy Castro for organizing and participating in the IPRH workshop for that chapter, and to Maryam Kashani, Krystal Smalls, and all of the other fellows for their comments on that draft. Chapters 3 and 4 benefited from comments in two separate LLS workshops, where many of the folks listed here participated. I must add to that list Yuridia Ramirez and Daniel Gonzalez, whose comments during my workshop for chapter 3 proved especially helpful. In addition to being furthered by wonderful colleagues, this book also benefited from the contributions of many bright undergraduate research assistants, including Sandra Rodriguez, Fatima Valerio, Kerime Alejo, and Armando Miranda. I received so much support from Jessica Kadish-Hernández during the last stretch of edits and am forever grateful to her for helping me with that final push. I also have to thank Aída Rosalia Guhlincozzi for her help in formatting the tables that appear in the book.

Scholars at many other institutions contributed their time and knowledge to this endeavor. I am so thankful to Miroslava Chávez-García and John McKiernan-González for reading and commenting on several versions of this manuscript. I owe many thanks to Julie A. Minich for her comments and for encouraging me to elaborate on my thinking on disability and reproduction. Several parts of this work started off as conference papers, and I thank my colleagues and friends René Esparza, Lina-Maria Murillo, and Nic John Ramos for organizing panels and offering comments on those papers. Thank you to the folks at the Department of American Culture and the Latina/o Studies Program at the University of Michigan, where I spent several years doing preliminary research for this book. I also appreciate Martha S. Jones for reading and offering her insight on a very early version of this work. I am so lucky to work with an incredible interdisciplinary group of scholars at the Sterilization and Social Justice Lab, including Siobán Harlow, Sharon Kardia, Johanna Schoen, Nicole Novak, Kate O'Connor, ToniAnn Treviño, Juan Gudino, and Marie Kaniecki. I am particularly grateful to Nicole and Kate, whose expertise in data collection and analysis far exceed my own and who offered generous advice and support over the years.

The research for this book would not have been possible without the assistance of many wonderful archivists. Thank you to everyone at the California State Archives for facilitating my many trips to the research room. Especially Sebastian Nelson, who helped me gain access to restricted files in the Lanterman Development Center accession. Francisco de Paula Castro Reynoso and Jorge Fuentes Hernández at the Archivo Historico Genaro Estrada in Mexico City were very helpful in coordinating permission to research documents from the Los Angeles Mexican Consulate. I am also thankful to Lois Lowe, who helped process several California Protection of Human Subjects applications for earlier research on sterilization in California.

It is an incredible honor to publish this book as part of the Reproductive Justice Series at the University of California Press, and I am grateful to Rickie Solinger for her incisive comments on the manuscript and for her transformative scholarship in the field. Thank you to Ruby Tapia and Naomi Schneider for believing in this book and for including it as part of this series.

I want to end by returning to those who sustained me with their love and friendship during this process. To my siblings Cindy, Juan, Omar, Tiffany, and Lenny—thank you for always checking on me and for making every Lira get-together a celebration. There are no words to express how important you all are in my life. I am blessed to have friends that are also like family and who have cheered me on. Rach, Aixa, Nichole, and Gaby, your friendship is a wellspring of joy and support. Last, but certainly not least, I want to express profound gratitude to my partner in life, Danny. Thank you for reminding me to be kind and patient with myself, for making sure I ate and slept during my long stretches of writing, and for taking over home and doggy care responsibilities so that I could focus all my time and energy on the book.

Note on Terminology

MEXICAN-ORIGIN AND SPANISH SURNAME

Following the lead of Elena R. Gutiérrez in *Fertile Matters: The Politics of Mexican-origin Women's Reproduction*, I use the term "Mexican-origin" throughout this book. Although the majority of the patients committed to and sterilized in Pacific Colony were born in the United States, others were Mexican immigrants, and so I use the term "Mexican-origin" to facilitate a discussion of their collective experiences. Furthermore, I find that the term best describes the way that state authorities in the various institutional, educational, legal, and public health settings I examine viewed Mexican Americans and Mexican immigrants. As Elizabeth R. Escobedo noted in her work on Mexican American women's encounters with juvenile authorities and reformers, distinctions in terms of citizenship were rarely made and authorities largely referred to second- and third-generation Mexican Americans as "Mexicans" (2013, 133).

In my analysis of the more than two thousand sterilization request forms processed by Pacific Colony, I used Spanish surname as an approximation for quantifying Mexican-origin. After reviewing thousands of patient records, family histories, and admission ledgers in the Lanterman Development

Center (previously Pacific Colony) archive that do record racial ascriptions, I was able to confirm that the large majority of the patients with Spanish surnames were in fact Mexican-origin, although a small number hailed from Spain and Puerto Rico. Although many of the records for Spanish-surnamed patients made mention of Mexican parents, many did not, so I continue to use "Spanish surname" whenever I talk about analysis of the sterilization requests and "Mexican-origin" or "Mexican American" when discussing cases that were explicitly labeled as such.

FEEBLEMINDEDNESS, MENTAL DEFICIENCY, AND MENTAL DEFECT

In the introduction and throughout this book I discuss how "feeble-mindedness"—a medical label that was used to refer to low intelligence or mental capacity—became a diagnosis and categorization of social worth. I illustrate the ways that IQ scores and economic status converged with racism, ableism, and sexism to shape diagnostic practices. By "ableism," I mean discrimination and prejudice against people with disabilities and practices that support the supremacy of nondisabled people. Through-out the book I use the terms "feeblemindedness," "mental deficiency," and "mental defect" interchangeably. The term "feeblemindedness" was most common at the turn of the twentieth century and through the 1920s, but by the mid-1930s the phrase "mentally deficient" started to replace "fee-bleminded" in diagnostic practices.

Psychologists and state authorities used the terms to describe the same symptom complex of low IQ score, economic status, and social deviance. Throughout the book I also describe the ways that psychologists diag-nosed individuals using the terms "moron," "borderline," "imbecile," or "idiot." Clinicians and other state workers used these terms to refer to dif-fering levels of supposed intelligence under the umbrella of "feeblemind-edness." My use of these terms throughout the book reflects the ways that social workers, legal authorities, and clinicians viewed the people in their care. As this research illustrates, the terms are much more reflective of the ableism, racism, sexism, and classism of the time than the disability status of the person in question.

Introduction

> They never told me that they were going to do that surgery
> to me. They said they were going to remove my appendix
> and then they did that other. They should have explained to
> me.... After they did that surgery to me, I cried.... I still
> don't know why they did that surgery to me. The steriliza-
> tion wasn't for punishment, was it? Was it because there
> was something wrong with my mind?
>
> —Unnamed eugenic sterilization survivor

> They shouldn't do that to people just because they are in
> that hospital. They never ask you! They just tell you after
> it's done.
>
> —Unnamed eugenic sterilization survivor

Reflecting on their painful experiences, the two unnamed survivors
quoted above underscore the violence, deceit, and disregard that pervaded
practices of confinement and sterilization in California during the first
half of the twentieth century. The two survivors were sterilized at Pacific
Colony—the Southern California institution at the center of this book—at
some point between 1931 and 1951. Their statements, collected as part of a
study published in the 1960s in *Eugenics Quarterly*, were printed without
their names. The authors of the study omitted all other information about
the lives and experiences of the two survivors, but their statements speak

volumes about what happened to them at the institution. The sterilizations were not wanted, officials did not ask permission, no one explained
the operation to them, and in at least one case institutional authorities
lied outright about the nature of the surgery. These statements point to
the survivors' stance on the legitimacy of what Pacific Colony clinicians
did to them while they were confined to the institution. Being committed to an institution did not, in their eyes, justify the operation. And if we
extrapolate from the second survivor's quote, having a disability label—
which was both the legal and medical basis for confinement and sterilization in Pacific Colony—did not amount to a sufficient justification to strip
a person of their reproductive capacity.

In this book I examine the experiences of people who, like the unnamed
survivors, were marked with a disability label, committed to Pacific
Colony, and forcibly sterilized between the late 1920s, when the institution opened, and the early 1950s. Combining insights from feminist scholarship on the politics of reproduction and Critical Disability Studies, I
analyze a vast range of archival materials to answer questions like those of
the first quoted survivor: Why were people committed to Pacific Colony?
Why were they sterilized? Were these practices punishment or treatment?
This book also seeks to answer broader questions: How did Pacific Colony
come to be? What motivated practices of institutionalization and sterilization? How did state workers and institutional authorities justify these
practices? How did disability labels organize power in this historical context? And what roles did race, class, and gender play in state practices of
confinement and reproductive oppression?

Although the authors of the study published in *Eugenics Quarterly* did
not include the racial or ethnic identity of the quoted survivors, this book
centers the experiences of young working-class Mexican-origin women
and men who were confined and sterilized at Pacific Colony at rates that
were disproportionate to their population in the state at the time. When
possible, I trace their experiences across sterilization requests, consent
forms, admission ledgers, newspaper articles, and any other available documents in order to glean a sense of what their experiences of institutionalization and reproductive constraint were like. In most cases, Mexican-
origin youths were confined to Pacific Colony for several years, forced into
unpaid labor in the institution, and sterilized before being discharged. My

research examines the principal disability label used to commit youths to Pacific Colony: feeblemindedness. I analyze institutional publications, legislative documents, surveys, master's theses, research journals, and various state department archives to situate feeblemindedness as a medico-social and historically constructed disability label and to understand how state authorities—including physicians, psychologists, educators, social workers, and juvenile court officials—used the diagnosis in the early twentieth century to establish Pacific Colony. I also detail the ways state authorities applied the label to facilitate and justify the confinement and sterilization of Mexican-origin youth. Excavating the history of Pacific Colony illustrates how state authorities combined ideologies of race, gender, and disability to render working-class Mexican-origin youth "mentally deficient," how the racial and gendered valences of feebleminded diagnoses were used by state authorities to justify punitive interventions, and the ways that residents of Pacific Colony confronted and contested these practices.

The book elaborates two arguments. The first is an empirical argument, based on both archival evidence and data analysis, about the discriminatory application of state practices of institutionalization and sterilization. I assert that state workers targeted Mexican-origin youth in Southern California in practices of disability labeling, decisions about who needed to be committed to Pacific Colony, and determinations about which Pacific Colony residents needed to be sterilized. The second is an epistemic argument about the roles that racism, sexism, and classism played in the development of theories of intelligence and feeblemindedness. I assert that scientific research on feeblemindedness conducted and circulated by California professionals in fields like psychology and juvenile delinquency established "mental defect" as a constitutive component of Mexican racial difference in ways that were gendered. This production of knowledge about Mexican mental inferiority added scientific validity to existing notions of Mexicans as sexually deviant, hyperfertile, criminally inclined, and economically dependent, naturalizing these stereotypes as inherent traits. This knowledge legitimized violent state efforts to manage the lives and reproduction of young Mexican-origin women and men.

During the first half of the twentieth century, California led the nation in eugenics-inspired efforts to prevent people deemed physically, mentally, or socially unfit from reproducing, sterilizing approximately twenty thousand people who were committed to state institutions. Performing about one-third of the sixty thousand sterilizations that took place under eugenic laws in thirty-two states across the country, California's sterilization program has received important attention from scholars over the years.[1] Historical analyses of California's sterilization practices have rightly focused on the eugenic aspects of the state's sterilization statute and the role that gender played in efforts to institutionalize and sterilize working-class women. The existing scholarship on this dark episode of California history offers crucial insights about the roles of gender and eugenic ideology; however, little is known about the demographics of who was sterilized. Scholarly research on institutions for the feebleminded in the East Coast, Midwest, and South outlines the ways that this diagnosis was applied in different regions of the country.[2] This analysis of Pacific Colony broadens that research, illustrating how race, disability, and gender converged to justify institutionalization and sterilization in ways that disproportionately affected working-class, disabled, and racialized people in Southern California, Mexican-origin youth in particular

Pacific Colony was one of two institutions for the so-called feebleminded in California. It was not the first nor did it sterilize the most people. Those distinctions go to the Sonoma State Home, which opened in 1891 and was located in Northern California. Sonoma State Home authorities sterilized more than five thousand people between the 1910s and the early 1950s. Pacific Colony, located near present-day Pomona in Southern California, was the second state institution built to confine, manage, and sterilize people labeled "feebleminded." Pacific Colony did not open until 1927, but white middle-class professionals who often identified as progressive social reformers commissioned studies and compiled research starting in the mid-1910s on what they viewed as a concerning population of nonwhite, defective, delinquent, and dependent people in the southern part of the state. They used this research to garner support for building Pacific Colony, which came to represent California social reformers' best thinking on how to manage populations they deemed undeserving of the rights and privileges of citizenship, including freedom and the right to reproduce.

Various state department officials from the juvenile courts, the Public

Health Department, and the Department of Social Welfare worked in tandem with Pacific Colony administrators, targeting Mexican-origin youth for commitment to the institution and sterilization. Between 1928 and 1952, Pacific Colony processed 2,090 sterilization requests and 533 of those—approximately 25 percent—were for people with Spanish surnames. Over the years the number of sterilization requests for Spanish-surnamed residents never dropped below 13.5 percent and peaked at 36 percent in 1939.[3] To be clear, Spanish-surnamed residents were disproportionately sterilized across the state. Analysis that compares data from sterilization requests processed by all institutions between 1920 and 1945 to U.S. census data on people living in individual institutions shows that institutionalized Latinas/os were at higher risk of sterilization than non-Latinas/os. Latino men were at a 23 percent higher risk of being recommended for sterilization than non-Latino men living in institutions, and Latinas were at a 59 percent greater risk of being recommended for sterilization than non-Latinas living in institutions.[4] While Latinas/os, most of whom were Mexican-origin, faced higher rates of sterilization across the state, Mexican-origin people faced the highest proportion of sterilization at Pacific Colony—especially Mexican-origin youth. Thus Pacific Colony represents an important case study on how race, disability, and gender were co-constructed in eugenic practices of population control during the first half of the twentieth century.

Honing in on this one institution, I highlight how professionals in various fields, including psychology, education, and social work, produced entire bodies of research that constructed Mexican-origin youth as inherently defective and prone to deviant behavior and economic dependence. I illustrate how this research was translated into state policies of confinement and reproductive constraint, and how officials collaborated across state departments to implement these policies. A vast web of powerful actors came together to convince the California State legislature to invest millions of dollars in Pacific Colony over several decades, and they worked together to identify, label, manage, and sterilize people who often already faced extreme social and economic marginalization. Examining the institution from the late 1920s to the early 1950s, this books shows that, in the face of overcrowding, allegations of abuse, and persistent rebellion on the part of residents, experts and state workers consistently argued that population control measures (segregation, confinement, and sterilization) were the most scientific and humanitarian approaches to large social issues like poverty and crime.

By analyzing the history of Pacific Colony and the experiences of Mexican-origin youth that lived there, we gain important insights on how social hierarchies are built and justified through notions of race, gender, disability, and class. We also see how these notions become embodied in violent and harmful ways. However, as my research illustrates, the power of the state in the lives of these Mexican-origin youth was not absolute. As the two survivors quoted at the beginning of this introduction make clear, Pacific Colony residents had strong views about institutional authorities' right to limit their reproduction. Many young people at Pacific Colony acted on their views, taking great risks to challenge, defy, and resist efforts to manage their lives, labor, and reproductive capacity.

"FEEBLEMINDEDNESS" AND THE CONSTRUCTION OF MEXICAN RACIAL INFERIORITY

From the late nineteenth and well into the middle of the twentieth century, psychiatrists, educators, social workers, and juvenile court authorities across the country relied consistently on one specific medical diagnosis to justify the institutionalization and sterilization of young people: feeble-mindedness.[5] This practice rested on a body of research that emerged in the late nineteenth century and proliferated in the era of eugenics. According to eugenicists and researchers in the fields of psychology, education, and juvenile delinquency, "feeblemindedness" was a hereditary condition of individual mental defect that gave way to a host of social issues including poverty, immorality, and crime.

Given the social and reproductive implications of this medical condition, researchers argued that individuals with this diagnosis required management, confinement, and reproductive constraint in order to stave off the negative social implications of their supposed defect. Historians have demonstrated the ways that, as a medical diagnosis, feeblemindedness was not the accurate, scientific, or objective measure of mental capacity that clinicians portrayed it to be.[6] Instead, as with other categories of disability, "feeblemindedness" was a socially and historically situated construct that was far more indicative of relationships of power than of inherent intelligence or any fixed condition of the mind. As this book demonstrates, ideologies of race, gender, and class were embedded in the formulation of this disability label and thus shaped the way feeblemindedness was determined, who would be marked with this label, and who would have to endure the most invasive forms of "treatment." In California, researchers repeatedly concluded that Mexican-origin people were more prone to feeblemindedness. As a result, state authorities often approached the behaviors of Mexican-origin youth through this lens of disability, labeling them feebleminded and targeting them for confinement and sterilization.

The idea of feeblemindedness was wedded to ideas about intelligence and its role in determining who was capable and deserving of full citizenship in the United States. When psychologists like Lewis Terman, whose work I examine in chapter 1, claimed to be able to measure a person's inherent level of intelligence, they did so in ways that tied a person's mental capacity to their role and value in society. In fact, in his book on the Stanford-Binet intelligence test, Terman wrote explicitly about the ways that the IQ score—a numeric representation of someone's intelligence— could be used to determine both who was a likely social menace and who had the capacity to be a valuable and productive citizen.[7] According to Terman, intelligence tests should be used in educational settings, to identify "delinquents" and determine "vocational fitness."[8] When used in schools, IQ scores could determine which youths would benefit from education and which youths should be excluded. When used in juvenile courts, IQ scores could determine which youths had the potential to be reformed and which were born criminals. When applied to industry, IQ scores could determine which individuals were fit for managerial and administrative roles and who should be relegated to low-status and low-wage labor. According to those who subscribed to this line of thinking, intelligence became a seemingly natural, logical, and even scientific way to organize society. People of normal or superior intelligence were the natural and most capable beneficiaries of rights, freedom, and economic success. People on the lower end of the intelligence spectrum, however, were a burden at best and a social menace at worst.[9]

To be sure, diagnoses of feeblemindedness relied on more than IQ scores, and people in charge of testing and labeling drew heavily from social data, family histories, and interactions with youth that were marked by unequal power dynamics. Thus diagnoses of feeblemindedness largely resulted from a combination of IQ scores and subjective assessments of social location and behavior. As psychologist Mark Rapley has described, clinicians formed diagnoses of mental deficiency through a "symptom complex" or an understanding of a group of symptoms that, when occurring together, characterize a certain biological defect.[10] The main components of this symptom complex were most often low IQ scores; poverty, which psychologists and other state workers interpreted as a manifestation of "economic incompetence," and socially disruptive or "deviant" behavior such as sexual promiscuity and criminality, which state workers read as symptomatic of low intelligence. In an attempt to add more specificity to their evaluative practices, psychologists created a rank list of diagnostic grades to go with their assessments of intelligence. The diagnostic grades purportedly represented a hierarchy of intelligence with the "idiot" at the very bottom, followed by "imbecile," "moron," "borderline," and "dull normal."

Clinicians often used IQ scores to assign a specific mental grade, but behavior and social location could also move a person higher or lower on the intelligence spectrum. In practice, general diagnoses like "feeblemindedness" and specific classifications like "idiot" or "moron" were applied as if they were distinct categories of personhood. For clinicians and state workers these diagnoses became a powerful "resource" or "way of talking" about people they identified as requiring management.[11] They had social meanings and became shorthand for how a person might or might not fit into society, and what type of bodily and reproductive interventions should be applied to that person. Clinicians and state workers involved in diagnosing feeblemindedness worked from a set of beliefs and standards that were premised on the superiority of white middle-class heterosexual norms and behaviors. That is, diagnostic judgments about mental capacity were made in comparison to an idealized American subject or "normal person" who, as Rapley writes, "just happens to bear a striking similarity to an upper-middle-class psy professional."[12]

In the late nineteenth and early twentieth century, American reformers and researchers in fields ranging from public health to juvenile delinquency established concepts of "normality" and "defect" to naturalize difference and inequality in ways that both legitimized and replicated existing racial, gendered, and class hierarchies.[13] Disability labels like feeblemindedness obscured the social and economic causes of issues like crime and poverty and, instead, made them outcomes of individual defect. Researchers and reformers sought to prove this point through statistics, surveys, and other scientific methods.[14] Doing so justified such interventions as institutionalization and reproductive constraint, which were framed as "treatment" and "prevention." At the same time, the emergence of compulsory education, state boards of charities, juvenile court systems, and institutions for the confinement of people labeled feebleminded created opportunities for a host of professionals to build careers, illustrate their expertise, and convince both the public and state legislatures that they had the knowledge and the technologies to ameliorate the social ills caused by defective individuals.[15] In the process, psychologists, social workers, educators, and juvenile court authorities engaged in the consolidation of categories of difference and the application of violent state interventions.

Laboratory of Deficiency examines how this process played out in California from the late nineteenth century and into the 1950s, with a focus on Pacific Colony and the various researchers and state workers connected to the institution. I contend that although Pacific Colony advocates couched their arguments for confinement and sterilization in science and humanitarianism, their efforts were largely about the management and control of certain derided populations and the production of laboring bodies in the name of economic progress and white racial fitness and superiority.[16] From its inception in a legislative bill in the 1910s and through the late 1950s, advocates of the institution asserted that the state needed to fund practices of labeling, confinement, and reproductive constraint as a way to manage people deemed feebleminded for the public good. Ideologies of race and gender were central to the definition and application of feeblemindedness and, as my work shows, researchers in California used Mexican-origin youth as subjects in their studies on intelligence and mental defect, thereby influencing the ways that state workers applied the label in their practices of policing, confinement, and sterilization.

Tracing the ways state workers used the label of feeblemindedness to mark Mexican-origin youth as defective and in need of management highlights the ways disability worked during the first half of the twentieth century to signify relationships of power and justify inequality for disabled people and other marginalized groups not traditionally understood as disabled.[17] In historical analyses of feeblemindedness and the institutions established to confine and manage people with that label, scholars often point out that people targeted for institutionalization in the past would likely not be considered disabled today. In this book I do not engage in arguments about whether or not the people discussed herein were actually cognitively impaired. My position is that intellectual or cognitive ability are not valid measures of social value, and disability is not a justifiable reason for restricting rights, bodily autonomy, or reproductive capacity. Instead, I assert that disability in the form of feeblemindedness legitimized subjective judgments about Mexican-origin youth as racially and socially inferior, and justified violating their bodily and reproductive autonomy.

As a concept, disability in the United States, and the exclusionary and oppressive work that this concept has historically performed, functions through ableism and notions of normality that are premised on the superiority of white middle-class able-bodied male heteronormativity.[18] In his classic essay "Disability and the Justification of Inequality in American History," the historian Douglas Baynton writes: "not only has it been considered justifiable to treat disabled people unequally, but the *concept* of disability has been used to justify discrimination against other groups by attributing disability to them."[19] This book shows how disability became the central rationalizing tool in decisions regarding institutional confinement and sterilization. That is, once a diagnosis of disability was applied, a host of interventions became available as rational options in the name of treatment.

DISABILITY AND THE MATRIX OF REPRODUCTIVE OPPRESSION

My analysis of Pacific Colony and the broader process of disability labeling, management, and justifications of violent state interventions draws extensively from the theoretical and methodological insights of Critical Disability Studies and feminist scholarship in the movement for Reproductive Justice. Scholars in both of these fields insist on an intersectional approach to power and the body that is essential for understanding how and why the reproductive and bodily autonomy of the young Mexican-origin women and men discussed herein was so easily violated by the state. A central facet of both the politics of reproduction and the politics of disability in the United States is the power to decide the meaning, value, and consequence of bodily difference (race, sex, disability) and (reproductive) capacity.[20] As historians of both reproduction and disability have illustrated, the meanings, values, and consequences ascribed to bodily difference and capacity have largely been shaped by historical context and subject position.[21] While differences in human biology and neurological function certainly exist, their social meanings and consequences have changed over time. Moreover, ideas about gender, race, class, sexuality, age, nationality, and ability play a fundamental role in this broader meaning-making process. I apply these insights to understand the ways that one disability label (feeblemindedness) was deployed in determining the meanings and values of certain bodies—and the harmful consequences of this practice.

Reproductive Justice is both an organizing framework and an analytical lens for examining reproductive oppression. In the 1990s a group of Black women and Women of Color developed the organizing framework of Reproductive Justice in response to the narrow focus of the mainstream reproductive rights movement on abortion. Keenly aware of the broader issues Women of Color have faced in living out the basic right to have children, the founders of Reproductive Justice asserted that any movement for reproductive freedom must go beyond the right to choose abortion. Reproductive Justice thus represented a paradigm shift that applied principles of social justice and human rights to reproductive politics. The Reproductive Justice paradigm is built on three principles: (1) the right to not have children using the method of one's choice; (2) the right to have children in safe conditions; and (3) the right to parent in safe environments. With these three principles the founders of Reproductive Justice underscored the bodily and reproductive autonomy of all people and families as fundamental to any transformative movement for freedom and justice.[22]

Activists and scholars have adapted this organizing framework as an analytical lens through which to examine and understand systems and experiences of reproductive oppression in the United States.[23] Reproductive oppression in the United States, to paraphrase activist and scholar Loretta Ross, refers to the management and exploitation of bodies, sexuality, labor, and fertility in order to maintain and legitimize unequal social and economic power within a broader system of white supremacy.[24] Instead of examining reproduction as a singularly gendered experience, a Reproductive Justice lens demands a broad and multifaceted analysis of the ways that power, historical context, and subject position shape people's experiences of sex, sexuality, reproduction, family, and labor differently and in relation to economic systems.[25] In practice, a Reproductive Justice lens analyzes how power works through intersecting ideologies of race, gender, class, ability, and sexuality to create and naturalize hierarchies of reproduction that legitimize and sustain a "complex matrix of reproductive oppression."[26] As *Laboratory of Deficiency* illustrates, ideologies of disability, race, gender, and class came together to construct both the feebleminded subject (disabled, dependent, racially inferior) in contrast to the ideal citizen subject (abled, middle- and upper-class, white). These constructs were mapped onto the bodies of people in different ways and structured the value and consequences of their lives, families, labor, and reproduction.

Adopting Reproductive Justice as an analytical lens, I offer a broad examination of what constitutes reproductive oppression during the period of this study. Certainly, forced sterilization was the most explicit expression of oppression in this context. But my analysis also considers confinement, the forced unpaid labor of residents in Pacific Colony, the process of labeling, the surveillance and policing of state workers, and the legal diminishment of parental authority by juvenile courts—which occurred when a young person was committed to Pacific Colony—as integral aspects of this matrix of reproductive oppression. I analyze this matrix in light of intersecting, structural, and individual relationships of power. Granted authority by the state, psychiatrists, social workers, and juvenile authorities were enlisted to engage in practices of surveillance and labeling to implement institutionalization and sterilization on people deemed inferior and unfit. They held decision-making power over both the body and reproductive capacity of Mexican-origin youths, but they also actively diminished the value and authority of Mexican-origin parents and families. Thus this books parses out the multifarious ways Pacific Colony advocates, clinicians, and collaborators established a system—supported by the state and much of the public—that legitimized the notion that some people do not have the right to reproduce, and some families do not have the right to raise their children.

Knowledge production was crucial to developing and legitimizing this matrix of reproductive oppression. The science of eugenics, research in psychology, and juvenile delinquency were all essential in legitimizing and naturalizing hierarchies of reproduction and practices of population control. By examining the role of science in these processes—namely the ways California researchers created knowledge about the relationship between race and disability and operationalized that knowledge in line with existing racial and ableist biases—we gain an understanding of the role knowledge production plays in upholding long-standing beliefs about social value in our society.[27]

Disability was the central component of this particular matrix of reproductive oppression and, as mentioned, this book builds on the work of Critical Disability Studies. Like the Reproductive Justice framework, scholars in the field of Critical Disability Studies emphasize an analysis of power in the production of disability labels, the oppression of people with disabilities, and the role of the state in concentrating disability in marginalized populations through neglect or violence.[28] Engaging Critical Disability Studies "as methodology rather than subject," my analysis of the concept of feeblemindedness illustrates how deviating from social norms of race, gender, class, and sexuality came to be read as disability, and how this particular form of disability became concentrated among working-class Mexican youth.[29] I make clear the ways that feeblemindedness as a medical diagnosis was not simply an old or ill-informed way of talking about intellectual disabilities (a mistake that lives in the past), but a social category within a larger system of power used to naturalize social hierarchies, categorize deviant populations, and justify population control measures.

My analysis draws on disability studies scholar Sami Schalk's necessary distinction between *(dis)ability* as "a system of social norms which categorizes, ranks, and values bodyminds" and *disability* as "a historically and culturally variable category within this larger system."[30] Using this important distinction, my analysis points out the ways that feeblemindedness functioned within a system of ableist medical, legal, and social norms—(dis)ability—that categorized certain working-class Mexican-origin youths as defective. Under this label working-class Mexican-origin youths became the targets of a number of normalizing and eliminatory interventions produced and justified by the same (dis)ability system. Instead of improving their lives, state intervention often caused Mexican-origin youths labeled feebleminded significant physical and emotional pain—and worked to funnel them into low-wage jobs, resulting in long-term economic exploitation and disadvantage.

The system of (dis)ability that the mostly white upper- and middle-class California reformers created with feeblemindedness drew on already existing ideologies of race, gender, and class. Here, disability studies scholar Nirmala Erevelles's theorization of disability as an "organizing ideological force" deployed to "organize social hierarchies in their respective historical contexts" is instructive.[31] Erevelles explains that disability operates as a naturalizing "ideological linchpin" in the (re)constitution of "social difference along the axes of race, gender and sexuality."[32] In other words, disability, or ableist logics, have historically worked to justify the organization of social hierarchies along racial, gendered, and class lines. The frameworks of Reproductive Justice and Critical Disability Studies work as guides in examining this historical process of social organization and (re)constitution of difference in relation to social *and* economic systems. As Erevelles points out, in the United State this (re)organizing process occurs in relation to capitalist economic systems that seek to parse out human value in the name of profit and progress.[33] Within these economic systems people with disability labels embody "the disruption of normativity that is symbolic of efficient and profitable individualism and the efficient appropriation of those profits produced within capitalist societies."[34] This book highlights how white middle-class social reformers and state agents, many of whom were ardent eugenicists, sought to manage the populations they deemed inferior and defective in line with capitalist logics of economic efficiency, profit, and productivity.

Like social reformers in other states across the country, prominent Californians involved in establishing and running Pacific Colony were interested in managing people labeled feebleminded in an economically strident way, displaying what historian Molly Ladd-Taylor has described as "professional self-interest, fiscal politics, political expediency, and deep-felt cultural beliefs about economic dependency, disability, and gender."[35] As my research asserts, race was a central component of this process in California. To be sure, scholars have long asserted the centrality of race in eugenics and as legal scholar Dorothy Roberts has written, "eugenic theory did not transcend the American racial order; it was fed, nurtured and sustained by racism."[36] Thus the scientific, efficient, and cost-effective way that California researchers, legislators, and state workers proposed to manage the "feebleminded" largely worked to reinforce and replicate the unequal racial and economic dynamics of the state. Research produced by advocates of Pacific Colony highlighted "mental defect" as the reason why the working class, people with disabilities, and racialized groups were impoverished, thereby obfuscating unequal and exploitative economic systems.

According to their research, this supposed mental defect also caused behaviors that California reformers judged deviant and dangerous. They asserted that the state needed to divest from and intervene in the lives and families of people labeled feebleminded. This divestment and intervention occurred at two levels. Politically, advocates of Pacific Colony asserted that public money meant to address issues of poverty were best used to fund institutionalization and sterilization as opposed to poverty-alleviating programs. At the institutional level, Pacific Colony administrators asserted that confined residents should be required to perform free labor as "training" for possible placement in low-wage jobs outside of the institution. At both levels the arguments were premised on making individuals less burdensome and more productive and, if possible, funneling people into exploitative labor positions that produced a profit for others. In effect, the project of Pacific Colony revolved around transforming purportedly defective, deviant, and dependent people into productive, but not *reproductive*, laborers.

Diagnoses of feeblemindedness and practices of institutionalization used the language of medicine and science to naturalize existing social hierarchies and the unequal economic impacts of the emerging industrial capitalist system. These processes empowered state officials to make decisions about the lives, labor, and reproduction of people labeled feebleminded. As Reproductive Justice scholars have extensively documented, however, practices of state-mandated reproductive constraint have consistently been met with strong resistance.[37] The power of the state in the lives of people labeled feebleminded was often overwhelming, but, as illustrated in chapter 4, confined youth, their families, and their allies found various ways to challenge, disrupt, and resist this power.

THE RACIALIZATION OF MEXICANS IN CALIFORNIA: IMMIGRATION, MEDICALIZATION, AND DISABILITY

Laboratory of Deficiency centers the experiences of Mexican-origin youth to illustrate the ways that racism shaped how the label of feeblemindedness was constructed and deployed. To be clear, Mexican-origin youth were not the only racialized group confined at Pacific Colony—Black and Native American youth were also labeled, confined, and sterilized. Experts on processes of racialization highlight the ways that racial categories are constructed relationally.[38] Although this book does not take up the relational ways that practices of labeling, institutionalization, and sterilization played out among youth categorized as Mexican, Black, Native American, and white, I bring the experiences of other racialized youth into this work because their presence and experiences in the institution matter. Here I provide historical context necessary to understand the specific experiences of Mexican-origin youth in Pacific Colony.

This book is indebted to the robust historical scholarship of Latinx and Chicanx scholars and builds on their invaluable insights on the racialization of Mexican-origin people in the United States. I make clear, however, that Mexican-origin youth endured the institution alongside youth that were racialized and marginalized in different ways. In Table 6 in the appendix I include a list of the different racial descriptors used to label people admitted to Pacific Colony between 1927 and 1947. My hope is that other scholars will pick up this book's loose ends and expand what we know about how other youth experienced and challenged these eugenic practices.

During the first three decades of the twentieth century, California was undergoing major demographic shifts, especially with regard to the state's Mexican population. Mexican immigration to California increased during the early twentieth century due to both the Mexican Revolution and the United States's need for industrial and agricultural labor.[39] By 1928, Los Angeles was the city with the largest population of Mexicans—both immigrant and American-born—in the country.[40] At the same time that Mexican labor fueled capitalist accumulation of wealth, most Mexicans in California faced racial discrimination in housing, education, and public spaces. Regardless of citizenship status and despite official racial designation as "white," Mexican-origin men and women were forced into low-paying and low-status jobs in agriculture, manufacturing, transportation, and the service industry, thus experiencing significant economic marginalization.[41] In California, as in much of the Southwest, Mexican-origin youth in particular faced discrimination in schools and persistent policing and harassment by law enforcement officials.[42]

Despite their long-standing presence in the United States and Mexican immigrant workers' significant contribution to the nation's economy, Mexican immigration was hotly debated throughout the first half of the twentieth century. Some saw Mexican immigrants as potential Americans who, after proper socialization and training, could find a place within the nation's social and labor system.[43] But others called for a closing of the United States–Mexico border and repatriation of immigrants and their American-born children. Nativist sentiment grew between the 1920s and into the Great Depression, and nativists repeatedly called for increased restriction on immigration from Mexico. Politicians in favor of restriction increasingly derided Mexicans as racially and culturally inferior, and Mexicans were frequently portrayed in newspapers and magazines as dirty, diseased, violent, and dependent on an already overburdened state. In the late 1920s the widely read *Saturday Evening Post* ran a series of articles calling for the restriction of Mexican immigration. In one such article, columnist Kenneth Roberts warned the nation of the "race problem" caused by unrestricted Mexican immigration. Significantly, his articles highlighted Mexican women's "reckless" breeding, which Roberts warned would result in the "mongrelization of America."[44]

Immigration legislation during the early twentieth century, particularly the creation of the Border Patrol and the introduction of national-origin and numerical quotas by the 1924 Johnson- Reed Act, remapped understandings of race and citizenship in the United States.[45] The Immigration Act of 1924 altered racial and ethnic categories, making European "ethnics" into whites and constructing Mexicans as "illegal aliens," thus marking all Mexicans—immigrant or American citizen—as foreign.[46] This new "immigration regime" reflected the predominance of a global racial logic that was theorized in then popular works of historian Theodore L. Stoddard and American lawyer Madison Grant. In their books *The Rising Tide of Color against White World-Supremacy* (1920) and *The Passing of the Great Race* (1918), the two authors divided the globe into "White / superior" and "Colored / inferior" races and argued that their mingling would result in the demise of white civilization. Staunch eugenicists, Stoddard and Grant used their racial theories to argue against unrestricted immigration and for the use of race and heredity in the creation of immigration policy. These measures posited racial exclusion, segregation, and population management as necessary means of ensuring progress and wealth for white Americans who were situated as naturally superior and thus the rightful beneficiaries of progress and wealth in the United States.

A major component of racial inferiority and otherness embedded in immigration restriction was disability. In fact, as Baynton's research in *Defectives in the Land: Disability and Immigration in the Age of Eugenics* illustrates, arguments about racial segregation and immigrant exclusion were often grounded in notions about certain racial and immigrant groups' tendencies toward dependency, mental illness, physical disabilities, and feeblemindedness.[47] To prevent the immigration of diseased and deficient newcomers, U.S. border enforcers sought the aid of physicians, public health workers, and other experts who claimed to be able to discern between the fit and unfit. This resulted in the medicalization of not just borders but processes of inclusion and exclusion.[48] Thus the concept of mental disability, backed by science and medicine, was a powerful tool for arguments of exclusion. Moreover, the notion that certain racialized immigrant groups were more prone to mental deficiency was instrumental to their construction as unfit for citizenship.

Race and disability, interpreted through eugenic notions of natural social hierarchies, shaped both efforts to restrict immigration as well as efforts to manage immigrant and racialized groups already in the nation. By the 1920s ideas about the need to restrict entry to immigrants of "bad racial stock" were published alongside policy proposals to institutionalize and sterilize "unfit" populations in the United States. In prominent eugenicist Harry Hamilton Laughlin's *Eugenical Sterilization in the United States* (1922) a significant amount of text focuses on the perils of unrestricted immigration. In the book's preface, Judge Harry Olson, chief justice of the Chicago Municipal Court, wrote: "America needs to protect herself against indiscriminate immigration, criminal degenerates and race suicide."[49] Olson concluded that in order to do so, segregation and sterilization should be enforced under the notion that "sterilization protects future generations, while segregation safeguards the present as well."[50] The Immigration Act of 1924 reflected these eugenic concerns—as historian Mae Ngai expertly documents, eugenicists proposed the act to limit the number of Eastern and Southern Europeans who were deemed racially undesirable.[51]

The lack of restriction on the country's southern border, however, resulted in restrictionist focus on Mexicans. As the historian Natalia Molina has written: "Brownness came to signify the most important new threat to the racial hegemony of white native-born Americans."[52] Often this threat was figured in medical terms as an immediate public health threat and a long-term form of "racial suicide" through reproduction.[53] Scholarship on the racialized medicalization of Mexican immigrants and Mexican Americans has laid the foundation for understanding the role that medical knowledge and discourse has played in reifying ideas about the racial inferiority of Mexicans. This body of work illustrates how "Mexican" as a racial category, as well as the U.S.-Mexico border as a racialized space, have been historically constructed and negotiated through discourses of disease, defect, and contagion.[54] Scholarship by Molina and John Mckiernan-González details at length the role public health officials have played in the creation of medical borders and the racialization of Mexican bodies and spaces.[55] Such scholarship brings to the fore how histories of race in the United States are tied to histories of medicine.[56] In effect, medical knowledge and public health have been used to justify exclusion and the policing and disciplining of bodies that exist at the intersections of race, class, disability, gender, and sexuality.

In California, and indeed across the nation, notions of Mexicans as not only racially inferior but also defective and more susceptible to disease worked to garner support for exclusionary and eliminatory policies. By the time the Depression hit, legislators drew on biologically based notions of Mexican inferiority to advocate for restriction and exclusion. For example, in 1929, California public health officials asserted that Mexicans were prone to tuberculosis, biologically less able to fight off the disease once infected, and therefore a drain on municipal governments because they filled county hospitals. As a result, the California Department of Public Health called for a "shutting off of the tide of [Mexican] immigration" to reduce tuberculosis rates and the cost of caring for sickly patients.[57]

In addition to being cast as biologically prone to disease, Mexican immigrants in California were figured as a problem to be dealt with by state institutions. With an eye already on the menace of unregulated immigration, the California Department of Institutions established a deportation office in the early 1920s to deport immigrants from state hospitals, relieving the counties of their care. Mexicans quickly became the target of these deportation efforts. In 1928, 47 percent of patients deported by the Department of Institutions were Mexican, and 62 percent of them came from Southern California, which was where "the problem of caring for the defective, delinquent and destitute of the Mexican race" was seen as "most acute."[58] In 1930 the deportation agent remarked that there was "a material decrease in the number of aliens deported" due to the 1924 Immigration Act, but he went on to highlight that "about fifty percent of the aliens [deported were] of Mexican nationality, a nation to which the quota law does not apply."[59] The deportation agent, however, was hopeful that a "tightening up along the Mexican border" would result in a "decided decrease in the number of Mexicans requiring care and treatment in our institutions."[60]

One of the ways that the California Department of Institutions dealt with the Mexican-origin population in the state was by ordering the deportation of Mexican immigrants. These deportations largely occurred among immigrants who were committed to state institutions for the mentally ill and not Pacific Colony. However, deportation was not the only tactic—nor was it a feasible measure when dealing with the American-born children of immigrants. Institutionalization and sterilization at Pacific Colony became an appealing option for dealing with this early generation of Mexican American youth. In fact, concerns over the "acute Mexican problem" in the southern part of California were front and center in the minds of the various physicians, educators, and social reformers who established the Pacific Colony. Once up and running, Pacific Colony was charged with managing what many viewed as the most concerning aspect of this population: their high rates of mental defect or "feeblemindedness," which was seen as contributing to poverty, dependency, deviant sexuality, and delinquency in the state. By committing Mexican-origin youth to Pacific Colony, state authorities combined carceral practices with population-control measures under the guise of "treatment" and "care" to deal with what they saw as a distinct racial and disability problem.

A NOTE ON METHODS

I apply the insights of Reproductive Justice and Critical Disability Studies to my historical analysis of a sprawling archive that includes several California State Department collections, institutional publications, newspapers, research journals, and social science theses, among other sources. In addition to archival analysis, I also collected data on race, gender, age, and economic status from California Department of Institutions reports and more than two thousand sterilization requests processed by Pacific Colony between 1928 and 1951—all of the sterilization requests available for that institution on the Sterilization Records reels.[61] I used this data to conduct quantitative and qualitative analyses in order to identify and discuss demographic patterns in Pacific Colony admissions and sterilization practices. I analyzed supplemental materials apart from sterilization requests that are available in that archive, including consent forms and interdepartmental letters that further explain the details of specific cases. I tracked individuals across the Sterilization Records archive and several sources available in the Lanterman Development Center (previously Pacific Colony) archive. To preserve the privacy of people who appear in medical or restricted use documents, I discuss most cases using pseudonyms, and in some instances I alter county and other identifying information. Real names and information are only used in cases where the sources come from newspapers, court documents, or other publicly available material.

I read the sources for this book "along the archival grain" to understand how power worked through ideologies of race, gender, and disability, but I also interrogate the legitimacy of some of these documents. This is particularly the case in my analysis of sterilization consent forms. If I had the names of the two sterilization survivors quoted at the outset of this introduction, I could look for their sterilization records and would likely find consent forms. Of course, their statements about sterilization at Pacific Colony would be enough to question the validity of extant consent forms, but these documents are also questionable for many other reasons. First, consent was not legally necessary in the sterilization approval process, and institutional authorities were explicit about the fact that collecting consent forms was primarily about protecting officials from liability as opposed to acquiring permission for surgery.[62] Second, the individuals being sterilized were not the ones asked to give consent. Parents and guardians were the designated consenters. Thus these forms don't reflect the wishes of individuals subject to the operation. Third, while some parents surely wanted to have their children sterilized, institutional practice and the unequal power dynamics that existed between state authorities and parents introduce a serious level of coercion in the process of obtaining consent.

As I discuss, Pacific Colony authorities endeavored to sterilize all residents before discharge, so parents could've been coerced into signing consent forms in exchange for the release of their children. Moreover, in several consent forms the witness signature is provided by a parole officer or some other legal authority, which places into question whether consent was given freely or by force. For example, the mother of Andrea Garcia, a young Mexican American woman confined to Pacific Colony in the late 1930s, went to court to try to prevent her daughter's sterilization. Yet sterilization records make no mention of this effort and include a signed consent form. I offer a more in-depth analysis of consent in chapter 4, but I bring it up here to point out that my use and analysis of these and other documents is methodically attuned to context and power.

In other chapters I upend pathologizing discourses that are rampant in the source base for this research. Inspired by the work of feminist historians like Saidiya Hartman, Emma Pérez, and Sarah Haley, who have expanded the disciplinary boundaries of history to draw on the power of speculation and fiction, I speculate on how people felt about living, laboring, and being sterilized in Pacific Colony.[63] Part of the violence that the label of feeblemindedness and the process of institutionalization enacted was the systematic dismissal of individuals' feelings and experiences, and the rendering of these feelings and experiences as merely symptomatic of defect. The narratives I construct in this book are based on institutional records and researchers' descriptions of people in Pacific Colony, but I make assertions about how confined residents felt and how they were impacted as a way to subvert the dehumanizing and pathologizing gaze of the archive. Where possible, I work in the words of people who experienced institutionalization at Pacific Colony, like the two survivors whose testimony open this introduction. I also draw from the testimony and experiences of people institutionalized in similar institutions across the country. While Pacific Colony is the central case study and was unique in the concentration of Mexican-origin youth among its residents, the institution was not exceptional in the conditions of abuse that were produced by confinement. The words of people who experienced labeling, confinement, and sterilization are an essential component of this book, and they move the analysis in ways that traditional archives simply cannot.

CHAPTER BREAKDOWN

This book consists of four chapters. Chapter 1 examines the research and arguments used to establish Pacific Colony, the goals of the institution, and demographic patterns of admission and sterilization. It narrates the construction of feeblemindedness as a "problem" that mobilized racism, ableism, and classism to create a broad matrix of reproductive oppression. Chapters 2 and 3 examine the gendered dynamics of feebleminded diagnoses, institutionalization, and sterilization. Tracing how social reformers

figured Mexican-origin youth as "sex delinquents" and inherent criminals, I present evidence that shows that institutional authorities sterilized
young Mexican-origin women and men at near equal rates, albeit for different reasons. Chapter 4 grapples with matters of agency and resistance
under conditions of confinement. This last chapter is dedicated to recu-
perating stories of youth confined to Pacific Colony and their families who
sought to prevent sterilization and challenge institutional power.

1 The Pacific Plan

RACE, MENTAL DEFECT, AND POPULATION CONTROL
IN CALIFORNIA'S PACIFIC COLONY

When Margarita arrived at Pacific Colony in the summer of 1938, she joined her sister, Sofia, in a bittersweet reunion. Committed at the age of seventeen, Sofia had been living and working at Pacific Colony for a full year before Margarita arrived. Margarita had just turned seventeen herself and was committed to Pacific Colony six months after giving birth. The sisters' confinement at Pacific Colony was based in part on the results of intelligence tests performed by state workers, Sofia's at a Los Angeles City high school and Margarita's at juvenile hall. Test administrators determined that the girls did not do well and asserted that their low scores signaled innate mental defect. To supplement what the scores purportedly represented about the sisters' mental ability, state workers also gathered information about their family. In their notes on the sisters, clinicians highlighted the fact that their parents were Mexican immigrants, that their father died of tuberculosis, that their mother was "illiterate and dull," and that they had a brother who was a ward of the court. State clinicians also noted the family's dire economic situation and the birth of Margarita's child, which happened outside the bounds of marriage. They cited all of these factors as supplemental evidence for what the intelligence test results indicated: that the girls were "feebleminded."

Figure 1. Photo of Pacific Colony, ca. 1939. Burton O. Burt, Works Progress Administration Collection, Los Angeles Public Library.

All of these factors—their test scores, their family history, their economic situation, the presence of a young unwed mother, and being the children of Mexican immigrants—played a significant role in the California Superior Court's decision to commit both sisters to Pacific Colony, Southern California's institution for the so-called feebleminded. According to state authorities, the girls were "in need of care and supervision." During a clinical meeting at Pacific Colony in November 1938, a few months after Margarita was committed, institutional authorities decided that the sisters were also in need of sterilization. By preventing reproduction, Pacific Colony officials believed they were fulfilling the ultimate goal of the institution—protecting California from the spread of degenerate family lines. Their version of care and supervision revolved around confinement, forced labor, and reproductive constraint.[1]

While at Pacific Colony, Margarita and Sofia lived in Cottage 6, a

Spanish-style building typical of California architecture. They were confined there with approximately sixty other young women, including Pauline and Carlotta, another pair of Mexican-origin sisters who were both described as "sex delinquents" and labeled feebleminded of the "familial type." Rosa, a seventeen-year-old Native American girl, was also confined to Cottage 6 with Margarita and Sofia. Rosa was transferred to Pacific Colony after a psychiatrist at the Sherman Institute administered an intelligence test and labeled her a "mentally deficient Indian girl" suffering from "familial deficiency (hereditary causes)."[2] Betty, a young Black girl, was also a resident of Cottage 6. Like Sofia, Betty was tested at a Los Angeles City School, where a psychologist described her as having "borderline" intelligence. All of these young women came from different parts of Southern California, they had different backgrounds and different life experiences—but what brought them to Pacific Colony were assumptions made by teachers, psychologists, and legal and institutional authorities about their bad heredity, low intelligence, and the danger that their behavior and reproduction posed to the state.

Cottage 6 was one of thirteen buildings on more than six hundred acres of land near present-day Pomona, constructed by the state to confine people deemed mentally and socially deficient by state workers. Between the 1920s and 1950s men and women were committed to Pacific Colony for a variety of reasons. The state confined infants and the elderly at Pacific Colony, but a majority of the population consisted of youth between the ages of twelve and twenty-five. Some lived in the institution for a short period, others for a lifetime. The two pairs of Mexican-origin sisters, together with Rosa and Betty, lived in Cottage 6 for about four years. Deemed unfit for education, the young women spent their days working in different parts of the institution, caring for young and incapacitated fellow residents in Cottage 2, working on laundry and kitchen details, and sewing sheets and pillows for the hundreds of institution beds. Pacific Colony authorities made their release from the institution contingent on sterilization, and during their time there all of the women were forced to undergo the surgery. Sofia and Carlotta were sterilized on the same day: March 1, 1939. These young women were among the approximately twenty thousand people sterilized in California state institutions between the 1920s and early 1950s.

When Pacific Colony opened in the late 1920s, confinement and sterilization was described as "necessary for the unfortunate child born into the
world lacking in the mental equipment necessary to develop into a useful
citizen."[3] Over the years Pacific Colony authorities and their advocates in
California politics, education, and social welfare used confinement and
sterilization to manage the bodies, labor, and reproduction of people
(namely youths) they deemed defective, deviant, and dependent. Ableism,
racism, and classism informed the construction of feeblemindedness as a
diagnostic label, the diagnostic process of labeling, and decisions about
who required institutionalization and sterilization. Researchers and officials involved in these processes established a system of state care that
largely worked to maintain Anglo-American social, political, and economic dominance in Southern California.

Indeed, the label of "feeblemindedness" worked to naturalize, maintain, and enforce the state's social and economic hierarchy, which positioned white Anglo-Americans at the top as stewards of the state's future
and the rightful beneficiaries of the state's resources, while the state's poor,
immigrants, the disabled, and racialized groups were to be managed—
ideally in profitable or productive ways. California researchers, educators,
and welfare authorities situated institutionalization and sterilization as
appropriate, effective, and economically efficient ways to manage people
they viewed as inherently inferior. At worst, the people confined would
have to remain in the institution through the reproductive period; at best,
they could be trained, sterilized, and released so that they could lead lives
of "usefulness and self-support in the community."[4]

This chapter analyzes the founding of Pacific Colony and the arguments used in favor of expending state funds on the institution with an
eye toward why the legislature thought institutionalization was necessary. I detail the institution's target population from its inception in 1927
through the early 1950s. This reveals how the work of the institution, institutional authorities, and the people who supported its efforts established
a system of (dis)ability that functioned as a blueprint for how to manage
poor, disabled, racialized, immigrant Californians—and those that existed
at the intersections of these identities—in ways that were profoundly violent and harmful.[5] The ideological architects of Pacific Colony used white
upper- and middle-class social norms as a basis for constructing this sys-

tem of (dis)ability, and drew on industrial and capitalist logic to highlight and reaffirm mental capacity, productivity, profit, and self-sufficiency as measures of social value.

THE THREAT OF FEEBLEMINDEDNESS: A NATIONAL MOVEMENT

In 1915, California's legislature gave the green light to a broad coalition of researchers, reformers, and professionals lobbying for an institution for the feebleminded in the southern part of the state. Chapter 729 of the 1915 legislature authorized state officials to conduct a "comprehensive study of the problem of feeble-mindedness" in California and prepare recommendations to establish an "institution for the care, training, confinement, discipline and instruction of defective persons."[6] Members of the State Board of Charities and Corrections, the State Board of Education, the State Board of Health, and the State Commission in Lunacy gathered in support of this effort and formed the State Joint Committee on Defectives in California. With Carrie Parsons Bryant, then vice president of the State Board of Charities and Corrections, at the helm this committee selected prominent researchers in education, juvenile delinquency, and psychology to study the scope and size of this supposed problem and provide input on institutional confinement as the appropriate solution.

Based on surveys and intelligence test results, the researchers highlighted feeblemindedness—alternately referred to as "mental deviance," "mental defect," or "low intelligence"—as the central problem in a broad range of pressing social issues including poverty, crime, and immorality. According to these researchers, not only did feebleminded people cause a plethora of social ills, they also represented an economic burden to the state and, by extension, an undue burden on the nonfeebleminded or "normal" public. The researchers described public education, charity, and state-funded social supports for people labeled feebleminded as a waste. In their expert opinion, public resources like these were squandered on people whose inherent defect meant that they were incapable of learning, destined for poverty, and biologically inclined to social deviance.

In his contribution to the studies, Stanford professor of education

Lewis M. Terman raised another more alarming point of concern. Not only were people of low intelligence social threats and economic burdens, their condition was hereditary. Terman wrote that not only was feeble-mindedness "incurable" but "in the large majority of cases it is caused by heredity."[7] Thus the reproductive capacity of people labeled feebleminded represented both a wellspring of social maladies and a never-ending economic liability. Terman and his fellow researchers in juvenile delinquency and psychology agreed that this multifaceted problem required a multi-pronged solution: identify and label the feebleminded with the help of intelligence tests (coincidently designed and calibrated by Terman himself), ideally at a young age; segregate people with the label into institutions to protect the public from impending crime and immorality; and prevent the feebleminded from reproducing either through confinement or sterilization.[8]

With the work of these experts in hand, Bryant and her colleagues on the State Joint Committee on Defectives in California furnished scientific evidence in support of the institution that would become Pacific Colony. Convinced by this work, the 1917 legislature appropriated funds to begin constructing Pacific Colony, thereby legitimizing two key positions that the researchers and leaders of the various California agencies adopted in their advocacy for the institution. First, that individual pathology, as opposed to structural inequality, caused large-scale social problems—that is, "defective" individuals were the primary source of crime, poverty, and immorality. And second, that state funds earmarked to address such social issues as poverty, crime, and immorality were best spent on efforts to manage these individuals. Specifically, population control measures like segregation, confinement, and reproductive constraint were upheld as policies necessary for the broader social and economic good.

I return to Terman, intelligence testing, the authoritative knowledge he and his colleagues produced, and how racism and classism were embedded in their research and policy recommendations around feeblemind-edness later in this chapter. Here, I place Pacific Colony's political and ideological beginnings in a broader national and historical context. The research gathered by state authorities in support of Pacific Colony represented the most up-to-date and cutting-edge science, but the core ideas and impulses were not new. Claims about low mental capacity or intel-

lectual disability have long been used by state authorities to justify under-
mining the freedom and bodily autonomy of people deemed "unfit" for
citizenship, including the disabled, the poor, and racialized others. Both
in theory and when implemented in state policy, the concept of disability
has worked to maintain white supremacy and unequal and exploitative
power dynamics.

The long-standing use of disability in general, and intellectual disability
in particular, as a basis for exclusion from the national body and a rationale for diminishing the freedom and bodily autonomy of certain people
made it possible for the authors of the 1915 California bill to start from the
premise that feeblemindedness was indeed a problem that required state
intervention. As early as the seventeenth century, colonial Poor Laws facilitated the exclusion and confinement of people who, for biological or other
reasons, could not labor or be self-sustaining. People deemed dependent
outsiders, the elderly, the disabled, and people labeled "idiots" were often
either expelled from colonial communities or confined.[9] Because these
practices were rooted in early European capitalism and Puritan work
ethic, class was paramount in these experiences. Many of these people
were confined under conditions of forced labor in poorhouses or work-
houses—practices that disability scholars situate as antecedents of modern carceral institutions.[10] As the sociologist Alison Carey has pointed out
in her work on intellectual disability, in early America so-called "idiots"
were seen as unfit for the rights and privileges of citizenship and were
legally subjected to confinement and restrictions, but their vulnerability to
these experiences was largely tied to their economic status, familial relationships, and access to resources.[11] That is, people with supportive families or economic resources could ultimately avoid legal punishments like
being confined to a workhouse. During this period disability and poverty
became legitimate reasons for social exclusion, the restriction of freedom,
and even forced labor.

Early Americans wielded a similar rationale to justify the brutal dispossession, exploitation, segregation, and confinement of Native Americans.
Claims about Native racial difference and inferiority legitimized land theft
and forced displacement in federally designated reservations in the name
of colonial expansion. European colonists justified these actions through
claims about the inherent mental and physical inferiority of Native

Americans, which served to dehumanize and situate Indigenous folks as outside the bounds of citizenship and rights.[12] In the mid-nineteenth century Anglo-Americans seeking to further diminish Native sovereignty decided to deal with the "Indian problem" by taking Native youths from their families and confining them to federal boarding schools on the premise that they were mentally and culturally inferior and thus required "care" by the American state.[13] At the turn of the twentieth century, the federal government established an institution called the Hiawatha Asylum for the sole purpose of confining Native people.[14] Native peoples' accounts of Hiawatha make clear that, in addition to confining people labeled "insane" or "mentally defective," federal authorities also confined Native people labeled "troublemakers" because they refused to comply with government demands.[15] For example, some were committed to Hiawatha after challenging federal agents' authority to kidnap and confine their children in boarding schools.[16] Moreover, because they were considered "mentally defective," people confined to Hiawatha were deemed unfit to reproduce and often confined for their entire lives to prevent reproduction.[17] From colonial settler expansion to the early twentieth century and beyond, the U.S. government has consistently relied on a confluence of racism and ableism to justify Native exploitation, segregation, confinement, and the overall diminishment of parental autonomy.

Indeed, assertions of biological difference and mental inferiority represent the bedrock of racism and have thus served as core rationales for the racial violence and exploitation of Black people in the United States. Supporters of slavery in the United States drew expansively on assertions about the bodily difference and inferior mental capacity of enslaved Africans. In the nineteenth century, supporters of slavery asserted that the people they enslaved had such low mental capacity that they could never be capable of proper citizenship.[18] In fact, enslavers perversely argued that their brutal system of confinement and forced labor was a benefit to the enslaved. According to them, a population with such low intelligence would be burdened by freedom and eventually fall into madness, ill health, or poverty. In this way, Black racial difference was made real through assertions about Black people's inferior "endowment of body and mind," as Thomas Jefferson put it.[19]

Not only did these assertions work to maintain white supremacy, but they also sustained a broader capitalist system built on free labor. As scholars like Dorothy Roberts and Deborah Gray White have documented, this racist economic system profoundly shaped the reproductive experiences of enslaved people.[20] Reproduction represented a potential for profit under a system where human bodies were likened to property. While enslaved women were sometimes encouraged to reproduce, parents had little control over what happened to their children, and thus their familial relationships and parenthood status were thoroughly degraded. Because enslavers sought to benefit financially from the birth of people who could be used for free labor, children born with disabilities were devalued, viewed as "useless," or a financial burden.[21] Not only did racism and ableism converge to justify enslavement and racial violence, but together these ideologies worked to denigrate Black parenthood, families, and reproductive autonomy.

In addition to justifying land theft, labor exploitation, and racial violence, disability was also a useful concept in immigration restriction. Since at least the nineteenth century, immigrants with "physical defects," "mental deficiency," or "insanity" were banned outright. Moreover, immigrants seen as less desirable because of their nationality or because they were racialized as nonwhite were often banned from entry on the basis that they were inherently more susceptible to mental or physical defect.[22] Not only did immigration laws cast these immigrants as unfit to be American, but they were also banned on the premise that their (potential) disability made them more "likely to become a public charge."[23] In effect, immigration laws in the nineteenth century and into the twentieth century combined racist, nativist, and ableist ideologies with a discourse of dependency to justify exclusion.

As this condensed history illustrates, long before efforts to establish Pacific Colony began in the 1910s, disability in the form of "low mental capacity" existed as a logic that, by itself or when embedded in racism, classism, and nativism, worked to legitimize limiting the freedom and degrading the bodily and reproductive autonomy of different populations. By the late nineteenth century, what disability studies scholar Susan Schweik has described as a "tensely conjoined ableism, biologized racism, and nativism" pervaded American society and culture, and points of connection were spuriously (re)drawn between disability, poverty, race, and citizenship.[24] As in the past, these connections worked to maintain white supremacy but were also constructed in the specific context of rampant immigration, urbanization, industrialization, and the overall expansion of a capitalist system that required, and thus placed value on, productive versus nonproductive people.[25] Disability became a useful shorthand for distinguishing between the two, but as sociologist Allison C. Carey has written: "While some of the 'non-productive' were easily identified, differentiation based on mental and intellectual disability proved more challenging."[26] To aid in this project of differentiation, Carey adds that physicians, psychologists, and educators "took on the task of sorting the productive from the unproductive (the unworthy from the worthy) and [deciding] their appropriate treatment."[27] In the 1870s a group of American physicians and educators formed the Association of Medical Officers of American Institutions of Idiotic and Feeble-Minded Persons (AMOAIIFP) to take up this broader effort.[28]

In 1876, Isaac Kerlin, then superintendent of the Pennsylvania Training School for Feeble-Minded Children, invited a handful of his colleagues from Connecticut, Illinois, and Ohio to Philadelphia to celebrate the nation's centennial and for a meeting that resulted in the formation of the AMOAIIFP.[29] Some were trained in medicine and others in education, but all of these men presided as superintendents over institutions for people labeled feebleminded. That year—as they celebrated the signing of the Declaration of Independence, a document that extolled equality and the right to life, liberty, and freedom—Kerlin and his colleagues asserted that their work in confining and managing individuals they labeled defective and inferior deserved greater prominence on the national stage. In the previous decade charity and corrections work had become a centralized facet of state governments, and the superintendents believed this work should include the establishment of large and specialized state-funded facilities led by professionals like them.[30]

Building the ideological framework that California reformers used to advocate for Pacific Colony in the 1910s, members of the AMOAIIFP asserted that poverty and the supposed increase in immorality and crime associated with urbanization and industrialization were caused, in part, by mental defect. Because of this, they cast people with "low mentality" as a combination of incompetent, deviant, or dependent and therefore unfit

for freedom and in need of management by the state. Notably, these assertions were made at the tail end of Reconstruction, after abolitionists had
succeeded in challenging the racial contours of American labor, citizenship, and political rights with the Thirteenth, Fourteenth, and Fifteenth
Amendments.[31] At a time when race was, at least at the federal level, being
challenged as a legitimate argument for forced labor and the denial of
freedom and citizenship, the AMOAIIFP—made up entirely of Anglo-
American professional men—situated disability as a more scientific and
thus more legitimate and precise tool for drawing the boundaries of citizenship and rights.

   In the late nineteenth century, AMOAIIFP members waged a national
campaign with three aims: (1) market feeblemindedness as a social problem, (2) situate large custodial institutions as a necessary social good, and
(3) build their professional power and status in both of these realms.[32] To
meet these ends, members harnessed the rationalizing power of science. By
1884, Kerlin succeeded in establishing a special committee on feeblemindedness within the National Conference of Charities and Corrections—an
annual meeting of legislators and social reformers who held sway in state-
funded work related to poverty, crime, immorality, and immigration.[33] At
the conference, AMOAIIFP members presented surveys and statistics that
represented their stance on the vast problem of feeblemindedness. With
this numeric evidence they drew connections between mental defect and
crime, immorality, and poverty.[34] To support their assertions about the
dangers of reproduction among the feebleminded, they cited widely read
family studies like Richard Louis Dugdale's *The Jukes: A Study in Crime,
Pauperism, Disease and Heredity* (1877). In all, the AMOAIIFP presented
a compelling case, particularly for the legislators, social reformers, and
charity workers already involved in privately and publicly funded efforts
to manage the poor, infirm, elderly, immigrants, and people confined to
jails and prisons around the country. In the minds of the AMOAIIFP
and their audience in state and national charities and corrections work,
the idea that a large proportion of these people were inherently defective
made sense, especially in the context of an increased belief in biological
determinism.

   The rise of eugenics in the late nineteenth century worked to bolster all
of the AMOAIIFP's claims. English statistician Francis Galton's theories

on the inheritability of traits like intelligence, criminality, and morality seemed to confirm what many upper- and middle-class Anglo-Americans already believed about the poor, the disabled, immigrants, and other denigrated groups in the United States—namely that social hierarchies were reflective and consequent of inherent biological inferiority that marked human difference. With financial backing from wealthy philanthropists, American eugenicists like Charles Davenport produced a bevy of scientific research including family pedigrees, surveys, and statistics in support of the notion that feeblemindedness was indeed a hereditary pathological mental condition and that this condition was tied to numerous social problems. Professionals in education, social work, medicine, and psychology adopted eugenic theories and called on local and federal governments to intervene and manage these social and biological threats in order to save the (white) American gene pool and pocketbook.[35]

In many ways the popularity of eugenics completed the project that the AMOAIIFP had started in the 1870s. Eugenicists argued that hereditary conditions like feeblemindedness were best addressed through "prophylactic institutionalization" or confinement for the entire reproductive period.[36] Large-scale institutional confinement became the "backbone of the system of control" that largely worked in favor of the social and economic interests of white upper- and middle-class Anglo-Americans.[37] In other words, by adding scientific weight to the work of the AMOAIIFP, eugenics helped naturalize and (re)enforce social inequality and a hierarchy of reproduction that both uplifted the status of white middle- and upper-class (able)bodies, culture, and futures, and legitimized the pathologization, institutionalization, and reproductive constraint of poor, racialized, and disabled people. Wielding state-mandated confinement and reproductive constraint against people deemed disabled, degenerate, and dependent became legitimate means of preserving American economic and social progress for the most deserving (white able-bodied) citizens.

In the 1910s, when Bryant and the Joint Committee on Defectives in California described their work in support of the institution that became Pacific Colony, they situated themselves as part of a "nation-wide awakening to the menace of the feeble-minded." This, according to the committee members, was "one of the most noteworthy movements of . . . public thought" at the time.[38] The long history of ableism in the United States, the advocacy work of the AMOAIIFP, and the scientific backing of eugenics made their framing of feeblemindedness as an issue that required state intervention intelligible and convincing to legislators. They were indeed bolstered by a national movement. Between 1904 and 1910 the institutionalized population in the United States increased by 44.5 percent. Between 1910 and 1923 it increased another 107.2 percent.[39] The number of institutions also grew exponentially: in 1890, fourteen states had institutions for the feebleminded; by 1923, forty states in the nation had at least one, and several states had multiple institutions.[40] Eugenic sterilization laws followed this trend, with the first being passed in Indiana in 1909. After the validity of eugenic sterilization was upheld by the Supreme Court in 1927, other states followed suit, and by the 1930s more than thirty states held eugenic sterilization laws on the books.[41]

CALIFORNIA AND THE CASE FOR PACIFIC COLONY

California legislators were early converts to the national AMOAIIFP campaign regarding feeblemindedness and the need for large state-funded custodial institutions across the country. In 1887 the state took over a small privately funded facility near San Francisco called the California Home for the Care and Training of Feeble-Minded Children. Over the next several years legislators funded relocation and expansion projects, establishing the first large custodial institution of its kind in California. In 1909 the institution was renamed the Sonoma State Home and remained the state's largest institution for the feebleminded through the middle of the century.[42]

Institutionalization fell in line with the ways that many California elected officials, reformers, and state workers viewed social problems. In the early twentieth century, members of the California State Board of Charities and Corrections approached their work in the "prevention and correction" of poverty and crime through a combination of humanitarianism, science, and economics. Composed of well-to-do Anglo-American women and men, the State Board of Charities described themselves as a "business society for the wise and economical administration of the charity funds," and they viewed it as their "business to see that the unworthy are not permitted under the guise of charity to impose upon the kind hearted."[43] That is, their primary goal in addressing problems of crime and poverty in the state was not to equitably distribute private and state funds to the needy. Instead, board members saw it as their duty, as "the kind hearted," to identify and differentiated between the "worthy" and "unworthy" poor and manage these individuals in ways that eliminated or at least reduced their burden on the state. Feeblemindedness was an important scientific tool in this project of differentiation, and institutionalization was often framed as the most efficient and cost-effective solution in this management scheme.

By the 1910s the State Board of Charities and Corrections along with a coalition of researchers, educators, and other state agencies asserted that the Sonoma State Home was "wholly inadequate to care for the large numbers of feeble-minded who should become wards of the state."[44] At the time, Sonoma had a capacity of roughly fourteen hundred, and institutional authorities consistently reported overcrowding. In addition to wanting to expand the number of institutionalized people by at least one thousand, advocates of Pacific Colony wanted to extend this practice of confinement to the southern part of the state. Efforts to establish a new institution in Southern California began in earnest at the legislative level in 1915. That year, California hosted the national AMOAIIFP meeting in Berkeley, the first time the organization's national meeting was held on the West Coast.[45] Acting on momentum created by the conference, California's state legislature formed the State Joint Committee on Defectives in California, which was tasked with compiling a report for the 1917 legislature on feeblemindedness in the state as a first step toward establishing Pacific Colony.[46]

Advocating for the appropriation of state funds to build Pacific Colony, prominent researcher Lewis M. Terman declared to the state legislature that while "feeblemindedness has always existed" California researchers and state workers were only beginning to recognize "how serious a menace it is to the social, economic, and moral welfare of the state."[47] Highlighting the fundamental problem, authors of the Pacific Colony bill asserted that the feebleminded were individuals whose mental condition prevented them from "ever become[ing] self-directing citizens." Because their condition was considered inherent and hereditary, the state needed to act on their behalf and impose confinement both to prevent them from becoming a "menace to society" and so "their defect" would not be "transmitted to future generations."[48]

To back up their assertions, advocates of this second state institution presented legislators with a collection of research on feeblemindedness at both the local and national level. The legislative report in support of Pacific Colony cited work from preeminent American eugenicist Charles B. Davenport on the topic of eugenics and euthenics. It also included a piece on "Feeblemindedness as a Social Problem" penned by psychologist and prominent eugenicist Henry H. Goddard, who was also director of research at the School for Feeble-Minded Girls and Boys in Vineland, New Jersey. For expertise on the California problem of feeblemindedness, the report furnished legislators with research by Terman and his former graduate student J. Harold Williams. Terman's research played a key role in the legislative push for Pacific Colony, making him one of the principal architects behind both the elaboration of feeblemindedness and how this diagnosis was applied in California. Terman's research underscored the centrality of race in notions about intelligence and mental inferiority. In California assumptions about the inherent racial and mental inferiority of nonwhite populations—namely Mexicans, Native Americans, and African Americans—were embedded in research on the "problem" of feeblemindedness in the state.

As historians have documented, the ideology of white supremacy structured the social, cultural, political, and economic dynamics of Southern California, Pacific Colony's new home.[49] Part of Mexico until 1850, Anglo-Americans worked to impose and maintain white supremacy in Southern California in various ways. In 1862 the federal government offered Americans up to 160 acres of land to encourage westward expansion that resulted in the dispossession of Native American land and Mexican American land grants. From the late nineteenth century and into the early twentieth century, the Los Angeles Chamber of Commerce attracted even more middle- and upper-class Anglo-American settlers through an extensive "booster campaign." The Chamber of Commerce circulated hundreds of thousands of pamphlets with images portraying Southern California as a racial and economic paradise for white Americans, encouraging them to take advantage of the area's weather, cheaper land, and new economic opportunities.[50] Significantly, these booster campaigns portrayed Mexicans in the areas as either a quaint aspect of a disappearing past or as a cheap and malleable labor source, a considerable selling point for manufacturers and businessmen.[51] Thus Anglo-Americans' early understandings of Mexicans in Southern California revolved around their diminishing power in the area and their availability as menial laborers.

Anglo-American settlers established racially segregated neighborhoods in order to live out their white racial utopia, but Southern California was diverse in the early twentieth century. Mexicans were the largest nonwhite population in Los Angeles, and their population grew during the Mexican Revolution. The Black population in Los Angeles was small during the early part of the century but reached thirty-nine thousand by 1930.[52] In addition to Mexicans and African Americans, there were considerable numbers of Japanese, Chinese, and Jewish people living in Los Angeles, and while they lived largely segregated from Anglo-American communities, other neighborhoods in Los Angeles were often racially mixed.[53] By and large, Black, Mexican, Japanese, Chinese, and Jewish city residents were not only spatially segregated from Anglo dwellers, they were also relegated to low-wage industrial and service work. The social and economic marginalization of nonwhite residents was the direct result of racial discrimination, and their prevalence in low-wage jobs worked to legitimize Anglo-American settlers' beliefs that these groups were racially inferior and thus naturally destined for inferior social and economic conditions.

Anglo-Americans like Terman and the other advocates of Pacific Colony held considerable social, political, and economic power in Southern California during the early twentieth century, and they often tied their social and economic prosperity to their own racial superiority. Moreover, they asserted that their continued success and stronghold over social and political power was fundamental to progress in the state. Nonwhites, if not wholly excluded, needed to be managed in efficient and productive ways—ideally, by harnessing their labor at a low cost. Of course, racialization, political exclusion, and social marginalization did not occur uncontested. In fact, historians have documented the many revolts, labor uprisings, and resistance to racial discrimination in arenas ranging from health care to housing in Southern California.[54] They also have documented the use of policing, incarceration, and other state forms of violence to quell rebellion and unrest.[55] These examples point to a willingness among Southern California political elites to draw on practices of confinement to protect the social and economic interest of Anglo-Americans. In many ways Pacific Colony expanded the carceral capacity of Southern California, and the label of feeblemindedness became a mechanism for managing the "unworthy" in alignment with the area's existing racial and economic hierarchy.

Terman arrived in Southern California in 1905 in the midst of these ongoing efforts to construct, solidify, and police racial categories and their social implications. Born into a wealthy rural Indiana family, Terman was one of many Midwesterners enticed by the "booster campaigns" financed by the Los Angeles Chamber of Commerce.[56] A graduate of Clark University and student of renowned American psychologist Granville Stanley Hall, Terman had a deep-seated interest in theories of intelligence.[57] Like other American psychologists at the time, Terman espoused ideas about intelligence that were shaped by eugenics. He believed that intelligence was hereditary, remained constant over a person's lifetime, and could be measured using the right methods. Moreover, he accepted assertions about the relationship between intelligence and a person's morality, behavior, and economic capacity. Because intelligence level played such a decisive role in a person's behavior and economic fitness, Terman bought into the idea that accurate intelligence testing could help determine a person's overall social value. Thus he spent much of his professional career furthering these theories and developing tests to measure and rank human intelligence.

In the 1910s, Terman gained national recognition for writing the Stanford-Binet intelligence test, popularizing the Intelligence Quotient (IQ) as a numeric representation of inherent intelligence, and for his role in army recruit testing during World War I. He is largely remembered for that work, but Terman's research in support of Pacific Colony during the same period makes clear how his theories of intelligence and its social significance were bolstered by racism, classism, and ableism in the context of California. His research supported a particular interpretation of racial and class dynamics in California—that Anglo-American professionals like him needed to identify, confine, and manage the labor and reproduction of racially, mentally, and economically inferior populations in the state.

Intelligence, if properly measured, could serve as a diagnostic tool for determining individual social value—who should be a manager and who needed managing. Terman's scholarship and advocacy for Pacific Colony worked precisely toward this end.

Terman lived and worked in Southern California for five years before accepting a professorship at Stanford University in 1910.[58] While at Stanford, Terman gained prominence after revising French psychologist Alfred Binet's intelligence test (the Binet-Simon) for use in the United States.[59] He published the Stanford-Binet along with his general philosophy on intelligence and the social application of testing in his widely read monograph *The Measurement of Intelligence* (1916). Entering an ongoing debate about whether intelligence was in fact an inherited unit trait of grand social significance, Terman asserted that his test and the IQ score that it provided offered a scientific way to prove his position. As a representation of a person's "original endowment" in mental capacity, the IQ score purportedly demonstrated the existence of a hierarchy of intelligence that ranged "from idiocy to genius."[60]

Working from the assumption that the IQ score accurately reflected a person's inherent intelligence, Terman declared that determining people's level of intelligence would help answer fundamental questions of the time. These included: "Is the place of the so-called lower classes in the social and industrial scale the result of their inferior native endowment, or is their apparent inferiority merely a result of their inferior home and school training? Is genius more common among children of the educated classes than among children of the ignorant and poor? Are the inferior races really inferior or are they merely unfortunate in their lack of opportunity to learn?"[61] Of course, Terman already had his mind made up about these questions. For him, "original endowment" in intelligence was a deciding factor in all of these issues. His phrasing of these fundamental social questions underscored an important point about the cause of problems and their solution. If "inferior native endowment" caused these issues, then the solutions would have to address individual defect. If "lack of opportunity to learn" caused these issues, then the solutions would have to be structural.

With his Stanford-Binet, Terman tied an existing theory of hierarchical intelligence to numeric scores. People who did well on his test (90 and above) were labeled with an intelligence level that was "normal" (90–110), "superior" (110–120), "very superior" (120–140), and "genius" (above 140). Terman established a numeric middle ground of intelligence for people who were "dull" (80–90) but not "classifiable" by testers as feebleminded. He also reserved a space in his scoring method for "border-line deficiency" (70–80) that could be used on its own or that testers could move up to "dull" or down to "feebleminded" depending on factors outside of testing. Finally, Terman's test classified anyone who scored below 70 as displaying "definite feeblemindedness." He buttressed the categories that other psychologists used to further classify people under the umbrella term of feeblemindedness with his IQ score system as well. People who scored between 50 and 70 were labeled "morons," people who scored between 50 and 20 were labeled "imbeciles," and people who scored below 20 were labeled "idiots."[62]

The practice of testing and producing a numeric score added scientific validity to this hierarchy of intelligence, but the IQ score alone did not define mental deficiency. In his book Terman defined a feebleminded person as someone who was "incapable, because of mental defect existing from birth or from an early age, (a) of competing on equal terms with his normal fellows; or (b) of managing himself or his affairs with ordinary prudence."[63] This definition was consistent with that of other psychologists at the time, including Henry Goddard, the New Jersey eugenicist whose work was cited in the research in support of the Pacific Colony bill. According to Goddard, feeblemindedness was "a state of mental defect existing from birth or from an early age and due to incomplete or abnormal development in consequence of which, the person is incapable of performing his duty as a member of society in the position of life to which he was born."[64] In addition to asserting the congenital nature of mental deficiency, both of these definitions highlighted assessments of behavior and social status as fundamental to the process of labeling. That is, in the process of determining whether someone was feebleminded, a clinician would have to assess whether a person's behavior reflected an ability to compete with "normal fellows" and whether a person was managing their life "with ordinary prudence"—what constituted "normal fellows" and "ordinary prudence" was largely up to test administrators to decide. Moreover, administrators were in charge of assessing the status of a person—"the position of life to which he was born"—and whether that person was "performing his duty" at the level and position decided by the clinician.

Because social encounters and assessments of behavior and status were key, non-normative behaviors and people already deemed inferior were pathologized in the process of intelligence testing. Criminalized behavior, sex outside of marriage, and even simply living in impoverished conditions were already established "symptoms" of feeblemindedness by the time Terman published his test and the standard definition for mental deficiency remained in effect after the IQ score became a diagnostic tool. In 1930 the social concept of feeblemindedness became enshrined in the General Laws of California, Act 3690, Section 16, which described the condition as pertaining to "anyone who is so mentally deficient that he is incapable of managing himself and his affairs independently with ordinary prudence." Labeling and classification remained a largely subjective and uneven practice. Terman's scoring method added a sense of precision and accuracy, but it did not eliminate the use of behavior and social status to inform labeling. In fact, Terman encouraged test administrators to draw on social data about a person's economic status, family, and behavioral patterns to inform their scoring and labeling practices, particularly when determining the "higher grade" feebleminded labels of "borderline" and "moron."[65]

American psychologists repeatedly called attention to the "borderline" and "moron" level of intelligence, which they cast as especially dangerous.[66] On the one hand, they asserted that people with "normal," very high, or very low levels of intelligence could be identified readily and accurately with intelligence tests. On the other hand, they cautioned that a population of feebleminded people existed that had a level of intelligence that was just high enough to allow them to "pass" in society undetected and to score fairly well on intelligence tests, despite their inherent (and potentially dangerous) defect. Like the contemporaneous science on sexuality, concepts that were central to race science like "passing" and "mixing" made their way into theories of intelligence and mental deficiency and effectively highlighted the need for expertise in diagnostic practices.[67] Because some feebleminded people could potentially "pass" as "normal," the IQ scores could help testers identify mentally deficient people whose seemingly "normal" behavior allowed them to "pass" undetected. Likewise, deviant behavior could be used to label someone "borderline" or "feebleminded" if their IQ score was higher than a test administrator expected. Factors like economic status, family history, emotional responses, and assessments of a person's morals were important. In fact, the social aspect of the diagnostic process not only made room for but implicitly summoned ideologies of race, gender, and class in the evaluative process of matching up and making sense of IQ scores and social data. In effect, poverty, gender deviance, and nonwhite racial status were used to calibrate IQ scores and often resulted in lowering a person's assessment of inherent intelligence.

This process of combining intelligence test results with evaluations of behavior and social status largely reified existing notions of what constituted normalcy and what constituted defect along racial and class lines. It also helped clinicians, social workers, and psychologists justify a range of interventions from school segregation, social exclusion, and institutionalization. In one example, Terman described a Portuguese youth who scored in the "border-line" range on the IQ test and whose family history and behavioral assessment led to an evaluation of being "moral" and "capable." Even though his score was low, Terman determined that his good behavior would likely allow him to "pass as normal." While institutionalization was not necessary for cases like the Portuguese boy, Terman nevertheless argued that youths who fell into this class should be segregated from school because education would never "make them intelligent voters or capable citizens in the true sense of the word." Instead, Terman advocated for training people at this level of intelligence for a future as "laboring men and servant girls."[68]

After going over this particular case and expounding on the social implications, Terman extrapolated on the topic of race. He asserted that this particular level of intelligence was "very, very common among Spanish-Indian and Mexican families of the Southwest and among negroes," adding that their "dullness seems to be racial, or at least inherent in the family stocks from which they come." Furthermore, Terman described the "extraordinary frequency" with which he and his researchers found this inferior level of intelligence among "Indians, Mexicans, and negroes," arguing that the question of racial difference in intelligence should be taken up by experimental methods (i.e., intelligence testing). These meth-

ods, Terman predicted, would undoubtedly reveal "enormously significant racial differences in general intelligence, differences which cannot be
wiped out by any scheme of mental culture."[69]

Terman was not shy about the implications of his research and made
clear policy suggestions in his book. According to him, intelligence was
the trait that determined social status and social value. Thus it was vital
to the social and economic future of the nation and should be used to
inform social policy. This assertion had significant weight in the context of the expansion of public schooling. If certain populations were
found to be "unable to benefit" from schooling, then they could justifiably be excluded from regular classes. Because the general intelligence of
"Indians, Mexicans, and negroes" was found to be inferior and unchange-
able, researchers and legislators could argue that they be excluded from
public school, or at least segregated into special classes that focused on
industrial training. Indeed, instead of advocating for complete exclusion,
Terman asserted that youths with low intelligence could be trained as
"efficient workers."[70]

Moreover, Terman argued that from a "eugenic point of view," people
who fell in this range of intelligence should not be allowed to reproduce
and that their reproductive capacity constituted a "grave problem because
of their unusually prolific breeding."[71] While not stated explicitly, it was
implied that individuals who fell below this range should also be prevented
from reproducing. Institutionalization was one approach to managing the
reproduction of the mentally "unfit," but Terman and his colleagues conceded that it would be impossible to confine all people who scored poorly
on intelligence tests for the reproductive period. Deviant behavior was the
most important factor in determining the need for institutionalization,
and Terman wrote that "as long as an individual manages his affairs in
such a way as to be self-supporting, and in such a way as to avoid becoming a nuisance or burden to his fellow man, he escapes the institutions for
defectives and may pass as normal."[72]

To be clear, Terman did not leave the upper level of the intelligence
hierarchy unexamined. In addition to describing mental defect and its
implications, he also described the role that people who scored well on his
test should play in society. Not surprisingly, Terman's section on people
with superior intelligence (IQ 120–140) consisted almost entirely of the

children of Anglo-American professionals and businessmen, or people who lived in "smaller cities of California among populations made up of native-born Americans."[73] This level of intelligence, Terman wrote, was found most commonly among people of "superior social status," and it was from these populations that the nation's leaders and professionals were bred. According to Terman, youths with this level of intelligence suffered by being educated alongside youths of lower intelligence. Therefore, removing youths of low intelligence was necessary to allow learners with "normal" and "superior" intelligence to benefit from education. Even in his description of people with high IQ scores, Terman thus relied on the contrasting image of the mental defective as a burden and a drain. His opinion was clear, people of low intelligence represented the "ballast" of democracy—"not always useless but always a potential liability." In order to address that potential liability, state authorities needed to figure out how to manage them and "make the most of their limited abilities, both for their own welfare and that of society."[74] More than tools for measuring intelligence or discovering mental defect, the process of labeling worked to naturalize the existing social order and justify exclusion and inequality based on racism, ableism, and class.

On the heels of *The Measurement of Intelligence*, and in the midst of great professional success, Terman became the state's go-to expert on feeblemindedness and he put his support behind the movement for Pacific Colony. Funded by the State Board of Charities and Corrections, Terman, his former student J. Harold Williams, and Grace M. Fernald, the head of the Psychology Department and the Los Angeles State Normal School, performed several surveys to assess the impact of feeblemindedness in California. In the surveys Terman and his colleagues applied his theories of intelligence to the specific racial and economic context of California. In addition to naturalizing California's existing racial and economic hierarchies, their surveys painted a dismal picture of groups that were already under the management of the state. The researchers collected information on the "mental deviation" of four populations under the management and surveillance of the State Board of Charities: prisoners, public school students, orphans, and unwed mothers. Using Terman's testing methods, the researchers concluded that there were high rates of feeblemindedness among these populations and that increased confinement and reproductive constraint was warranted. Approaching crime, poverty, and immorality (i.e., unwed motherhood) through a population-control lens, their surveys illustrate the ways that racialized, gendered, and ableist logic structured the categories of "normal"/"defective" and "deserving"/"undeserving."

Among these populations, African Americans, Mexican-origin people, Native Americans, and newly arrived Irish, Italians, Spanish, and Portuguese were described by the researchers as exhibiting higher incidences of feeblemindedness than Anglo-Americans. Based on this data, the researchers concluded that California had drawn "a large proportion of immigrants of an undesirable type" and that "the ratio of feeble-mindedness was far higher among Mexicans, Negroes, and recent immigrants from Europe than among those of Native American [white] stock."[75] Terman, Williams, and Fernald described these populations as largely working-class and the feebleminded groups as dependent on state aid, highlighting the economic burden that mental defect represented.

Describing a California county he labeled "county x," Terman estimated that the cost of mental deficiency among poor and racialized groups amounted to $60,000 per year in "poor relief," the maintenance of juvenile courts, the cost of deportations, and the "waste" of educating feebleminded pupils.[76] Making clear that this was merely the financial cost of feeblemindedness, Terman listed social costs, including "vocational unfitness, alcoholism, general disease, and prostitution among the defective population," which he asserted were just as concerning as the financial cost.[77] Moreover, because feeblemindedness was hereditary, Terman argued that any state aid that helped this "defective population" survive economic hardship amounted to "a subsidy for the breeding of feeblemindedness."[78] All of the surveys tied population changes in California—namely the growing number of Eastern and Southern European immigrants, Mexican-origin people, and Black migrants—to the claim that there was a growing number of "socially incompetent" and fiscally burdensome people in the state. Thus the surveys highlighted for the readers—legislators, social reformers, educators, psychologists, physicians, and other interested parties—the supposed problem of feeblemindedness in California: the high proportion of mental deficiency among working-class racialized populations in the state, their deviant behavior (caused by mental deficiency), their undue economic burden, and their reproduction.[79] According to the researchers, Pacific Colony would be the most effective and efficient solution to this sprawling population problem.

In his contribution to the report that accompanied the Pacific Colony bill in 1917, Terman cited the surveys as supporting evidence and emphasized the economic cost of feeblemindedness in the state. Combining the collective cost of crime, alcoholism, pauperism, prostitution, and disease, Terman asserted that it was "reasonable to conclude that the mentally defective inhabitants of California entail a burden upon the rest of the state far in excess of $5,000,000 a year." This astronomical figure, which today would amount to approximately $110 million, became a compelling economic argument for the need to establish Pacific Colony. In fact, Terman wrote that constructing Pacific Colony would prove to be an economic investment, and confinement would "serve the state every year more than the outlay for such an institution." This cost-benefit analysis represented a eugenic argument about the way the state should manage funds allocated for the needy. State supports such as cash payments or programs that provided for the well-being of those in need were seen as contributing to the "survival of individuals who would otherwise not be able to live and reproduce." While humane, these state programs, according to Terman, resulted in an ever-increasing population of "physically unfit individuals." From the point of view of Pacific Colony advocates, the social and economic problem of feeblemindedness could only be addressed by placing individuals under the type of "state care" that could "curtail the reproduction of defectives."[80]

In order to reduce the social and economic costs of what Terman described as "nests of feeblemindedness" in Southern California, the legislature needed to fund Pacific Colony and ensure that the southern part of the state could confine at least one thousand "morons during the reproductive period" at any time.[81] Pacific Colony advocates were clear that the institution represented a long-term investment in prevention, meant to avert "the birth of several thousand of their kind within the next fifty years."[82] In a statement that foreshadowed the Supreme Court opinion in *Buck v. Bell* (1927) a decade later, Terman wrote that a "single family of 'Kallikaks,' 'Jukes,' 'Nams,' 'Hill Folk,' 'Pineys,' 'Zeros,' 'Ishmaelites,' or 'Vennams' in three or four generations costs the state in which it resides more than is asked for by the measure herein proposed. If we would preserve our state for a class of people worthy to possess it, we must prevent, as far as possible, the propagation of mental degenerates."[83] While advocates of Pacific Colony were not always explicit about who was a member of the "mental degenerate" class and who was a member of the "class of people worthy" of possessing the state, Terman's research makes clear that ableism, racism, and classism informed the construction of these two groups.

Of course, gender also played a crucial role in the push to establish Pacific Colony. Women were involved in both research and lobbying efforts on behalf of the institution. Suffragists in California were among the earliest to succeed in winning the franchise in the country, and advocating for Pacific Colony played a role in many women's efforts to forge professional and political identities as well as power for themselves.[84] The Women's Legislative Council of California (WLCC), an organization consisting of seventy-five thousand members, advocated and sponsored the 1917 Pacific Colony Bill. In addition to establishing Pacific Colony, the WLCC advocated two other propositions during that legislative session—changing community property laws to increase women's power within marriages and an amendment to state laws that would allow women to serve on juries.[85] At the same time that the WLCC worked to consolidate rights for propertied, married, and privileged white women, they were also arguing for the need to manage the freedom and reproduction of people they deemed defective and undeserving.

This dynamic characterized the relationship between upper- and middle-class white women and individuals committed to the institution in the years to come. Prominent women in Los Angeles political circles continuously threw their support behind the institution.[86] Mrs. Marie C. Flint, member of the WLCC and the well-known Club Woman, acted as chair of the committee to locate a site for Pacific Colony and later became head of the institution's board of directors. She remained active in the effort to establish the institution until she passed away in 1920.[87] Cora L. Haynes, the daughter of a prominent physician, was also active in the effort to establish Pacific Colony. Later, she went on to found the Psychopathic Association of Los Angeles and held meetings in her house to discuss the most recent scholarship on feeblemindedness and epilepsy.[88] Various women's groups including the Friday Morning Club and the Women's City Club hosted lectures on feeblemindedness and on work being conducted at Pacific Colony.[89] No doubt, these lectures and the women's positionality relative to the feebleminded—who were all mostly working class, recipients of state aid, wards of the state, and often people of color and immigrants—served to consolidate their identity as intelligent, capable, and worthy of the civic and social recognition they desired.

Women's involvement in establishing Pacific Colony and their continued involvement in the institutions' projects not only worked to affirm how they thought of themselves but also led to public service positions, career opportunities, and financial independence. As nurses, social workers, psychologists, and attendants, white middle-class women were the ideal workers to facilitate the practices of the institution. These women were often figured as especially capable for these positions and as possessing the skills necessary to collect information on patients through social work interviews, analysis of homes and neighborhoods, and by building rapport with youth in mental testing situations. This work helped establish (white) women as legitimate professionals in the helping fields, "eugenic enforcers," and as intelligent, competent, and necessary actors in protecting society and producing a better future.[90] Ideas about mental defect have historically been integral to arguments about women's inferiority to men, and claims about weak minds and bodies have long been used to justify men's dominance over women and women's exclusion from civic society.[91] No doubt aware of these stereotypes, upper- and middle-class white women in California effectively distanced themselves from categories of defect and disability through their work at Pacific Colony while maintaining other inequalities and relationships of power. In chapters 2 and 3, I expand on the role that gender played in practices of institutionalization and reproductive constraint. Next, I examine the way that advocates of Pacific Colony imagined the institution's goals and who in Southern California was subjected institutional practices of confinement, forced labor, and sterilization.

CONSTRUCTING THE COLONY

In February 1920 the state purchased 1,000 acres of land in Walnut, a small community about seven miles west of Pomona and thirty miles from

Los Angeles. By May of 1921, thirty-three young men—including sixteen-year-olds Louis Maldonado and Willard Williams, seventeen-year-old Joe Rivera, eighteen-year-old Clarence Parker, and twenty-one-year-old John Hernandez—were confined to a single building deemed by one reporter as "not in shape for patients."[92] Described as "workers from the moron and epileptic groups," and alternately referred to as "inmates" and "patients," these young men were forced to labor under the supervision of Dr. Willard C. Rappleye, a clinician from the University of California–Berkeley and Pacific Colony's first superintendent. Louis, Willard, Joe, Clarence, John, and the twenty-eight other young men paved roads, tilled the land, and became "helpers" in the construction of institutional buildings meant to confine young Californians like them.[93] These young men's confinement and labor on the construction site signified the early realization of several years of advocacy work by the men and women who backed the establishment of Pacific Colony.

Following the passage of the 1917 Pacific Colony bill, local newspapers celebrated the forthcoming institution, describing it as a place where the feebleminded would be granted the opportunity to "do something of a productive nature, according to [their] ability" and where "inmates of both sexes" would be trained "in the manual arts and domestic science."[94] This became an often lauded aspect of Pacific Colony. Columnists celebrated the notion that "inmates" who required segregation because of their inferiority and because they posed a social and biological threat would not just be confined but would be given something productive to do and might possibly obtain some sort of education, rehabilitation, or treatment. Laboring for free at the institution was one of the few ways these youth could be seen as productive and deserving of care. Unwilling to go along with this plan, however, Louis, Willard, Joe, Clarence, and John ran away from the construction site, eschewing the implications of the labels "feebleminded," "helper," "inmate," "worker."[95] The Walnut land was also unwilling to comply—or the Pacific Colony advisory board made a bad choice in site selection. The local water source did not support the large-scale institution dreamed up by Pacific Colony proponents, and the site's distance from existing rail lines meant that water and supply transport would be too costly to maintain.[96] Unfit for expansion, the institution closed in January 1923, but the push for Pacific Colony in Southern California did not end there.[97] Members of the Psychopathic Association, the State Board of Charities and Corrections, the Department of Institutions, and authorities involved in Southern California juvenile courts urged the state to fulfill the promise of the 1917 bill. In 1927 their persistence paid off and Pacific Colony reopened in a small town called Spadra, also near Pomona.

The institution's beginnings highlight two themes that remained consistent in the history of Pacific Colony into the 1950s. First, the forced labor of residents was central. Arguments about the need for Pacific Colony revolved around assertions about the social and economic burden of feeblemindedness. The institution represented an investment through reproductive constraint but advocates also asserted that, through training, some feebleminded individuals could be made productive through unpaid labor during the period of confinement. By the time the institution opened in its permanent location in 1927, institutional authorities and the public accepted that residents would be trained as institutional workers and would provide unpaid essential labor to sustain Pacific Colony. Second, the initial failure and resuscitation of Pacific Colony marked the start of what would be an ongoing insistence—despite serious concerns over abuse and overcrowding—on using public funds to confine populations in Southern California that state workers regarded as defective, burdensome, and a social menace, and to manage their labor and reproduction. An analysis of the Pacific Colony population during the first two decades of existence shows that Mexican-origin youth were disproportionately impacted by this state practice.

More than one hundred people were confined in the new Pacific Colony site by the end of 1927, and in the 1930s, despite economic uncertainty caused by the Depression, the state spent a significant amount of money building out the institution. According to leaders in juvenile research, special education, the Department of Institutions, and then Governor James Rolph, the physical expansion of Pacific Colony was not only practical but an important "investment on the part of the state."[98] In 1930 the institution grew onto an adjacent 41-acre tract and the state funded the construction of six ward buildings, a powerhouse, two residence buildings for employees, a commissary unit with a kitchen, a dining area, a store, a laundry unit, an auditorium, and a school building.[99] A year later, $652,000 of federal money was allocated to fund additional buildings, including a new hospital, an administrative building, two employee quarters, three more ward buildings, a horse barn, and a blacksmith shop.[100] By the mid-1930s the institution rested on a total of 640 acres, 100 of which were under cultivation by the people confined in the ward buildings. This massive construction took place during a time when people in need were denied social services, and state authorities in Southern California conspired to deport Mexican and Filipino immigrants accused of overburdening the state's budget.[101] Thus the choice to use scarce state and federal funds to augment Pacific Colony underscores the approach that state officials took in managing people in need who they considered undeserving, undesirable, and unproductive.

Thanks to the investment of the state, Pacific Colony, with its new buildings and modern hospital facilities, became a source of pride for proponents of institutionalization in Southern California. In March 1932, Governor Rolph joined the director of the Department of Institutions for what were described as "impressive dedication ceremonies" to celebrate the new Pacific Colony buildings.[102] Local residents, celebrities, and Southern California civic leaders came together around the state's investment. The new facilities were impressive. The hospital maintained a fifty-bed capacity with x-ray equipment, a complete specimen lab, a surgery department, a psychologist's office, and a room for periodic dentist visits. The buildings used to confine residents were referred to as "cottages" and described as "attractive one-story buildings."[103] Institutional authorities used them to segregate individuals along gendered lines and in accordance with diagnosis and age. The cottages had similar layouts, each with a large room that served as a dormitory, a shower room, a dining room, and a room meant for recreation. Whereas the individuals confined to Pacific Colony ate, slept, and showered together, the paid staff, most of whom lived on the property, had more comfortable and private accommodations. Staff lived and dined in their own building and enjoyed individual bedrooms. The superintendent, business manager, and resident physicians had entire houses to themselves with private lawns and garages where they lived with their families. Given the large tract of land and the fact that the institution had its own power source, farmland, bakery, butcher, laundry facility, hospital, and school building, Pacific Colony functioned very much like a small town, governed by the authority of the superintendent and paid workers, and sustained by the labor of confined individuals.[104]

People that visited Pacific Colony in the mid-1930s were likely impressed by the enormity of the institution, the brand-new buildings constructed to reflect a distinct "California style of architecture," and the large expanses of greenery. As one graduate student writing about the institution for her degree in social work put it: "Pacific Colony [did] not have the customary appearance of an institution."[105] Indeed, the architecture and design of Pacific Colony was drastically different from late nineteen- and early twentieth-century institutions that often consisted of large and looming multistory, corridor-style buildings. Advocates of Pacific Colony were no doubt aware of the nightmarish reputation of abuse, neglect, and overcrowding that marked these earlier asylums and state institutions. By adopting a more spread-out, cottage-style design, and by presenting an "attractive appearance," proponents of Pacific Colony tried to align themselves with a more modern, evolved, and humane approach to institutionalization. This novel architecture and layout were also a point of distinction between Pacific Colony and California's northern institution, the Sonoma State Home. Instead of subjecting inmates to confinement in large overcrowded buildings with barred windows, the structural and ideological architects of Pacific Colony settled on confinement in a more "informal and interesting" setting with single-story cottages and a strategic placement of buildings to maintain "no suggestion of crowding."[106]

While the buildings at Pacific Colony may not have suggested overcrowding to visitors looking in, the cottages were constantly used to confine more people than official capacity mandated. Despite the addition of new buildings and efforts to place inmates on parole outside of the institution, Pacific Colony authorities consistently crammed more than one hundred individuals into living quarters meant for eighty.[107] In 1936 the patient population was listed at 900, despite an official capacity of 720.[108] In 1937 institutional authorities lobbied state legislators for more funding to increase the number of cottages and address issues of overcrowding. Instead of questioning the efficacy of the institution or the need to confine so many people, the state legislature responded by allocating more than $1 million in state and federal funds used to make room for even more inmates, adding a new hospital wing, eight ward buildings, three residence buildings for employees, a mortuary, and buildings for vocational training.[109] Even with this addition, overcrowding persisted into the next decade. In the mid-1940s, Pacific Colony had a capacity of 1,250 but was confining approximately 1,500 people.

Despite state claims of benevolence, treatment, and care, the residents and their family members often charged institutional authorities with abuse and neglect. In 1946 journalist Al Ostrow published a damning exposé in the *San Francisco News* that revealed dehumanizing living conditions endured by the people confined to California state institutions.[110] In the multipart publication, Pacific Colony was among the state institutions exposed for inflicting rampant neglect on the people confined there. Photos taken by the *News* staff cameraman, Robert Warren, depicted youth sleeping on mattresses on the floor and rows of beds crammed tightly together in the dormitories. The photos showed that rooms originally meant to provide space for recreation in the ward buildings were being used as overflow for additional beds.

While Ostrow's series certainly placed into question California's treatment of people deemed mentally ill and disabled, the practice of institutionalization itself was not critiqued in any substantial way. Instead, the series' call to action and the state's response was to, yet again, increase monetary investment in practices of confinement. Despite the fact that Pacific Colony received substantial funding in the 1930s and 1940s, then governor Earl Warren responded to Ostrow's exposé by situating neglect as an unfortunate outcome of a lack of investment due to the Great Depression and World War II. Under Warren's administration, the governor promised more than $57 million to build more buildings, hire more staff, implement treatments, and expand the overall capacity of all of California's state institutions. As a result, in 1949, Pacific Colony gained two additional ward buildings and increased capacity to 1,500, but overcrowding persisted. The next year, the state purchased a 240-acre adjacent plot, and the legislature appropriated $4.7 million to double Pacific Colony's facilities and produce a 50 percent population increase.[111]

Each wave of investment into Pacific Colony during the 1930s and 1940s was sold to the public as a move toward a more enlightened approach to caring for the disabled, helping the needy, and making the unproductive earn their keep. For advocates of institutionalization, Pacific Colony symbolized scientific progress from earlier custodial institutions, framed as a "great humanitarian project" and poised to become the "finest institution of the kind in the world."[112] Although the persistent call for additional funds was cast as an effort to move away from the "asylum era" of the nineteenth century, the state was ultimately investing in the same core practices of segregation and confinement for people deemed unfit for freedom, citizenship, and parenthood. The persistence of overcrowding and neglect might have called these practices into question. But instead of questioning whether the confinement of thousands over time was a necessary solution to social problems like poverty, crime, and a lack of disability accommodations, advocates lobbied for more buildings. Once established, additional buildings created opportunities to bring even more people under the scope of state control.

POPULATING THE COLONY

Just as the young men confined to the initial Pacific Colony site laid the groundwork for literal buildings, Terman and the advocates of Pacific Colony laid the groundwork for who would be confined to them. As described earlier, researchers like Terman and Goddard drew on theories of intelligence and eugenics to establish feeblemindedness as a broad and flexible diagnosis that not only represented mental capacity but also signaled an individual's social value, whether they posed a potential threat to society, and a justification for institutionalization and sterilization. Given their estimates of the frequency of feeblemindedness in California, Terman and his colleagues conceded that it was impossible to confine everyone who performed poorly on IQ tests. Thus IQ scores and physical impairments alone did not necessarily lead to institutionalization at Pacific Colony. In fact, families who were financially well-off were rarely compelled by the state to commit their children to Pacific Colony if they scored poorly on IQ tests or were diagnosed with a disability. Certainly physicians and psychologists recommended institutionalization to parents of disabled children, and the social stigma of having a child with a disability swayed parents with means to choose institutionalization.[113]

However, their economic status made it so that they could choose insti-

Table 1   Economic status of Pacific Colony residents, 1926–46

Economic status descriptor	Number of residents	Percentage of total population
Dependent	1,003	34.3
Marginal	1,531	52.4
Comfortable	331	11.3
Unknown	57	2
Total	2,922	100

SOURCE: Author's compilation from Biennial Reports of the Department of Institutions (Sacramento: California Department of Institutions), Third-Fifth; and Statistical Reports of the Department of Institutions of the State of California (Sacramento: California Department of Institution), 1936–46.

tutionalization in smaller and well-staffed private hospitals instead of the state option of Pacific Colony. Or, if they had the means, they could provide care and therapies in the home. Class status often meant that people could preserve the autonomy of their families. In fact, the economic profile of the Pacific Colony population shows that the majority of the people confined to the institution were indigent, working-class, or of low economic means. Institutional authorities documented the economic status of 2,922 people confined to Pacific Colony between 1927 and 1946 and more than half (or 52 percent) were described as "marginal," meaning of low economic means. One-third (or 34 percent) of the residents were described as "dependent," meaning that they were receiving some form of state aid. Only 11 percent of the people committed during the almost twenty-year period were described as economically "comfortable," and the economic status of the remaining individuals was "unknown." Thus poverty was instrumental in practices of institutionalization at Pacific Colony.[114]

Needing state aid often exposed families to interactions with state authorities such as social workers who would often make judgments about the mental capacity of people in their caseload. This was not the only path to Pacific Colony. Interactions with educators, police officers, and juvenile court officials were also events that could lead to institutionalization. As California social worker Winifred Wardell noted in his study of institutional care for the feebleminded in the state: "The simple fact of feeblemindedness does not usually involve outside agency."[115] What largely determined need for institutionalization were assessments about "delinquent conduct against society," whether an individual was brought "to the attention of the juvenile court, [or] social agencies," or if state workers deemed someone a threat to society. As a different social worker described it in her study of feeblemindedness in California: "Some form of overt rebellion against society was necessary to bring the problem of mental deficiency to the attention of interested agencies."[116]

The primacy of contact with state workers in decisions regarding institutionalization is evident in the fact that the principal pathway to Pacific Colony was the Southern California Superior Courts system. County probation officials, social workers, and juvenile court agents used the power of the court system to mandate institutionalization and most were committed to Pacific Colony in this manner.[117] Others were already wards of the state, also mandated through the courts, and were transferred to Pacific Colony from reform schools, orphanages, or boarding schools. Sometimes, transfers from these state facilities to Pacific Colony occurred because of medical concerns or beliefs that a youth would receive more appropriate care in an institution for the feebleminded. For example, Martha, a fourteen-year-old who spent much of her life in foster homes and orphanages, was transferred to Pacific Colony in 1935 after "several serious episodes of menorrhagia."[118] Because many of these youths had no parents or came from families of little means, Pacific Colony was one of few options for medical care. In a study by Florence Frisch, the social work student describes multiple cases in which parents sought out medical care in settings outside of the institution but were unsuccessful or could not afford the cost of such care.[119]

In other cases, transfers to Pacific Colony followed a disruptive incident such as fighting or challenging authority figures and were thus framed as punishment for bad behavior. Unsurprisingly, given the ways delinquent behavior was racialized, transfers to Pacific Colony from California state juvenile reform schools occurred along racial lines. In her monograph on Mexican American youths in California reform schools, historian Miroslava Chávez-García demonstrated that delinquent youth of Mexican-origin represented up to 25 percent of all children and adolescents transferred from state reformatories to state institutions for the feebleminded, concluding that youths of Mexican-origin who were placed in reform schools "were disproportionately being identified as defective delinquents who were in need of permanent care and sterilization in Sonoma or the Pacific Colony."[120] Again, parents certainly initiated commitment procedures to Pacific Colony, but the overcrowded condition of the institution meant that there was always a waitlist that often numbered in the hundreds. These waitlists, according to Wardell, had "no meaning" because "commitments filed by parents or guardians [were] rarely actualized."[121] Indeed, commitments through the Superior Courts and institutional transfers were often prioritized, enacting institutional efforts to confine individuals not on the basis of needy parents but on the basis of state desires to confine perceived threats.

That poverty and behavior shaped diagnostic patterns and the lived implications of being labeled with a disability underscores the social construction of feeblemindedness as a category of disability. Not only were subjective assessments about economic competence and social threat used to define the condition, but they were also used to determine who should suffer the most severe consequences of the diagnosis—the complete stripping of bodily and reproductive autonomy through confinement and sterilization. The role that social factors played in determining diagnosis and institutionalization evinces disability theorist Tobin Siebers's point that "disability is not a pathological condition, only analyzable via individual psychology, but a social location complexly embodied."[122] To be clear, California state authorities were not unique in their use of disability labels to confine people deemed economically and socially incompetent. Institutions in Illinois, North Carolina, and Minnesota likewise targeted the working class, the disabled, and people deemed socially deviant.[123] Pacific Colony's demographic patterns of commitment make evident the way that the racial dynamics of Southern California shaped ideas about who among the supposed feebleminded required confinement and sterilization in a state institution. A demographic analysis of who was committed to Pacific Colony clearly indicates how the racialization of Mexicans as inferior came together with feeblemindedness, resulting in the targeted confinement of Mexican-origin youth.

Available data on the age of the 2,505 residents of Pacific Colony confined between 1927 and 1945 shows that youths in their teens were primary targets for institutionalization, and 67 percent of the population confined during this time was between ten and nineteen years old. Youths in their mid- to late teens (between fifteen and nineteen) made up 39 percent of the total population confined during this period. The targeting of youths for confinement aligned with efforts to identify and institutionalize the feebleminded during the reproductive period and was also the result of a reliance on educators and juvenile court authorities to identify individuals who represented a social menace. However, not all Southern California youths were equally impacted, and Mexican-origin youths were targeted for confinement at rates that were disproportionate to their population in the state.

Faith Barber, a graduate student in education studying under Norman Fenton of the California Bureau of Juvenile Research, documented this targeted institutionalization in her 1935 study of Pacific Colony with a table labeled "Race Distribution of the Population." This table showed the "White" population in California at 88.8 percent and the "White" population in Pacific Colony at 80.2 percent. In contrast, individuals with the racial label "Mexican" represented 15.3 percent of the population confined to Pacific Colony but only 6.5 percent of the population in the state.[124] This targeting of Mexican-origin youths for institutionalization continued well into the 1940s. In 1947 the psychology department at Pacific Colony made a survey of the "racial background or nationality" of the population, finding 72.3 percent of the institutionalized to be "Whites (exclusive of Mexicans)," 21.2 percent "Mexicans," 5 percent "Negroes," 0.8 percent "Japanese & Chinese," and 0.7 percent "Indians."[125]

An analysis of the racial categories used to classify individuals committed to Pacific Colony between 1927 and 1947 shows that out of the 4,165 people admitted during that period, 907, or approximately 21 percent, were labeled with an "M" to indicate Mexican.[126] Clearly, Southern California state workers considered the Mexican-origin population in the state mentally and socially inferior to such an extent that they required confinement at Pacific Colony at rates that were disproportionate to their population in the state. Moreover, the fact that a large majority of these youths—more than 90 percent—were born in the United States indicates a primary concern over American-born citizens of Mexican descent in the state.[127] The demographic and diagnostic patterns of admission to Pacific

Table 2   Age of Pacific Colony residents, 1936–46

Age	Number of residents	Percentage of total population
Under 10	409	16.3
10–14	693	27.7
15–19	986	39.4
20–24	189	7.5
25–29	91	3.6
30 and above	137	5.5
Total	2,505	100

SOURCE: Author's compilation from Biennial Reports of the Department of Institutions (Sacramento: California Department of Institutions), Third-Fifth; and Statistical Reports of the Department of Institutions of the State of California (Sacramento: California Department of Institution), 1936–46.

Colony reflect the ways in which ideas about race, class, citizenship, and disability came together to target certain bodies for confinement in the institution. Once confined, these youths were often subjected to forced labor and sterilization under the guise of "treatment" and "care."

THE PACIFIC PLAN: MANAGING THE LABOR AND REPRODUCTION OF THE "UNFIT"

In the summer of 1932, the same year that Governor Rolph celebrated the new construction at Pacific Colony, the institution hosted the Fourth Annual Conference of the California Bureau of Juvenile Research. This was an opportunity for experts and authorities across the state in the fields of education, psychology, social work, and juvenile justice to tour the new facilities and witness the scientific progress being made in Southern California. During this meeting, Dr. Norman Fenton of the California Bureau of Juvenile Research, presented a paper outlining what institutional authorities named the "Pacific Colony Plan." According to Fenton and the audience, the "Pacific Plan" represented a novel, "humanized," and "scientific program of treatment" that marked a "new era" in practices of institutionalization.[128] Aware that the state was experiencing "times of economic duress" because of the Great Depression, Fenton framed the Pacific Colony plan as a worthy investment that balanced idealism and practicality through an efficient use of education and training.[129]

In his presentation Fenton described individualized educational programs for each person committed to Pacific Colony with the goal of developing their abilities and maintaining their happiness. He contrasted this plan with what was occurring in institutions for the feebleminded in other states, which he described as "depressing custodial places" where people were "merely fed and clothed."[130] At Pacific Colony, Fenton asserted, the "eternal children" confined to the institution received education consistent with their level of ability and staff maintained the "well-being and happiness of these inmates." While the Pacific Plan emphasized individualized education and the contentedness of the confined, the reality of life in the institution from the 1930s into the early 1950s was drastically different. The training and education that most residents received revolved around unpaid labor in the institution. For those deemed capable enough to eventually be released, vocational training meant creating a pipeline into low-wage labor outside of the institution. Moreover, complete discharge, was made contingent on being sterilized. Far from education and contentedness, "care" in Pacific Colony was premised on managing the labor and reproduction of residents.

While the Pacific Plan presented by Fenton in 1932 was novel in its centering of education, it also replicated the vision of institutionalization that members of the AMOAIIFP described in the late nineteenth century. Referring to their ideas simply as the "colony plan," AMOAIIFP members like Dr. George H. Knight of the Connecticut Training School for the Feeble-Minded touted an institutionalization model that rationalized the mass confinement of people with different physical and mental abilities in one institution. This "colony plan" drew on the principles of imperialism and took advantage of the deliberately broad and flexible application of the label of feeblemindedness to justifiably confine "all grades of feeble-minded" and extract labor from "inmates."[131] Under the model people with severe physical or mental disabilities, often referred to as "custodial cases," could be institutionalized in large numbers as long as "high-grade" able-bodied individuals were confined in the same institutions to help care for them. In addition to providing care for physically impaired inmates, "high-grade" individuals (who were considered "children no matter what the age") were also tasked with maintaining facilities and grounds, thereby facilitating the expansion and upkeep of the institution.

At the International Congress of Charities, Correction and Philanthropy held at the World's Columbian Exposition in Chicago in 1893, Knight asserted that the "colony plan" offered the "high-grade feebleminded" a "market for [their] labor" and offered "custodial cases" an opportunity for development and care. According to the AMOAIIFP, this nineteenth-century "colony plan" was a scientific achievement in both humanitarian and economic respects and appealed to the interest of people on two sides of an ongoing debate: reformers who believed it was the state's responsi-bility to care for people in (medical, economic, social) need and reformers who believed supporting these people was a waste of public funds. As one proponent of the colony model wrote: "Any successful plan for the care of these unfortunates which makes for their well-being, increases their economic value and consequently reduces their cost to the State should be of vital interest to the humanitarian and the taxpayer. Such a plan is the so-called colony system."[132]

The 1917 Pacific Colony bill included a piece by Joseph P. Byers, exec-utive secretary of the National Committee on Provision for the Feeble-Minded, that described the colony plan as the appropriate model for the Southern California institution (and this model likely inspired its name). Byers's piece displayed keen awareness of the economic cost of establish-ing an institution, writing that mass confinement of people "both for their own and for society's protection" would "make large demands on the revenues of the state." If the "humanitarian" aspect of this effort was not enough to convince legislatures to make this investment, then Pacific Colony needed to design "public care" such that the confined would be "usefully employed" and "economically housed."[133] To highlight this point, Byers compared institutionalization to industry, writing that "no manu-facturer of today has let the by-product of his plan go to waste as society has wasted the energies of this by-product of humanity." Revealing his clear disdain for the people he sought to have confined, Byers asserted that the colony plan represented an opportunity for states to make people labeled feebleminded productive so that society could "stop paying for their keep ... without getting any return, and put them in colonies at useful employment."[134] Thus, far from acting on a mere moral or humanitarian impetus to provide care for people who were suffering from physical, mental, or economic hardships, the colony plan was squarely about devising a way to make people productive or at least less burdensome on the state.

The "Pacific Colony Plan" outlined by Fenton in 1932 followed through on the general "colony plan" and emphasized admitting individuals along a spectrum of impairment and ability in order to use residents as sources of labor. In his presentation he described the three main purposes of the institution: (1) to provide custodial care and treatment for the "helpless and ill"; (2) to create a community in the institution, supervised by paid staff, consisting of people who were "able to work and to be useful yet lack the capacity to live adequate lives in the community on their own responsibility"; and (3) to train "high-grade defectives, usually of the moron level for placement in the outside world."[135] This third effort—to train and release certain individuals—likely represented the most novel departure from the standard colony plan. Proponents of institutionalization in the late nineteenth century imagined that people labeled feebleminded would have to remain confined through the reproductive period, but with the advent of sterilization in the early twentieth century, release without the fear of reproduction became a possibility. At Pacific Colony institutional authorities took as a given that some of the "helpless and ill" would require confinement for most of their (if not for their entire) lives, and that some "higher-grade" residents were needed in the institution to help provide that care. But the idea that some "higher-grade" residents could be trained and released through a process they referred to as "social regeneration" was often highlighted and celebrated as proof that the institution could implement education, treatment, and even produce self-sufficient and productive citizens.[136]

The Pacific Colony Plan shaped the commitment efforts of institutional authorities, who tried as much as possible to orchestrate an appropriate balance of differing abilities among the people they confined. They tried to keep the "helpless and ill" population lower than the number of purportedly "high-grade" residents so that there were enough laborers to maintain the institution. They also sought to maintain a steady stream of "high-grade" inmates who they regarded as eligible for release, flowing through the institution so that they could reach as many people as possible. This way, institutional authorities not only managed people who were confined to the Pacific Colony property but also the "high-grade" people who were placed on parole outside of the institution.

Implementing this plan depended on assigning the residents membership in one of three groups: the "custodial class," who required medical care and would likely live in the institution for the rest of their lives; the "institutional workers," who would also likely live in the institution for most of their lives but who were physically able to perform work in the institution; and the "vocational class," who represented the "high-grade" population that could potentially be trained and placed in a low-wage position outside of the institution. Upon commitment, individuals endured a long process of physical and psychological exams to help determine their placement at Pacific Colony and the institution's physician administered medical treatments if necessary. Their classification often determined which ward they would live in, whether they were given any academic schooling at all, and the type of labor they were expected to perform in the institution. On Friday afternoons the medical staff and the heads of the school, social service, and psychology departments met to make decisions about the course of action for new inmates, who might be eligible for parole from the institution, and who required sterilization.[137]

In many ways classification in one of these three groups represented the individualized education that Fenton described in his Pacific Colony Plan, and an individual's classification dictated what their experience at Pacific Colony would look like. An individual assigned to the "custodial class" likely remained confined to their cottage most of the time and was cared for by both paid staff and unpaid institutionalized laborers. Individuals classified as eligible to work spent a large portion of their day doing so—in fact, they performed almost all of the labor in the institution. A typical day for them consisted of waking up around 5:30 a.m. and being shuffled to the bathroom to get dressed for breakfast at 6:30. By 8:00 a.m. they had to report to their work detail, unless they worked in the kitchen or bakery, which meant that they had to wake up earlier than the others to help prepare and serve breakfast. Some might spend a couple of hours in the school building before or after lunch, depending on what their work detail demanded and whether institutional authorities thought they could benefit from schooling. Dinner was served at around 5:00 p.m. and then residents were given a couple of hours of recreation, if they weren't working, before an early bedtime around 8:00 p.m.[138] Some of the ward buildings had their own radios that provided entertainment in the evenings. People who were confined to Pacific Colony in the mid- to late 1930s were allowed a weekly motion picture that played the newsreel and feature movies from the Motion Picture Exchange. There was also a weekly dance during which staff played phonograph records over a public-address system and supervised the residents in attendance.[139]

In the mid-1930s, Pacific Colony depended on the labor of almost half of the people confined there.[140] Labor assignments were often segregated by gender. About fifty young women worked in the laundry building washing, sewing, and ironing all of the clothes and bedding. Groups of young women were charged with caring for the "helpless and custodial patients." Young women were also charged with serving employees as "waitresses and pantry helpers" in the employees' dining room. Institutional authorities made several women work as domestics in the houses of the superintendent, business manager, and resident physician. About fifty young men tended to the farm and the vegetable garden and were in charge of maintaining the landscaping of the vast expanses of green space that made the institution look so welcoming to visitors. Both men and women were assigned to cleaning details to maintain their own living spaces. There were also separate work details for the bakery, butcher, and blacksmith shop.[141] Through their labor these young women and men fulfilled the ideal proposed by the AMOAIIFP in the late nineteenth century, supporters of the Pacific Colony bill in 1917, and Dr. Fenton in 1932. Although the argument for the existence of Pacific Colony rested on the notion that the dependent and "unfit" required institutionalization, in effect the institution was dependent on residents.

Not only did Pacific Colony depend on the unpaid labor of the confined, but institutional authorities viewed this labor as "useful training" for those in the "vocational class" who, if managed appropriately, could build on that training and "go out and take their places in the world after leaving the institution."[142] Among the most celebrated parts of the Pacific Colony Plan was the placement of individuals from the "vocational class" on what was called "industrial parole."[143] These were parole placements in low-wage jobs outside of the institution. Eligibility for industrial parole relied largely on good behavior, assessments of emotional stability, and adequate performance of labor in the institution. In large part, industrial parole resulted in placements laboring on local ranches or working as domestics in the homes of local physicians or middle- and upper-class families in the area. Others provided child care for these same households. Sometimes residents would be sent to work as attendants in local hospitals and sanitariums. Placements were negotiated by one of the institution's social workers and the employer, and if residents made any trouble they were sent back to Pacific Colony.[144]

In her 1935 thesis on Pacific Colony, graduate student Faith Barber remarked that the industrial parole program was one of the most important features of the institution, and that individuals who were successfully discharged represented proof of the effectiveness of their plan. Society benefited from an "economic standpoint" because, upon release, individuals became "self-sustaining members of society."[145] What this particular institutional practice reveals, however, are the ways that people who were institutionalized were trained for and funneled into low-wage and often coercive work situations that were justified on the basis of their supposed inferiority. In order to set up this institution-to-low-wage-work-pipeline, institutional authorities denied many school-age inmates basic educational experiences in favor of making them labor in the institution as training for service and industrial jobs.

The testimony of people who were committed to Pacific Colony highlights the exploitative nature of forced labor in the institution and the lack of individualized education described by Fenton in the early 1930s. Martha, who was committed to Pacific Colony in 1935, described her confinement as "a rotten deal," stating: "I had my freedom taken away." She recalled: "Nobody paid me anything. I did all that work every day and never got one cent. They just kept us smarter patients there because if it wasn't for us who'd do the work? The employees wouldn't do it. They just stand around and make the patients work." Martha's recollection of her experience evinces a clear awareness of the fact that she was being exploited by institutional authorities at Pacific Colony.[146] She also points to a disturbing practice of keeping residents confined to meet labor needs as opposed to reasons of treatment and care.

Another person who was committed to the institution cited the lack of education he experienced while confined as negatively impacting his life once he was released. He stated: "All my problems in making good on the outside is due to just one thing—I didn't get no schooling at all in that colony. How can you make good without no schooling?" Another former Pacific Colony resident stated that she worried about not being able to "talk as good as other people. You know, like numbers and reading and all that. But how can I? I was in that hospital for eight long years and I didn't learn nothing about how to think or act on the outside."[147] Their testimony exposes how the institution's focus on labor at the exclusion of education shaped the experiences of former Pacific Colony residents in ways that were harmful and disabling.[148] That is, by denying residents education and segregating them from society for such a long time, state authorities actually prevented them from developing the skills necessary to participate in economic and social life outside of the institution.

The focus on industrial training in Pacific Colony went hand in hand with institutional practices of sterilization. An integral part of institutionalization was preventing reproduction in an effort to manage and eliminate "unfit" populations. This went in line with eugenic notions of mental deficiency as hereditary, but sterilizations were performed even when the inheritability of defect was questionable. People diagnosed as feebleminded were cast as unfit to parent regardless of heritability, and parenthood was often framed as an impediment to self-sufficiency. In California institutional authorities enthusiastically supported sterilization for people confined to state institutions. In 1909 a eugenic sterilization law was passed that granted institutional authorities the power to perform sterilizations at their discretion and without consent. Significantly, the 1917 Pacific Colony bill included a sterilization provision that made any person committed to the institution eligible for sterilization. At the level of the institution, however, sterilization did more than prevent reproduction. It was also seen as a necessary component of industrial parole and of any plans for release from the institution. It was the general policy at Pacific Colony to sterilize all patients prior to placement on parole, which was described as "in the line of preventative medicine."[149] In this way the institution could "safely" parole residents, making room for others to be committed, trained, and sterilized. According to California eugenicists

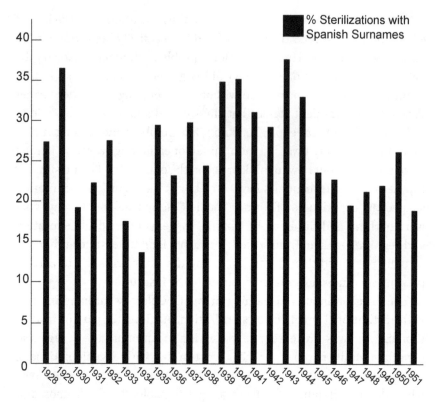

Figure 2. Sterilization requests by Spanish surname per year, 1928–51. See Table 4 in the appendix for the yearly sterilization request counts.

and institutional authorities, even if a purportedly feebleminded person did not properly adjust economically or socially once released from the institution, they were, at the very least, unable to propagate more "unfit" children.[150]

At Pacific Colony practices of sterilization mirrored the racial patterns of commitment. An analysis of more than two thousand sterilization requests processed by Pacific Colony between 1928 and 1951 reveals that Mexican-origin inmates were subject to sterilization at a rate that was disproportionate to their population in the state. From 1928 to 1951, Spanish-surnamed patients made up approximately 25 percent of all of the Pacific Colony sterilization requests processed during this period, and Mexican-origin youths in particular were targeted for sterilization. The average age for Spanish-surnamed patients over the twenty-two-year time span was eighteen for women and sixteen for men. When broken down by year, a review of the sterilization requests reveals that Spanish-surnamed youths consistently represented a high rate of inmates deemed in need of sterilization. In 1943 they made up 37.5 percent of all of the sterilization requests processed by Pacific Colony. Over the entire twenty-three-year period their requests never fell below 13.6 percent of the total number of requests.

The economic, reproductive, and social futures of the people committed to Pacific Colony were determined by institutional authorities who viewed them as fit for labor, fit to reproduce the institution, and potentially able to become self-supporting and productive citizens—but resolutely unfit for reproduction. Chapter 2 examines the racial and gendered aspects of confinement and sterilization and details the ways that concerns over working-class Mexican-origin women's sexuality and fertility came together with ideas about mental defect in Southern California.

2 The Mexican Sex Menace

LABOR, REPRODUCTION, AND FEEBLEMINDEDNESS

Valentina Cordova wore her best dress, deep red lipstick, and perfectly coiffed hair for her Saturday night date. She mastered the hairstyle during her downtime with the other girls in Cottage 3 at Pacific Colony, where she had been confined for five long years. When they weren't working on the laundry detail or taking care of infants in the nursery building, these young women talked about romance, fashion, hair, and makeup. They shared stories about Pacific Colony staff and the young men in the boys' cottages. They made hopeful plans for life outside of the institution.[1]

It was a beautiful Southern California fall evening in 1943 when Valentina readied herself for this date. By this point, she had been on parole from the institution for about three months. She was working as a live-in domestic at the house of Dr. Smith', a prominent physician in the area. The social worker at Pacific Colony coordinated Valentina's work arrangement and those of all the other residents deemed sufficiently "stabilized," "trained," and ready to become "self-supporting and useful members of society" by the clinicians in charge.[2] Most often these jobs meant long hours, low wages, and close supervision, reflecting institutional authorities' limited vision for the "social regeneration" of the young people they confined, managed, and sterilized. In their view, low wages were

Figure 3. Laundry Building at Pacific Colony, ca. 1921. Courtesy of the California History Room, California State Library, Sacramento.

appropriate given the intelligence level of Pacific Colony residents, the long hours kept them busy, and constant supervision was needed to keep them out of trouble. Psychologists, juvenile authorities, and social workers agreed: young women like Valentina should be put to work and closely watched both in and out of state institutions. After spending most of her teenage years in Pacific Colony, Valentina wanted to be free from that life.

Like many nineteen-year-olds, Valentina was excited about the prospects of a new romance, and she didn't want her employer interfering in her love life. When Dr. Smith asked her where she was going in her best outfit on her only day off, Valentina lied. Years of personal experience taught her not to trust doctors or state authorities. Her mother, a Mexican American woman, was born in Southern California in 1881, when Los Angeles was becoming a significant point of attraction for wealthy white Midwesterners. Valentina's mother was young when she married a handsome Mexican immigrant, and they had six children together. When Valentina's father abandoned their family amid the Great Depression, her mother did what so many other Americans had to do: she asked for help from the local welfare office. In exchange for that help, social workers demanded access to Valentina's house, tracking and judging every move her mother and siblings made. When Valentina's older brother and sister got into trouble, local parole officers worked with the family's state-appointed social worker to send them four hundred miles north to the Sonoma State Home for the Feebleminded.

Around the same time, Valentina's aunt Elena was committed to Pacific Colony, labeled a "moron" and sterilized. In their notes on Elena, clinicians stated that she had a "history of sexual promiscuity" because she had three children outside of marriage. Then, when Valentina was thirteen, the social workers came for her mother, who was also committed to Pacific Colony. Because her mother and siblings were imprisoned in different state institutions, Valentina became a ward of the court, and juvenile authorities sent her to St. Vincent's, a Catholic reform school for girls. Valentina was furious. The labeling and the family separation built up a wave of anger in her, and it came out violently. Eventually the Sisters at St. Vincent's gave up on Valentina; they assumed that the fighting signaled some sort of mental defect or disorder instead of trauma and pain. Her family history supported this assumption and authorities at St. Vincent's petitioned the court to have Valentina transferred to Pacific Colony, where she joined her aunt and mother.

In less than a decade, state social workers, legal authorities, and clinicians labeled and institutionalized two generations of Valentina's family. Then, the summer right before she went to live and work at Dr. Smith's, a physician at Pacific Colony sterilized Valentina against her wishes. Thus Valentina was keenly aware of the power state authorities had over her life and future, and she knew Dr. Smith was their surrogate. Even while his family benefited from Valentina's labor, Dr. Smith replaced Pacific Colony as Valentina's custodian. He was charged with supervising her and reporting details about her life and work to Pacific Colony authorities. In the 1940s certain populations of young people in Southern California enjoyed increased leisure time and were allowed (and even encouraged) to engage in youthful romance, but Valentina's situation was drastically different. A first date could have severe consequences for a young Mexican American girl who was labeled "feebleminded." A first date was ripe for analyses and assumptions about her mental state, her sexuality, and whether she deserved freedom. Lying to Dr. Smith was a form of protection. Valentina didn't want to get sent back to Pacific Colony over a date. A month later, she went a step further. Tired of being overworked, underpaid, and denied privacy, she left. Without permission or notice, Valentina escaped from the surveillance and control that had marked her and her family for most of her teenage years.

Valentina's experience both in and out of Pacific Colony is demonstrative of the ways that Southern California state workers tried to manage and control working-class Mexican-origin women's sexual and reproductive lives. In their invaluable research Chicana scholars have detailed the ways that young working-class Mexican-origin women negotiated systems of sexual, reproductive, and economic oppression both in the home and in American society during the early to mid-twentieth century.[3] I build on their work to illustrate how California state authorities, including social workers, educators, and Pacific Colony attendants and clinicians, applied the concept of disability through the diagnosis of feeblemindedness to young Mexican-origin women's sexual and reproductive lives. The concept of feeblemindedness situated the sexual and reproductive lives of young working-class Mexican-origin women as legitimate sites of control. In framing their sexual and reproductive behaviors as symptomatic of mental defect and labeling them feebleminded, state workers were able to bring young Mexican-origin women under their "care." Backed by the scientific weight of a psychological diagnosis, state authorities ordered the institutionalization and sterilization of hundreds of Mexican-origin women at Pacific Colony, including generations of women within families, like the Cordovas. Bringing working-class Mexican-origin women's sexual and reproductive behaviors under this lens of defect and deficiency, state authorities were able to justify the policing of entire working-class families and intervene in the lives of Mexican-origin women, denying them freedom, privacy, and reproductive autonomy.

The beliefs and policies that motivated state workers to surveil, institutionalize, and sterilize Mexican-origin women like Valentina and her family were grounded in profoundly gendered ideologies of race and disability. California eugenicists produced research on mental deficiency that created a gendered symptomology for diagnosing feeblemindedness wherein low mental capacity was correlated with deviant sexual behavior and hyperfertility among women. In California this symptomology went in line with the ways that Mexican-origin women were already racialized as culturally backward and inferior. Moreover, efforts to manage young Mexican-origin women's sex and reproduction were tied to ideas about their role in the state's economy as low-wage workers.

The expressed purpose of institutionalization and sterilization was to facilitate young working-class Mexican-origin women's entry into low-paid domestic, industrial, and care work. Their successful release from the institution was contingent on their sterilization and performance of labor in the institution, after which they would be assigned to work placements. Extending historian Sarah Haley's analysis of Black female deviance in the criminal legal system in the South to the Pacific Colony context, casting Mexican-origin women as sexual deviants who could labor but not reproduce moved the purpose of labeling and institutionalization beyond segregation and reproductive constraint to the ideal goal of training able-bodied Mexican-origin women to enter a "system of gendered and racialized economic exploitation and social control."[4] In addition to establishing a larger labor pool, this process also legitimized the superiority of white authorities in the "helping professions" and naturalized social and economic hierarchies of race, gender, and ability. As a result, state agents held considerable power over the lives, labor, and reproductive future of young Mexican-origin women who were committed to Pacific Colony. While this power was often overwhelming, when we examine the experiences of Mexican-origin women in Pacific Colony and upon their release, we get a sense of how they negotiated this power in an attempt to live and love on their own terms.

RACE, SEX, AND REPRODUCTION IN THE CONSTRUCTION OF MEXICAN-ORIGIN WOMEN'S DIFFERENCE

Valentina and her family's experience with state workers and institutions underscores the way that disability labels like "feeblemindedness" reified age-old stereotypes about Mexican-origin women's sexual and reproductive behavior. Sex and reproduction have long been sites of oppression and control for the working class, Women of Color, and people with disabilities in the United States.[5] Cast as deviant in ways often tied to crime and poverty, the sexual and reproductive lives of marginalized populations have historically been "marked for management" by state authorities.[6] Mexican-origin women have negotiated negative stereotypes about their sexuality and reproduction in California since at least the nineteenth century, and these stereotypes have largely worked to fit Mexican-origin women into the political economy in a particular way. As Chicana historians have demonstrated, sexual and reproductive deviance were some of the first ways that American imperialists discussed Mexican women as different, "other," and inferior.[7] Claiming ownership over California after the U.S. war with Mexico, Anglo-American men wrote and consumed literature that drew on racism and sexism to construct Mexican women as racially and morally inferior. Stereotypes of Mexican women as sexually immoral worked to rationalize the dispossession of land and the social and economic subordination of Mexicans who remained in California under Anglo-American settler expansion.[8]

Mexican women's sexual and reproductive otherness carried additional weight in the context of American xenophobia, nativism, and immigration restriction. Nativists have framed nonwhite immigrant motherhood as a threat to the nation both in racial and economic terms since at least 1890.[9] Historian Martha Gardner has written that fear over "the threat of immigrant women's reproduction" was so prevalent at the turn of the twentieth century that it became a "clarion call to those seeking to shore up the nation's defenses against the inassimilable and unwanted."[10] This threat was both a matter of racial degeneracy and a matter of rights and citizenship, as concerns over birthright citizenship and the Fourteenth Amendment erupted in the early twentieth century.[11] Understood as racially inferior, Mexican immigrant women's reproduction in the United States was often derided as contributing to "race suicide."[12] In addition to fears over the dilution of Anglo-American racial purity, nativists asserted that immigrant mothers and their American children represented an undue burden on the nation's economy because they were "likely to become a public charge."[13]

The racial and economic threat that Mexican immigrant women's sexual and reproductive behaviors posed to the nation was further compounded by assertions that Mexican-origin women were "hyperfertile." The characterization of Mexican-origin women's reproduction as hyperfertile was prevalent in late nineteenth-century literature and, as sociologist Elena Gutiérrez's seminal research has shown, hyperfertility became a constitutive piece of Mexican-origin women's supposed racial difference.[14] This stereotype persisted in early twentieth-century social science scholarship. These early sociological studies, Gutiérrez writes, were foundational in figuring Mexican-origin women's sexual and reproductive behaviors as irrational, premodern, out of control, and inefficient. In this way the constitutive aspects of their racial difference (irrational reproduction) marked Mexican-origin women as not only inferior but antithetical to white American behaviors, which, by contrast, were viewed as modern, prudent, and responsible.

The stereotype of Mexican-origin women as hyperfertile circulated well beyond social science circles, shaping the ways that California state authorities described Mexican-origin residents and the significance of their existence in the state. Gutiérrez describes a 1930 report prepared by the Mexican Fact-Finding Commission in California that stated Mexican-origin births equaled one-sixth of the total births in the state. Similarly, a Los Angeles County Health Department report form the same time period described Mexican-origin births as growing exponentially. As Gutiérrez asserts, studies like these communicated a false notion that the Mexican-origin population would outnumber the white Anglo population in the state, thereby stoking racist concerns over a decline in white economic, political, and cultural dominance.[15]

These reports took on additional significance in the context of the Great Depression, when state authorities sought to deny state aid to Mexican-origin residents who were already seen as inherently foreign and thus undeserving of aid meant for "real" Americans. The economic ramification of the supposed increase in the Mexican birth rate was an issue for several Los Angeles agencies, including the county welfare system, where officials often accused Mexican families of burdening the state's resources.[16] In a 1934 article in the *Los Angeles Times* titled "Aliens Load Relief Roll," the author expressed clear disdain over the number of Mexican families receiving aid. Discussing a report issued by Earl E. Jensen, the county superintendent of charities, the article stated that with sixty-three thousand Mexicans on relief, twenty-three thousand of whom were American citizens, Mexican "aliens" were "placing an extremely heavy burden upon the taxpayers of Los Angeles county."[17] According to Jensen, the support of these "Mexican aliens" added up to a financial burden to Los Angeles taxpayers of $2.4 million a year. Indeed, the widely accepted notion that Mexican women's reproductive behaviors were out of control and caused racial degeneration was compounded by assumptions about the financial dependency of Mexican families. All of this influenced the ways that Southern California officials approached the "Mexican problem." This "problem" was distinct from early twentieth-century concerns over the (in)ability of Mexicans to assimilate to American culture.[18] This was a problem of racial demographics, reproduction, and economics.

As historian George Sanchez's study of Americanization programs in California from 1915 to 1929 illustrates, the racial and economic rationale that state authorities used to justify their attempts to manage Mexican-origin women's reproduction were not just about excluding them from state aid. Americanization teachers—authorized by California law to enter the homes of Mexican families—attempted to manage the reproductive behaviors of mothers and daughters as a way to maintain a broader economic industrial order.[19] During this period Mexican-origin women were targeted to fill a growing demand for domestic and service industry workers.[20] The idea was that by teaching Mexican-origin women white middle-class American home and hygiene practices, Americanization teachers were both showing these women how to mother "efficiently" *and* training them to enter a specific labor market. According to Sanchez, the strategy was to "use the Mexican woman as a conduit for creating a home environment well-suited for the demands of an industrial economy."[21] In this way Mexican women's value to American society was tied to the labor they could provide to industries or to upper- and middle-class white families as domestics, while their reproductive behaviors were devalued as excessive and burdensome.

Compared to nativist calls for deportation and immigration restriction, Americanization efforts examined in Sanchez's study represented an arguably less drastic approach to the so-called "Mexican problem" in Southern California. Americanization teachers believed that Mexican-origin women could become a useful part of Southern California society, but the role they envisioned for these women was one of subservience. Furthermore, these teachers' approach to the problems that Mexican-origin families faced—poverty, hunger, and disease—was inherently racist. Americanization teachers believed Mexican cultural backwardness was the root cause of many of their problems, completely ignoring the structural forces including labor segmentation, wage theft, exploitation, and lack of access to health care.[22] Thus teachers approached Mexican-origin women through a framework of cultural pathology, believing that if these women changed backward behaviors and adopted American norms their problems would be resolved. Americanization programs were part of a broad range of interventions California state authorities made into the lives of Mexican-origin families as part of a Progressive Era impetus to address issues like poverty, immorality, and crime. Americanization teachers sought to reform behaviors in the home on the basis of cultural pathology, while social workers, juvenile court authorities, and clinicians at Pacific Colony intervened in more drastic ways into the private and reproductive lives of young Mexican-origin women on the basis of disability.

During the Progressive Era the sexual and reproductive behaviors of young working-class women were interpreted through the racist, classist, and ableist lens of eugenics. At the turn of the twentieth century, upper- and middle-class Progressive reformers adopted medical language in their efforts to more scientifically police and manage the behaviors of young working-class women whom they viewed as immoral and "sexually delinquent."[23] Some of these reformers understood so-called immoral behavior, like sex outside of marriage, as the result of inherent mental defect. Because immoral behaviors were framed as the outcome of defective individuals, Progressive reformers across the nation asserted that state authorities needed to identify, diagnose, and manage these sources of immorality.[24] The idea that young working-class women were a concerning source of social pathology was largely the result of middle- and upper-class reformers' impressions of turn-of-the-century changes. Urbanization and the heightened visibility of young working-class women in urban centers, increased immigration, and a growing industrial labor force created a context that triggered reformers' fears of racial degeneration and challenged their notions of gender roles and sexual propriety.

Psychologists played a significant role in legitimizing the concerns of reformers and medicalizing concerns about young working-class women's sexual behaviors. American psychologist Granville Stanley Hall, for example, identified an age period that he labeled "adolescence" during which youth were particularly susceptible to negative influence. According to Hall, this period was key in the successful transition from childhood to adulthood, and thus Hall and his supporters advocated strict supervision as well as concerted efforts to educated adolescents in proper morals and behaviors. Of course, the types of behaviors that Hall and his supporters deemed proper and normal were modeled after white middle-class standards. Setting white middle-class supervision and behaviors as the norm against which all other families should raise their children was problematic and had serious consequences for young working-class women.[25]

Having a stay-at-home parent to watch over young women and ensure their abstinence until marriage was a luxury that was simply unavailable to many working-class families. Moreover, many adolescent working-class women were laborers themselves and were thus working outside of the home. Sometimes these young women lived independently away from their families, which meant that they made their own decisions about their sex lives. Furthermore, some parents were simply not interested or invested in managing the sex lives of their daughters. Thus Hall's theory of how to properly manage adolescents cast working-class families as either deficient if they could not meet these standards or immoral and irresponsible if they simply chose not to. As a result, working-class families were often accused of depriving their daughters of "safe" and "moral" upbringings and were in turn pathologized as irresponsible and immoral.[26]

According to Progressive reformers, the supposed "sexual delinquency" of young women—whether framed as the outcome of inherent mental defect or the unfortunate result of deficient upbringing—became a thing to be managed and, if possible, prevented by state workers. Analyses of the nascent juvenile court system during this period show that these courts operated under a gendered notion of deviance whereby young women were almost exclusively tried for "moral offenses"—real or suspected illicit sexual behavior.[27] Young women who had children outside of marriage, engaged in sex (or were suspected of engaging in sex), or who were in any way associated with immoral behavior like running away from home, staying out late, or even being a the victim of sexual violence were tried and punished under the juvenile court system. Analyses of these juvenile courts offer empirical evidence that young women targeted for "moral offences" and "sexual delinquency" were largely immigrant and working class.[28]

In California, Progressive reformers established vice committees, juvenile court systems, and state social work agencies to address the perceived lack of supervision among working-class families and to identify defective or potentially immoral individuals. State authorities developed a system of classification and differentiation that attempted to parse out root causes (mental defect or lack of supervision) and dictate interventions. Educators, social workers, parole officers, judges, and sometimes even parents collaborated to try to control the sexual and reproductive behaviors of young women by having them committed to one of several state institutions. Juvenile court judges sentenced runaways, girls engaging in illicit sex, or young women considered on the route to immorality to the Ventura School for Girls, a state reform school, or one of many other public and private boarding homes and reform facilities in the state. Unwed mothers were sent to the Florence Crittenton Home or the Salvation Army, where they were often forced to place their children up for adoption.[29] Young women who were considered both delinquent *and* mentally deficient or who created too much trouble in an initial placement, like Valentina, were often sentenced to confinement at either the Sonoma State Home for the Feebleminded in Northern California or Pacific Colony. Given the predominance of working-class status among Mexican-origin women and the persistent ways their sexual and reproductive behaviors were viewed as deviant from white middle-class norms, they were often targeted by state authorities that had the power to sentence them to one of these institutions.

Despite the widespread efforts of state authorities to police and manage the sexual behaviors of young Mexican-origin women, they were persistent in their assertions of sexual agency throughout the first half of the twentieth century. Mexican-origin women engaged in flapper culture in the 1920s and challenged efforts to control their sex lives both in the home and on the streets.[30] By the 1940s young Mexican-origin women in Southern California asserted their sexual autonomy and economic independence while engaging in rebellious working-class youth culture as *pachucas*. Dressed in knee-length skirts and broad shouldered jackets, red lipstick, and high bouffant hairstyles, young working-class Mexican American pachucas came to symbolize "aberrant femininity and sexuality" in California and across the nation.[31]

At the same time that young Mexican-origin women were becoming essential to the Southern California war industry during the 1940s, these women were often seen as threats to the racial and social order by juvenile courts and institutional authorities in particular.[32] In fact, in her retelling of the international scandal that came out of *People v. Zamora*—wherein a group of young Mexican American men were unjustly charged with murder—historian Catherine Ramírez details the little-known stories of the young women who were picked up by legal authorities in connection with the case. At least five of these young women were sentenced to the Ventura School for Girls—known for its "draconian disciplinary measures"—without ever being tried or convicted of any crime but for simply "having consorted with bad company."[33] Some of these young women were confined until the age of twenty-one; others were released but remained wards of the court.

In the 1940s juvenile authorities continued to approach the behaviors of young working-class Mexican-origin women through a lens of racism and ableism. State authorities and much of the public accepted research by psychologists convinced that deviant sexual behaviors were often symptoms of low intelligence. This body of research made intelligible claims by psychiatrists like Ralph S. Banay, who asserted that youths engaging in pachuco culture were exhibiting "a psychological manifestation of chaotic sexuality."[34] According to Banay, the behaviors of working-class youth of color should not be read in light of "racial and economic discrimination" but should be seen "in most cases" as the result of "deeper psychological elements" including "chaotic sexuality, immaturity" and "aggression real or imaginary."[35] These psychological perspectives worked to further pathologize the behaviors of young working-class Mexican-origin women and legitimized long-standing notions of their sexual and reproductive behaviors as deviant and potentially dangerous. As a result, they fit more readily under the broad rubric of mental defect and feeblemindedness that marked them for commitment in Pacific Colony.

DEVIANCE AND DISABILITY: CONTROLLING THE SEX AND
REPRODUCTION OF "MENTALLY DEFECTIVE" WOMEN

By the 1910s psychologists, physicians, educators, and court officials
subscribed to the notion that immorality and sexual deviance could be
symptomatic of low intelligence and an inherent inability to comprehend
or abide by moral codes.[36] Since the late nineteenth century, psychologists asserted that low intelligence in the form of feeblemindedness—and
its various diagnostic grades including "idiot," "moron," "imbecile," and
"borderline"—could cause non-normative sexual behaviors. In the early
twentieth century, they devised intelligence tests in an effort to identify,
label, and properly manage women whose deviant sexual behaviors were
the outcome of "defective mentality." In most cases labeling was the first
step toward confinement. Once committed, these young women were
assessed regarding the type of jobs they could perform; whether they
could be trained and placed in domestic, service, or care work outside of
the institution; and whether they should be sterilized. This process played
out nationally, and working-class women were disproportionately labeled
"defective sex delinquents" and sentenced to confinement, forced labor,
and reproductive constraint.[37]

In California research produced by well-respected psychologists Drs.
George and Louise Ordahl legitimized theories that connected feeblemindedness with sexual deviance. The Ordahls began their career working
with the juvenile courts and institutions for the feebleminded in Illinois.
While there, they conducted hundreds of intelligence tests on young
women brought before Illinois juvenile courts. The Ordahls turned these
test scores into data that pointed to low intelligence as the primary factor
in the young women's sexually deviant behavior.[38] In the 1910s the Ordahls
moved to California, and George became the resident psychologist at the
Sonoma State Home around the time that Pacific Colony was being built.
In 1917, George Ordahl published a study on "mental defectives" in the
juvenile court in San Jose, California, in the *Journal of Delinquency*—a
journal that disseminated scientific research on "problems related to
social conduct" published by the Department of Research at the Whittier
State School, a juvenile reform school in Southern California. In that article he asserted that half of the young women brought before the juvenile

court were "either foreign born or of foreign born parentage" and that "the wards of this court belong to the lower levels of human intelligence."[39] Moreover, the article highlighted the fact that the "chief offense" among young women was "sex immorality."[40]

In an article published in the same journal a year later, the Ordahls drew from their extensive collection of IQ scores and social data collected during their time in Illinois to conclude that "the fundamental factor" at play among girls engaged in sexually deviant acts was "lack of general intelligence."[41] In the thirty-two page article, replete with charts and graphs, the psychologists asserted that "the problem of delinquent girls is perhaps without question the most serious one confronting society" and that the need to find ways to address this problem was paramount.[42] Intelligence testing, labeling, institutional confinement, training in industrial and domestic labor, and sterilization were repeatedly offered as scientific solutions to this social problem.

In his discussion of policy options to deal with these "foreign" wards of "low human intelligence," George Ordahl highlighted institutionalization and sterilization as available options. In 1917 he was skeptical about sterilization, largely because he feared the operation would give young women the license to have sex without fear of pregnancy. Although he was hesitant about sterilizing young women at first, Ordahl was a longtime advocate of segregation during the reproductive period. He also advocated sterilization for the parents of delinquent children so that the state could be "relieved of the burden of the feeble-minded children they are rearing."[43] Working in Sonoma, however, George Ordahl became complicit in the sterilization of thousands under the direction of superintendent Dr. Fred O. Butler, an enthusiastic proponent of eugenic sterilization.[44]

Studies like those conducted by the Ordahls provided corroborating evidence for the beliefs that middle-class professionals working in the fields of social work, education, juvenile delinquency, and psychology already had about the sexuality of young working-class women, some immigrants, and nonwhite people in general—namely that their sexual and reproductive behaviors were abnormal and largely representative of their inherent inferiority of mind, morality, and overall biology. This type of research amplified gendered understandings about the symptoms and scope of mental defect and constructed a particular archetype of female

sexual deviance—the feebleminded sex delinquent. The figure of the feebleminded sex delinquent invoked already existing contemptuous notions
about the sexual behavior of various marginalized groups including disabled people, immigrants, Women of Color, and the working class, and
their engagement in unwed motherhood, illicit and nonheteronormative
sex, promiscuity, and sex work. Already understood as inferior, dangerous, and distasteful, this behavior was now understood as an outcome, or
symptom, of hereditary mental defect. Under this framework individuals whose defect resulted in deviant behavior required state and medical
intervention—namely confinement in an institution. Eugenic ideology
provided further language and logic for linking the sexual and reproductive behavior of women to racial degeneracy, and proposals to use institutional confinement in conjunction with sterilization to address the issue
of mentally deficient and sexually delinquent women became a popular
intervention in California as well as several states across the country.[45]

In addition to being the resident psychologist at Sonoma, George
Ordahl served as the educational director, making decisions about who
could benefit from school or industrial placements and who was well
suited to be trained as a domestic worker. Ordahl was not optimistic about
the trainability of youth confined to Sonoma and expressed excitement
over the building of Pacific Colony, which could be used to improve and
expand training efforts so that after training and sterilization, certain
inmates could be "returned under extra-institutional supervision, as useful members of their communities."[46] In other words, Ordahl recognized
the Pacific Colony project as one that was aimed at administering education in the form of industrial training and treatment in the form of sterilization so that youth could be discharged as low-wage laborers under the
supervision of social workers and employers outside of the institution.

Making up a growing proportion of the immigrant and working-class
population in Southern California during the early to mid-twentieth century, young Mexican-origin women's sex and reproduction was increasingly labeled as deviant, dangerous, and in need of control. Already cast
as sexually deviant, backward, hyperfertile, and dependent on state aid,
Mexican women were easily brought under the broad category of feeblemindedness. In their 1938 study of sterilization in California institutions
titled *Twenty-Eight Years of Sterilization in California*, prominent eugen-

icists Paul Popenoe and E. S. Gosney of the California Human Betterment Foundation asserted that the sterilization of feebleminded women, many of whom "had illegitimate children" and were committed "largely because of their promiscuity," was among the most important and successful components of the state's sterilization program.[47] That feebleminded sex delinquents were dysgenic and unfit for full citizenship in the state was already assumed given their "low intelligence," struggles with poverty, and "inability to adjust" in the community.[48]

Moreover, the eugenicists described hyperfertility as a trait that was common among so-called feebleminded women. Popenoe and Gosney made this a point of observation and statistical calculation, writing that most feebleminded individuals came from families that had a mean size of "five living children." This number was situated in contrast to a specific type of "normal family." The eugenicists wrote that according to "statistical calculations" the "stock" of feebleminded families was "multiplying nearly twice as fast as the native-white population."[49] Although Popenoe and Gosney did not mention the racial or ethnic background of the women they were referencing, they make a clear distinction between their "stock" and reproductive behaviors and those of "native-whites" in California (i.e., Anglo-Americans). In addition to framing Anglo-Americans as the desired norm in California, this cementing of hyperfertility as a trait of feebleminded women also points to the fact that in California the feebleminded sex delinquent population was already correlated with foreignness and racial others. The two eugenicists situated poverty, sexual deviance, and non-normative domesticity as a sign of feeblemindedness among women. Popenoe and Gosney highlighted the impoverished conditions endured by the women they studied and took every opportunity to deride their "broken homes," "immoral mothers," and "unskilled laborer" fathers.[50] Furthermore, like Mexican families, feebleminded sex delinquents and their families in California were also figured as economic burdens. Popenoe and Gosney wrote that they were "in most instances on the borderline of economic self-sufficiency at best."[51]

In their discussion on available treatments and interventions, Popenoe and Gosney highly recommended sterilization, which they asserted was integral to the successful rehabilitation of people diagnosed as feebleminded—sexually delinquent women in particular. Not only would sterilization prevent the reproduction of additional "defective" and potentially delinquent children, but the operation was also discussed as a first step to economic productivity and the lessening of state support. Popenoe and Goosey made this clear in their assertion that 90 percent of people sterilized in the state's institutions for the feebleminded were "satisfactorily employed" once released from the institution, noting particular success among women placed in jobs in canneries, factories, or as domestic workers.[52] The two eugenicists pointed out that most of the women adjusted well in the community—and, most important, they were not "producing children who [would] be a burden to society and to posterity."[53] As in the case of Mexican women who were encouraged to limit reproduction in order to enter the low-wage labor market, women labeled "feebleminded" were only conferred social value through their potential in the industrial and domestic labor market. Their reproduction was seen as both a barrier and a burden.

The parallels that exist between the construction of Mexican-origin women's reproduction as problematic and the sociomedical construction of the sexually delinquent feebleminded woman were clearly premised on gendered, racial, and ableist ideology and the economic context. Although Popenoe and Gosney do not specifically mention Mexican-origin women in their analysis of sterilization in California institutions, their descriptions of feebleminded sex delinquents were undoubtedly based in part on a review of cases that likely included Mexican-origin women committed to and sterilized at both Sonoma and Pacific Colony. All were described as dysgenic, hyperfertile, and plagued by familial pathology. All were seen as potential economic burdens whose social value depended on their ability to engage in productive labor. Moreover, the parallels between the way Popenoe and Gosney described feebleminded women in California and the way that Mexican-origin women were cast as hyperfertile and sexually deviant indicate how state agents like social workers drew on the same set of eugenic beliefs and assessment rubrics.[54]

These descriptions of the economic and domestic experiences of women labeled "feebleminded" reflected the ways that state workers were actively assessing the conditions and experiences of the people they worked with. Family history, the conduct and economic status of the parents, and the home environment were seen as important factors for social workers who entered the homes of young women charged with "sexual delinquency."

Social workers adopted this same pathologizing lens, often "suspecting" the presence of feeblemindedness and judging home conditions to be lacking.[55] Their evaluations were then used to make recommendations regarding institutionalization and sterilization. State agents, including officials working in the juvenile courts and women working in the Department of Social Welfare, played important roles in institutional processes of commitment and sterilization. Women working in the Department of Social Welfare in particular positioned themselves as experts, facilitators, and mediators in state interventions into the lives of working-class women. Several women who worked in that state agency played direct roles in advocating for the institution before it was built and in shaping its future. Margaret Sirch, the woman in charge of the Los Angeles Department of Public Welfare, made several visits to the institution during the final stages of its construction in 1927, reporting on the number of cottages completed and the need for storage and additional places for residents to live and sleep.[56]

Through their positions in the department, women like Sirch were given the power of oversight and played direct roles in recommending and committing young women to Pacific Colony. They also played direct roles in facilitating the admission of inmates of color, including young Native women and men who were taken from their families by the federal government. For example, in early 1931, Sirch corresponded with Pacific Colony authorities regarding the admission of Florida LaChappa and Juan Hilquemup, two Native American youths with epilepsy who were committed to the institution. In their cases the Department of Social Welfare helped make arrangements through San Diego County to have the federal government pay the institution directly to confine them. This allowed the county to avoid the monthly charge from Pacific Colony and prevented the state from having to enter into a contract with federal authorities.[57]

Women reformers and social workers like Sirch were seen as necessary co-conspirators by prominent eugenicists and high-ranking men in other state departments. In November 1930, for instance, Fred O. Butler of the Sonoma State Home and the eugenicist E. S. Gosney were working on amending the sterilization approval process in order to protect institutions from litigation. The men wanted to strengthen and legitimize the sterilization request process by including multiple state department approvals. The directors of the Department of Institutions and the

Department of Health were already included in this process, and they systematically signed off on sterilization request forms during this period. Butler and Gosney wanted to add a third "lay person" as signatory to form a California eugenics board like the ones in North Carolina and Iowa. Signaling the authority and esteem that these men had for the women at Social Welfare, Butler and Gosney proposed adding the director of that department to this potential eugenics board, given that workers of the agency were known to be "conversant with all state problems." Butler supported the decision because he believed that the women of the department understood that California had a "type" of people that constituted "such a social problem" that they required reproductive constraint. The women of the department declined the position of lay person and signatory, and a formal eugenics board was never established in California. Instead, the law entrusted institutional authorities and the Department of Institutions with the power to approve sterilizations and enacted a practice of collecting signatures of consent from family members or guardians. Although these signatures were not required for sterilization, they were collected in an effort to protect institutional authorities from litigation.[58]

Although the women of the Department of Social Welfare did not seem to want to be involved in the procedural approval of all individual sterilization cases, they did look at the institution's power to perform sterilizations as an asset in their efforts to manage the sexual and reproductive lives of women they deemed defective, deviant, and burdensome. They often played a role in sterilization approvals as witnesses in the consent process. Many sterilization requests show the signatures of social workers in the "witness signature" section. This points to both their complicity in these practices but also suggests possible coercion and intimidation in the process of obtaining consent from parents and guardians.[59]

These women also worked with institutional authorities to have women committed for the primary purpose of sterilization. In 1936, Sirch communicated with Dr. Butler, Dr. Thomas Joyce (then the superintendent of Pacific Colony), and representatives of the city Health Department about "assistance in the matter of the sterilization of mentally deficient cases." Sirch was specifically interested in getting help with having five women sterilized at Pacific Colony. The only problem was that women had to be formally committed to the institution in order to be sterilized, even though Sirch planned on having the women return "to the community after the operation [was] done." Dr. Joyce was happy to "cooperate on all of them," as long as they were not "too delinquent," or likely to cause problems in the institution. In a phone call with Sirch, Joyce told her that he was more than willing to cooperate with the "sterilization of child bearing age mentally deficient women in Los Angeles," which they both agreed would be "a very great benefit to the community." When expressing her gratitude to Joyce, Sirch added that "Miss Agnes Talcott, director of Nursing Division, City Health Department; Mrs. Logan, Chief director of Social Service Division of the Bureau of Indigent Relief; and other workers in similar fields of service feel very grateful to you and Dr. Butler in making it possible to receive these patients for the short time period necessary for sterilization."[60] This exchange reveals both that women were committed to Pacific Colony for the sole purpose of sterilization and how effectively white professionals at various state departments drew on their influence and authority to work around the official commitment process in order to sterilize people who might not be considered eligible for the operation under state law.

An analysis of the sterilization requests processed by Pacific Colony points to several cases in which young Mexican-origin women were committed to the institution "for sterilization only." In 1936 a twenty-year-old Mexican American woman whose parents were dead (and was thus rendered a ward of the state) was "committed primarily for sterilization" by Judge Chas. L. Allison. In 1937 two women from the Los Angeles Health Department worked to admit a twenty-eight-year-old Mexican American woman who had three children outside of marriage to Pacific Colony "for sterilization." Pacific Colony sterilization requests reveal additional patterns about the ways that race, disability, and gender converged to shape Mexican-origin women's experiences at the institution.[61]

BY THE NUMBERS: MEXICAN-ORIGIN WOMEN AND STERILIZATION AT PACIFIC COLONY

Pacific Colony sterilization requests processed between 1928 and 1951 suggest that young working-class Mexican American women were more likely to be severely scrutinized and punished for engaging in sexual activity deemed deviant and delinquent by state workers. An analysis of these requests confirms that notions of sexual delinquency that emerged at the turn of the twentieth century played a significant role in determining which residents needed to be sterilized at Pacific Colony well into the 1940s. Almost a third, or 32 percent, of all residents targeted for sterilization during this period were characterized as sexually delinquent. Clinicians labeled these residents "sex delinquent" in the diagnosis section of their sterilization requests and often described the sexually deviant acts that residents were charged with in other parts of the requests.[62] The emphasis on sex acts makes clear that clinicians relied on these descriptors to rationalize sterilization. That notions of sexual delinquency were associated with female sexuality that deviated from white-middle class norms of sexual propriety is also supported by the data. A full 73 percent of individuals described as sex delinquents in their sterilization requests were women. Concerns over extramarital sex and pregnancy are also reflected in the records; 92 percent of individuals described as sex delinquents were single, and 25 percent had at least one child.

Descriptive data from Pacific Colony sterilization requests reveals the racial aspects of sex delinquency in California. More than half of the records for Spanish-surnamed women make reference to sexual delinquency. Sex outside of marriage was an important factor in these cases, given that 90 percent of these women were single. Reproduction also appears as a significant factor. An analysis of the records of "sexual delinquents" with Spanish surnames reveals that 20 percent had given birth at least once and 22 percent had more than one child. In approximately 36 percent of Spanish-surnamed women's sterilization requests, clinicians make a mention of "illegitimacy"—they were identified as illegitimate or they had a child outside of marriage.

Although the majority of sterilization requests that cited sexual delinquency as evidence of a need for reproductive constraint were for women, 27 percent were for the cases of young men. Analyzing the data derived from the records of these young men reveals noteworthy patterns. Approximately 80 percent of these cases were for non-Spanish–surnamed males. In fact, Spanish-surnamed males were slightly *less* likely to be characterized as sex delinquents, and 15 percent of their requests mention sexual deviance while almost 19 percent of requests for non-Spanish–surnamed patients mentioned sexual deviance. In his comparative study of "Anglo-white" versus "Mexican-white" male patients at Pacific Colony, graduate student Arthur Lawrence Palace remarked on the differences in reasons for commitment. Palace wrote that for white male residents of the institution, behaviors that immediately preceded commitment were "largely manifested in miscellaneous sex acts and incorrigibility."[63] Mexican male youth, however, were more likely to be committed following charges of criminality such as petty theft. I discuss the institutionalization and sterilization of young Mexican-origin men and their construction as inherently criminal in chapter 3, but this data suggests that more work needs to be done in terms of analyzing how race, gender, and sexuality intersected in institutional discourses on "delinquency" and "feeblemind-edness" in the cases of men. Importantly, of the 341 Spanish-surnamed patients sterilized at Pacific Colony from 1935 to 1951, 316 were born in the United States (92.7 percent), while only 25 were born in Mexico (7.3 percent). The majority, more than 70 percent, were born in California.[64] This data suggests connections between rationales for sterilization and overarching concerns regarding the reproduction of these young Mexican Americans in particular. It also points to the persistent construction of Mexican Americans as foreign and to efforts to constrict their rights as full citizens of the United States.

As the quantitative data indicates, more than half of the Mexican-origin women sterilized at Pacific Colony were single adolescents without children who clinicians labeled sexual delinquents or potential sex delin-quents. Their sterilization requests were often short and straight to the point. For example, a Pacific Colony official described seventeen-year-old Lilia Lara as a "mentally deficient girl, habitual truant, sex delinquent" and a "behavior problem."[65] California reformers were concerned about the sexual agency of young women and often read their sexual experiences as evidence of mental deficiency—and the sexuality of young Mexican American women in California was placed under particular scrutiny. Thus, in addition to being simply described as sex delinquents, many young Mexican-origin women's sterilization records point to their will-ingness to engage in nonmarital sex acts to "prove" their deviance and mental deficiency. Statements that reference Mexican-origin women's

willingness to engage in "voluntary acts of sexual intercourse"—a phrase
pulled from nineteen-year-old Gabriella Gomez's sterilization request—
underscore the ways that these young women's assertions of sexual agency
were used as both evidence of mental defect and a reason for reproductive
constraint.[66]

While engaging in sex outside of marriage was reason enough, Pacific
Colony clinicians also used unwed motherhood as evidence of sexual
deviance and mental deficiency. Unwed motherhood was by no means a
new phenomenon, nor was it something that occurred more often among
young Mexican American women. Yet the ways in which unwed mothers were treated by society and state authorities was shaped by race, disability, and class. In her work on single pregnancy, Rickie Solinger illustrates how young single white women who became pregnant were sent
to maternity homes and forced to give their children up for adoption,
while Black unwed mothers by contrast were not forced into adoption
but were subjected to general state neglect and left to struggle with low-
wage jobs.[67] If they received assistance from the state, it was often tied to
intrusive policing that put them at risk of having their children taken or
being coerced into reproductive constraint. Mexican American women fell
into both categories, and Vicki Ruiz's oral histories reveal that their fates
were often tied to the economic status and the general reactions of their
families.[68] Some were disowned by family or sent to institutions for unwed
mothers, while others were supported through their experiences of single
motherhood.

The sterilization requests reveal yet another consequence for Mexican
American women who became pregnant outside of marriage, especially
working-class women who were reliant on the state for support. Pregnancy,
IQ tests, and poverty combined to turn their reproduction into a symptom
of mental defect and a reason for confinement and sterilization. For example, single and in her twenties, Rafaela Sanchez was admitted to Pacific
Colony on December 5, 1939, because she had "three illegitimate children." Rafaela had contracted gonorrhea and syphilis, which was taken as
further evidence of her sexual deviance and feeblemindedness. A clinician
noted that she was "committed for sterilization" and on December 7, 1939,
just two days after she was admitted to the institution, the director of the
California Department of Institutions approved her sterilization request.

A Pacific Colony official noted that Rafaela was "apparently negative for nervous and mental diseases," making it even more clear that her reproductive behavior was the primary reason she was committed and sterilized.[69] Her records indicate that she was confined to Pacific Colony for the specific purpose of preventing her from having more children.

Pregnancy was also an important factor for sixteen-year-old Inez Moreno, who was previously housed in a boarding home before being committed to Pacific Colony in 1939. At the boarding home, she became pregnant "following relations with two gardeners" who were employed there. The gardeners "admitted intercourse" with Inez, and as a result she was sent to Pacific Colony where she was diagnosed as a "moron" of "familial type," a "sex delinquent," and a "behavior problem." Being diagnosed as mentally deficient and having "one illegitimate child" marked Inez's reproduction as out of control and threatening, leading institutional authorities to conclude that the "operation should be done for the girl's protection and that of the community."[70]

In addition to signaling the ways that young Mexican-origin women's single motherhood was pathologized and punished, Inez's sterilization request points to the role that sexual violence played in the commitment and sterilization of working-class Mexican-origin women. While her record does not describe her sexual relations with the gardeners at the boarding home as rape, it also does not indicate consent on her part. Moreover, sex with state workers in the context of confinement in a boarding school would, at the very least, be complicated by coercive and unequal power dynamics. As historian Michael Rembis has written in his work on institutionalization in Illinois, many young women committed to institutions were victims of sexual assault, but they were rarely cast as victims.[71] In fact, the perverse way that state authorities used confinement and sterilization to further punish sexual assault victims is enshrined in the landmark Supreme Court case *Buck v. Bell* (1927), which legalized state mandated eugenic sterilization. In that case, Carrie Buck's pregnancy, the result of rape, was a principal factor in her commitment and sterilization.[72]

In several of the Pacific Colony sterilization requests I reviewed, young Mexican American women clearly indicated that they experienced sexual violence, and clinicians documented these women's mentions of "attacks." Some were victims of sexual violence by strangers, but many experienced sexual violence in their homes. Institutional authorities were aware of these incidents of sexual violence and often cited them in their disparaging descriptions of the young girls' family and home life. These descriptions were then used to justify removing young women from their parents and making them wards of the state, which social workers and judges asserted was an act of care or in their best interest, but the revelation of sexual violence was also used to support confinement in Pacific Colony and sterilization. In one twenty-year-old Mexican American woman's records, a clinician noted that she was a ward of the state, a "rape case," and "committed primarily for sterilization."[73] In several cases Pacific Colony authorities actively collaborated with abusers to secure approval for sterilization. For example, Pacific Colony officials asked the stepfather of a young woman who was charged with raping his stepdaughter to sign a consent form for her sterilization.[74] In 1935 the father of a seventeen-year-old Mexican American girl who was convicted of her rape and serving time at San Quentin was subsequently allowed to sign off on the girl's sterilization from the prison.[75] Thus, even when their experiences were recognized as rape, these young women were still labeled "sexually delinquent." Their cases point to the ways that they were doubly victimized both through the initial sexual violence and additional violations of their bodily autonomy by the state under the guise of "care."

Although most of the Mexican-origin women sterilized at Pacific Colony were young and single, others were older women who struggled to care for their children and thus came to the attention of the authorities. Monica Alvarez, a "Catholic, Mexican woman," married when she was twenty and had a baby with her husband. A few years later, they divorced and she moved back in with her parents, who provided Monica with childcare while she worked outside of the home. Over the years she had a relationship with "a Portuguese" and had three children with him. In her sterilization request a clinician wrote that Monica then had a child with a "Swiss-Italian" and gave birth to "another illegitimate child" after that. Describing Monica's relationships with men and the birth of her six children, the clinician declared confidently that she was "sexually promiscuous." Monica was thirty-six when she was committed to Pacific Colony and had been doing "housekeeping on ranches" to support her family.

In her sterilization request the clinician described the "socio-economic state of the family" as "low" and made a note about the "intermittent relief" that Monica relied on to survive, thereby figuring her and her family as social burdens. Recounting her sexual experiences, reproductive past, and struggles with poverty, the Pacific Colony clinician cast Monica as the embodiment of the stereotypical Mexican woman—a reckless breeder who not only created an economic burden on society but whose promiscuity crossed racial lines and thus threatened the racial purity of the nation. The description put her squarely in line with the archetype of the feeble-minded sex delinquent and supported the clinician's diagnosis of Monica as a "High Moron." The clinician wrote that "because of this woman's past difficulties" Monica should be sterilized, and the Pacific Colony clinical staff "unanimously approved" the operation on March 4, 1938.[76]

In 1940 a Pacific Colony clinician referenced thirty-nine-year-old Laura Ramirez's sexual history, family size, and economic struggles as evidence of mental deficiency, sexual delinquency, and a need for reproductive constraint. When she was admitted to Pacific Colony in January of 1940, Laura was the single mother of thirteen children, four by her first husband and nine by her second partner (who Laura's record indicated had "deserted" her and their children). The clinician wrote in her sterilization request that Laura was a "mentally deficient woman" who had "neglected her home and children" and who could not "adjust." In addition to describing Laura as feebleminded and an irresponsible mother, the clinician mentioned that she was diagnosed with gonorrhea, labeled her "promiscuous," and said she was a "community menace." The staff at the clinical conference at Pacific Colony "unanimously recommended" sterilization in February 1940, a month after Laura was committed. Since Laura's parents had passed away and her most recent partner was no longer involved in her life, hospital officials determined that no one was available to sign her consent form. Having been legally committed to Pacific Colony, Laura was determined to have "no legal guardian other than the state" and so her case was presented to the Department of Institutions "for consideration of sterilization without consent of relatives" because Pacific Colony authorities believed the "operation should be done for her own protection and that of the community."

Monica and Laura's cases illustrate how Pacific Colony clinicians used women's sexual and reproductive histories as evidence of mental defect.

Clinicians used their struggles to provide for their families as evidence of irresponsibility and an inability to "adjust" to their circumstances. Furthermore, Laura's case illustrates how after identifying her as a social threat, institutional authorities were able to diagnose her as feebleminded, have her committed to a state institution, and effectively render her powerless, diminishing her right to reproductive autonomy and bodily integrity.[77] In this way state workers' power extended beyond the scope of juvenile courts and engaged in a legal processes that rendered adult women "incompetent" in order to commit them for sterilization.

While many of these women were sterilized because of their diagnosis as "sexually delinquent," others were sterilized because of mere association with delinquency. That is, they were not found to be engaging in sexually illicit conduct, but their familial circumstances were figured as so negative that they should be sterilized anyway. Literature on the development of the social work method of collecting family histories to support the commitment of sexually delinquent girls reveals how descriptions of mental and social deviance among parents, siblings, and even extended family worked to mark young girls as feebleminded and in need of state intervention.[78] This was often the case for young Mexican-origin women. Alicia Rios, for example, was committed to Pacific Colony in June of 1940 when she was fifteen. In her sterilization request, Pacific Colony staff simply described her as a "mentally deficient girl" whose mother had abandoned her when she was an infant.

In her family history section, however, the clinician wrote that Alicia's father was an "alcoholic" and a "dope addict" with a "long criminal record" who never married Alicia's mother, making her an "illegitimate child." The staff member described Alicia's mother as an "alcoholic" and a "prostitute" with a "long record of arrests for prostitution." Other than the fact that Alicia had become a ward of the court after being abandoned by her parents, no other description was given about her conduct that might justify a need for sterilization. The clinician did not describe Alicia as engaging in delinquent behavior in any way. Instead, the clinician simply described the young girl as a "High Moron, Familial Type" and stated that the clinical committee deemed that sterilization was "advisable for her." The operation was approved on June 15, 1942.[79] This decision, made on the assertion of deviance and pathology by association, illustrates the ways that racism and ableism came together and functioned as a predictive tool—predicting future deviance and defect—in order to legitimize sterilizing young Mexican-origin women.

In California ideas about the relationship between sexual deviance and mental defect were informed by already existing beliefs about the inferiority of Mexican bodies, behaviors, and minds and their unfitness for citizenship or social membership in the state. These beliefs mobilized racist and ableist logics in gendered ways, casting Mexican-origin women as pathological sex deviants who were hyperfertile and thus problematic—even threatening to the racial and economic health of the state. The consequences of this convergence are represented in the implementation of eugenic sterilization practices at Pacific Colony. The sterilization requests processed by Pacific Colony offer a glimpse into the ways in which working-class Mexican-origin women's sexuality was pathologized and how their bodies were subject to state interventions. In the requests clinicians presented descriptions of Mexican-origin women's sexual and reproductive experiences in an effort to construct them as immoral and pathologically sexual. In this way, sterilization requests reveal how gender, race, and (dis)ability came together to situate already marginalized women as "pure body."[80] In her essay "Integrating Disability, Transforming Feminist Theory," disability studies scholar Rosemarie Garland-Thomson writes that this "sentence of embodiment is conceived as either a lack or an excess."[81]

The women committed to Pacific Colony were often figured as both—lacking mental capacity, intelligence, and inhibitions and thus excessively sexual and fertile. Thus they were targeted for interventions meant to alter their bodies and behaviors. The most obvious intervention in the case of Pacific Colony was sterilization. While institutional authorities understood that sterilization did not impact sexual desire, it was nevertheless used to manage and control the bodies of those displaying deviant sexuality to prevent the consequences of sex and, ultimately, reproduction. In a report on the sterilizations he performed at the Sonoma State Home, Dr. Butler discussed an added benefit of the operation with regard to "the feeble-minded." He asserted that the operation "appears to make them more amenable to discipline and more easily controlled."[82] The role that sterilization played in making young women more "amenable to discipline" and control offered institutional authorities another excuse to implement the practice, particularly in their efforts to make these women more productive. Not having children certainly made them more available for labor.

Not everyone who entered Pacific Colony was sterilized. In fact, the "custodial cases" (people with severe physical or mental impairments who were committed as permanent residents) were rarely sterilized. Decisions not to sterilize "custodial cases" were grounded in two assumptions about the severely disabled. The first was that they lacked sexual desire and thus did not pose the same problem as "sexual delinquents." And second, that they would remain in the institution their entire lives and would therefore be "protected" from sex. In the records of several "custodial cases," clinicians often wrote the phrase "sterilization unnecessary," indicating the assumption that they would be confined for the entirety of their lives and would therefore be "protected" from reproduction.[83]

Although women who were labeled "custodial cases" were rarely sterilized, institutional authorities devised other ways to make their care at the institution more manageable. For example, in 1963 three male physicians began administering norethynodrel and mestranol (Enovid) to "profoundly retarded patients" in an attempt to suppress menstruation as "a hygienic measure in the care of mentally retarded patients."[84] Their study discussed a number of side effects, including the exacerbation of seizures in one resident, but in the end the physicians were optimistic about the use of these drugs to make it easier to care for menstruating residents in custodial institutions. This treatment did nothing to improve the health of these people, and in some cases caused them harm. This study illustrates how Pacific Colony—even after undergoing extensive administrative shifts, eliminating the practice of eugenic sterilization, and changing its name to Pacific State Hospital—continued to view the bodies of women with disability labels as burdensome problems to be managed. For all the effort that state workers put into controlling these young women, they still managed to find ways to assert their own agency and desires. In various ways, institutionalized women established meaningful platonic and romantic relationships within the confines of Pacific Colony.

SEX, CARE, AND LABOR IN PACIFIC COLONY

Rosie Zavella was so distraught over the death of her charge in the infirmary that she couldn't even talk about it. She suffered from depression from time to time. She couldn't remember if the sadness was always there or if it started with Pacific Colony. Either way, eight years in the institution wasn't helping, and the death of the young child that she cared for every day put her over the edge. The pain was unspeakable.[85]

Rosie was seventeen and sick with tuberculosis when she was committed to Pacific Colony in the 1940s. She spent two years healing in the communicable disease ward of the infirmary and learned so much while she was there that when they moved her to a regular cottage, administrators had her return to the ward every day to work as a "helper." Rosie was a multifaceted young Mexican American woman who played basketball and volleyball and liked to skate. Clearly, Pacific Colony staff found Rosie skilled enough to work in the infirmary and capable enough to feed, bathe, dress, and comfort a sick child whom she grew to care about deeply. Rosie was generous. At one point she volunteered her limited free time to contribute to a research study conducted by a social work student named Elizabeth Brainard from the University of Southern California. Rosie joined Brainard's "social club for girls" and let the aspiring social worker observe, take notes, and ask questions for her master's thesis. While Brainard might not have recognized it, eight years at Pacific Colony made Rosie an expert in surviving the institution and understanding how to handle institutional authorities. She knew which ones to avoid and which might be trusted. When Brainard overheard Rosie sharing sage advice with her friends in the social club, she called it "gossip," but that was how Rosie helped protect her friends.

Despite clear condemnation, constant surveillance, and threats of punishment from Pacific Colony's staff, Rosie insisted on experiencing romance and pleasure. She had multiple lovers. One was Alice, a blond girl who had been in Pacific Colony for four years and lived in the same cottage. When Rosie and Alice were caught engaging in "homosexual acts," institutional authorities placed them in isolation as punishment and then moved them into separate cottages. Rosie had a boyfriend for a while, and Pacific Colony workers didn't seem to mind that as much as her relationship with Alice. Brainard wrote in her study that Rosie seemed to be "adjusting to heterosexuality," but Rosie still liked spending time with women more than men. The several "Special Incident Reports" that Brainard mentioned in her study point to Rosie's continued sex with women.

Rosie and the other young women confined to Pacific Colony navigated confinement, sterilization, physical and emotional punishment, and institutional authorities who saw their bodies, minds, desires, and futures as pathological and in need of control. Nevertheless, these young women asserted their desires and tried to find pleasure and joy during their forced confinement. In their positions as unpaid caregivers and as young people looking to experience romance and explore their sexuality, some residents of Pacific Colony formed a range of sexual and platonic relationships throughout their confinement. Based on their experiences, many developed their own analyses about sexuality and disability and waged incisive critiques of the prohibitive, contradictory, and cruel treatment they received at the institution.

Throughout the 1930s and 1940s, Pacific Colony authorities made concerted efforts to control and manage the romantic and sexual lives of residents. On the one hand, institutional authorities worked to prevent sexual relationships. Residents were confined to cottages segregated by sex, and staff were empowered to discipline and punish residents caught engaging in sexual acts. On the other hand, Pacific Colony administrators were permissive and sometimes encouraging about heterosexual romantic relationships, as long as they did not become sexual. In some ways administrators took on the task of educating residents on what they viewed as proper heterosexual relationships and created opportunities for romantic heterosexual behaviors. For example, part of Brainard's social work study involved inviting young men to visit and interact with her "girls social club"; she wrote approvingly of the boyfriend-girlfriend relationships that some of the young women in her study developed.

Pacific Colony administrators also attempted to impose proper heterosexual relationships through weekly dances in the auditorium. These staff-organized dances began in the mid-1930s and were routinized and controlled.[86] Like other institutions across the nation, Pacific Colony staff viewed dances as an opportunity to model appropriate romantic—but nonsexual—heterosexual behavior. Staff in attendance required youths to dance with members of the opposite sex, commanded them to dance at a distance, and kept a watchful eye over all of the participants. These limited opportunities for heterosexual romantic contact largely reflected the expectations that institutional authorities had about the social and sexual lives of Pacific Colony residents. Inside the institution residents were "allowed" casual emotional relationships, but anything nearing sex was strictly prohibited.

While paid staff tried to prevent sex among confined residents, Rosie and many other young women and men found ways to explore their sexuality and desires. In his study of Pacific Colony, anthropologist Robert Edgerton found that romance was an important aspect of young people's lives in the institution.[87] Young couples exchanged gifts, spent free time together, and found ways to spend time alone when possible. For some young women these relationships were about love. Others were uninterested in long-term romance and pursued relationships purely for pleasure. Despite their best efforts, institutional authorities could not be everywhere, and young couples found ways to engage in sex without being caught. They memorized staff schedules, found secluded locations on institutional grounds, and enlisted each other's help by asking friends to "look out" while they snuck away.[88]

As Rosie's story documents, young institutionalized women also engaged in same-sex relationships with each other. This was well known at the institution and documented in Brainard's social work thesis. In group contexts many of these young women spoke openly about their relationships with other women and with young men at Pacific Colony. They made several references to "Ward 40" as one in which sexual encounters between women were well known and openly discussed.[89] While boyfriends were tolerated, same-sex relationships were wholly discouraged and even punished. Not only were same-sex couples like Rosie and Alice separated, residents caught engaging in "homosexual acts" were placed in solitary confinement in the locked ward. Additional punishments included deliberate changes in work assignments ("working in the kitchen rather than with nursery babies"); taking away "privileges" such as attending weekly dances, occupational training, and recreation therapy; and revoking their "campus cards," which allowed them free range of the grounds.[90] In addition to condemning these relationships, institutional authorities cited them as clear evidence of mental, emotional, and sexual defect and inferiority; interracial same-sex relationships were deemed particularly concerning.[91] Some clinicians and staff discussed same-sex relationships as "pseudohomosexuality"—sexual behavior that would not occur outside of the institution and was either forced onto heterosexual residents by sexually deviant aggressors or chosen out of a lack of options.[92]

Despite punishment, nonheteronormative romantic and sexual relationships existed in Pacific Colony and in similar custodial institutions across the country throughout the twentieth century.[93] While residents of custodial institutions were subjected to this pathologizing and punishing interpretation of nonheteronormative sex, they developed their own stance on sexuality and insisted on much more expansive sexual and emotional experiences. Rosie continued to pursue same-sex relationships, and Brainard study indicates that these relationships were widespread. In his anthropological study Edgerton refers to "two active homosexual girls."[94] In addition to asserting their own sexual desires, formerly institutionalized people developed understandings about the significance of same-sex relationships that went beyond pathology, violence, and circumstance. To be sure, former residents of Pacific Colony and other state institutions have long described sexual violence by residents and staff.[95] And while one formerly institutionalized person described "stages of homosexuality you go through simply because you are there," he also described homosexuality as "a fact of life." [96] Reflecting on her experience at a different institution, another person described "homosexual girls" like this: "It wasn't a freak-like thing. I guess it was just to meet their own needs and satisfaction."[97] Describing "female homosexuality" at Pacific Colony, Edgerton wrote that the young women in his study were "much more tolerant of female homosexuality."[98] That is, they accepted each other and the vast spectrum of sexuality that existed among their peers.

Without a doubt, queer people of color with disability labels, like Rosie, did what they could to not only survive but to experience pleasure and romance in the context of confinement. Looking closely at Rosie's experience, Edgerton's observations, and the comments made by people institutionalized in other places reveals that they also developed nuanced views of these encounters and relationships. In contrast to institutional authorities, who saw same-sex acts as evidence of pathology and "poor sexual adjustment," some people who experienced institutionalization were more accepting of non-normative sex, seeing it as a "fact of life" and decidedly *not* "freak-like."[99] Thus not only are these experiences part of a long his-

Figure 4. Pacific Colony nursery cribs jammed together due to overcrowding, 1950. *Los Angeles Times* Photographic Archives, Collection 1429, Library Special Collections, Charles E. Young Research Library, University of California–Los Angeles.

tory of the violent pathologization of queer sex, but they also represent a long history of queer defiance in the face of this pathologization.

In addition to exploring sex and romantic relationships, young women in Pacific Colony also developed profound platonic relationships in their roles as unpaid caretakers. Confined residents performed the majority of the day-to-day labor of the institution, including cleaning, growing and preparing food, sewing and laundering clothes and bedding, and even washing the cars of physicians and other workers.[100] This work was highly gendered, and young women were assigned unpaid positions in janitorial details to learn "sweeping, dusting, and cleaning" or were assigned to work in the dining facilities of paid staff to learn "setting the table and waiting on the table."[101] Other young women were forced to work in the onsite homes of Pacific Colony physicians and administrators, who benefited from the free domestic and childcare services.[102] All of this labor fell under the notion of "vocational training," and women's performance in this free work was used to assess whether they could be placed on "industrial parole" in similar "low-skilled" and low-paid work outside of the institution, much like Valentina mentioned in the beginning of this chapter.

Like Rosie, women also provided the care work needed to sustain an institution that confined infants, young children, and people with physical impairments or severe cognitive disabilities. Pacific Colony authorities referred to them as "custodial cases" because it was assumed that they would spend their entire life at the institution. In the 1930s, Pacific Colony administrators tried to keep the number of "custodial cases" low and focus on so-called "high-grade" feebleminded people. By focusing on that specific demographic, clinicians could reach a wider population because "high-grades" could ideally be treated with "vocational training," sterilized, and placed on industrial parole as low-wage workers outside of Pacific Colony, thereby creating room for other people inside. However, parents and social workers in Southern California demanded that the institution also confine people with more severe physical and neurological impairments. Many of these people were infants or young children committed to Pacific Colony at the recommendation of a physician or social worker, because parents had no means to care for a sick child, or because parents were already primed to believe that having a disabled child was shameful or would cause an undue burden on the family. Regardless of the reason for commitment, infants, young children, and severely disabled residents required hands-on care, and care of "the helpless" was "done by patients who are trained as ward aids."[103]

In their positions as caregivers, women developed platonic caring relationships with the children and adults they cared for. Some, like Rosie, took care of sick children and young adults on the communicable disease ward. Others worked in the nursery wards, where immobile and bed-ridden young children were confined. Given the variety of needs that existed across these infants, youths, and adults, women in caregiving positions acquired specialized skills. They performed much of the bathing, feeding, and dressing, for example. In many cases, they tried to meet the "emotional needs" of the people they cared for, often treating them with more

tenderness and attention than paid staff.[104] Although they were trained
by paid nurses and attendants to provide specialized care, these women
were never paid themselves. They were expected to transfer these caregiving skills outside of the institution and apply them in low-wage positions in sanitariums, state hospitals, and in the homes of middle-class
Californians, where they were expected to care for other people's children
after being prevented from having their own.

Young women who were placed in these work arrangements outside
of the institution expressed clear discontent. Valentina, for example, left
her job at a physician's house. Another young woman, Mary, was placed
in multiple private sanitariums "baby-sitting" or working as a "mother's
helper" when she was discharged from Pacific Colony. She had to be
repeatedly moved after having "serious difficulties with her employers"
because they were overworking her.[105] Not only was Mary angry about
being forced into exploitative working conditions, she was "disturbed over
being sterilized at Pacific."[106] She wanted to have children and therefore
experienced sterilization as a profound and long-term harm. This no
doubt led to her refusal to merely comply with the childcare positions that
Pacific Colony authorities placed her in upon release from the institution.
Another woman highlighted this painful reality in her reflection on being
sterilized at Pacific Colony, stating: "I'd like to have one or two kids but not
a whole lot. I take care of everybody else's kids and everybody tells me I'm
good with children and they ask me why I don't have one of my own and I
just say that I can't have one."[107]

The coupling of sterilization with funneling women into low-wage
childcare positions underscores the contradictory and cruel ways that
Pacific Colony administrators framed disability, motherhood, and reproduction. Disability labels marked these women as unfit for motherhood
and justified diminished freedom and reproductive constraint through
sterilization. Yet institutionalized women were regarded as capable
enough to care for the physical and emotional needs of a number of children in the institution, many of whom had specialized needs. Women
who stayed in the institution for many years or all of their lives not only
performed work necessary to sustain the institution, but likely cared for
infants into adulthood and formed familial bonds with them. Aware of the
importance of these emotional bonds, institutional authorities used them

in cruel ways such as switching work assignments as punishment for bad behavior, separating caregivers from their charges on purpose. Although these relationships exposed women to emotional manipulation and pain at the hands of paid staff, the fact that the women enjoyed and cherished the caring relationships they built with their charges is evident. As Rosie's story illustrates, she developed feelings of tenderness for the infant she cared for and was deeply impacted by the child's death.[108]

Pacific Colony was not unique in having residents care for each other, and confined residents drew on these experiences to claim and affirm the humanity of the people they cared for. The deep emotion that Rosie displayed after the death of her young charge represents her recognition of the child as valuable and worthy of love and care. Reflecting on his experience caring for fellow residents and witnessing abuse by paid staff in a different state institution, one man concluded that "we can't just judge by appearance. There is a brain. They know when they are being abused. That is a human being. They have a heart, there is tissue that makes them a human being. They are creatures of god, regardless. If you take away the label they are human beings."[109] In the context of institutions built on the dehumanization, segregation, and ultimate elimination of people with disability labels, Rosie's emotion and this man's perspective challenged state and institutional authorities' assertions that the lives of people with disability labels were inferior and unworthy. Insisting on sexual pleasure and developing caring relationships with the residents they were charged with looking after, young Mexican-origin women and their peers confronted dehumanizing disability labels and efforts at controlling their sexual and reproductive lives, seizing joy, pleasure, humanity, and dignity wherever possible.

3 The Laboratory of Deficiency

RACE, KNOWLEDGE, AND THE REPRODUCTIVE POLITICS
OF JUVENILE DELINQUENCY

A sign reading "We Are Testing Please Come Back Later" hung on the closed door of a Los Angeles Juvenile Hall room where Mildred Malm, a state psychologist, detained fifteen-year-old Raul Martinez. This was a different type of questioning. In the room Malm administered an intelligence test, observing and analyzing Raul while he responded to prompts, interpreted sentences, organized wooden blocks, and completed a series of math problems. Based on this single interaction and his brief legal record, Malm assigned Raul a low IQ score and labeled him "mentally deficient." Maybe adrenaline from the "knife fight" that Raul was allegedly involved in made it hard to focus. Maybe the thought of how his father would react to his arrest—the second in a matter of months—distracted Raul from answering Malm's questions correctly. Maybe Raul didn't feel like cooperating with yet another juvenile court authority. Maybe he just didn't know the answers. Or, maybe the fifteen-year-old, separated from his parents and alone with a state psychologist in juvenile hall, was too scared to concentrate on sentence structures, shapes, and math.[1]

Raul had reason to fear what might happen to him at Los Angeles Juvenile Hall. It was December 1942 when he was forced to take this intelligence test alone and without parental consent. In August of that same

Figure 5. Pacific Colony, Cottage for Boys, ca. 1921. Courtesy of the California History Room, California State Library, Sacramento.

year the Los Angeles Police Department used the death of twenty-year-old José Díaz to throw hundreds of young working-class Mexican American men like Raul in jail, accusing them of José's murder.[2] By October, twenty-two young men were charged with Díaz's death in what became the largest murder trial in California history, *People v. Zamora*. News about José's murder, the roundup of young Mexican-origin men, and the drastic approach of the Los Angeles Police Department was widely publicized to prove that city authorities were tough on juvenile delinquency. So when Raul was tested by Malm, he was no doubt aware of the swift and punishing practices juvenile court officials waged against young men like him. Malm must have been similarly aware of what her colleagues—officers, social workers, psychologists—thought about the inherent delinquency of young working-class Mexican American men like Raul. She was, after all, an integral part of the Southern California system involved in the racialized criminalization of Mexican-origin youth.

During World War II, local and national press derided Mexican American youth, particularly pachucos who wore zoot suits, many of whom were working-class. The press, juvenile court authorities, and many upper- and middle-class Americans associated zoot suits—the elegant oversized suit coat paired with wide-legged and tight-cuffed trousers—with gangs, violence, and a lack of wartime patriotism. In 1943, Mississippi House Representative John E. Rankin described youth that wore zoot suits as "a bunch of marauding criminals" that needed to be "obliterated."[3] Psychologists offered their own interpretations of this "repugnant" and "bizarre attire." As one New York psychologist put it, zoot suits and the entire culture surrounding this working-class youth of color aesthetic—including the clothes, the dancing, and the slang—were likely evidence of "adolescent neurosis."[4] This was the backdrop against which Raul's behaviors were being interpreted by state workers. Shortly after testing Raul, authorities at Los Angeles Juvenile Hall coupled Malm's mental assessment with Raul's legal record and decided to have him committed to Pacific Colony. A charge of being "intoxicated in one of the local pool halls," another for being "involved in a knife fight," and a low IQ score were enough to have the fifteen-year-old taken from his family and confined in a state institution for an indeterminate amount of time.

On December 11, 1942, just a few days after Malm's test, Pacific Colony authorities moved Raul into Cottage 15, which was already overcrowded with least eighty other young men. A few months later, on March 18, 1943, Pacific Colony clinicians processed paperwork to have Raul sterilized. His father protested the sterilization, refusing to sign a consent form for the operation. Consent, however, was not a legal requirement, and Pacific Colony superintendent Thomas Joyce simply sent a letter to the California director of institutions outlining the case for approval without the father's consent. In his letter, Joyce recounted Raul's two arrests, claiming Raul was "involved with a local gang of marauding Mexicans." Discrediting the clear refusal to sign off on Raul's sterilization, Joyce described the boy's father as feebleminded and "a constant alcoholic who failed to provide for his family," thereby diminishing the grounds of his parental authority. Joyce also informed the director of institutions that a social worker familiar with the family alleged that Raul's four siblings were also feebleminded or at least of "borderline" intelligence. Hitting all of the major components under the medico-social rubric of mental deficiency, including social deviance (crime), poverty, hyperfertility, family pathology, immigrant stock, and low intelligence, Joyce presented a medically and socially grounded case for Raul's sterilization. Indeed, the entire clinical staff agreed that the fifteen-year-old should be sterilized "on account of his being a mental defective with strong "criminal tendencies." Convinced by the medical narrative offered by Pacific Colony staff, the director of the California Department of Institutions approved Raul's sterilization on March 22, 1943.

Within a span of six months, Los Angeles juvenile court authorities labeled fifteen-year-old Raul mentally deficient, committed him to a state institution, and sterilized him despite his father's protest—all because of his supposed "criminal tendencies." The rapid pace at which Raul was drawn into this web of state actors, pathologizing discourse, and punitive interventions illustrates how precarious life as a young Mexican American boy from a working-class family could be in Southern California in the 1940s. It's also indicative of how entrenched ideas about the inherent criminality of young Mexican-origin men were and how effective disability labels were in justifying bodily state interventions. This chapter traces the origins of these ideas to uncover how fifteen-year-old Raul Martinez's life and reproductive future could be so dramatically altered in such a short period of time. Examining early twentieth-century scholarship on juvenile delinquency, I contend that California researchers and state agents working with youth targeted by state workers and juvenile court authorities wed ideologies of disability and race to construct young Mexican-origin men as pathologically criminal or "defective delinquents." Doing so meant that these youths were seen as less redeemable and more dangerous because their deviance was both inherent and hereditary. As Raul's experience demonstrates, this labeling resulted in more severe consequences for Mexican-origin youths who engaged in behavior deemed deviant or delinquent.

This chapter hones in on the experiences of young Mexican-origin men like Raul to understand the role that disability in the form of feeblemindedness played in processes of racialized criminalization. Diagnoses

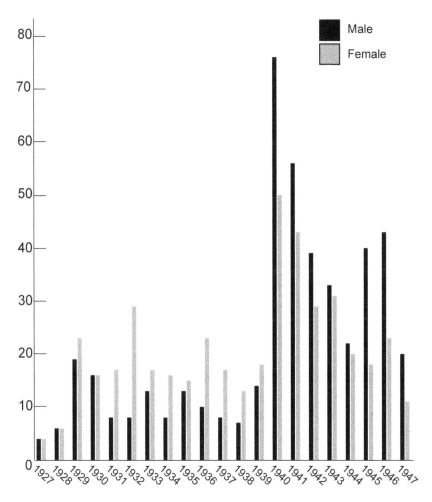

Figure 6. Admissions to Pacific Colony: Mexican-origin by sex, 1927–47. See Table 5 in the appendix for yearly counts.

of feeblemindedness largely followed gendered ideologies of deviance wherein women's pathology revolved around sexual immorality, while young men were labeled following charges of truancy, theft, some other form of petty or status crime. Young Mexican-origin men were sterilized at Pacific Colony at rates that were nearly equal to those of young Mexican-origin women. Bringing their experiences into the fold works to broaden the gendered scope of literature on the history of sterilization abuse in the United States as well as our overall understanding of the roles that race, gender, and disability have played in reproductive politics.

When Raul was committed in the 1940s, he was part of an overall increase in the number of youths being funneled into Pacific Colony. This was in part a function of the material expansion of the institution—the state invested hundreds of thousands of dollars to build more cottages to confine youths like Raul. It was also part of a larger effort on the part of Southern California state authorities to police, punish, and confine young Mexican American men in particular. Chicano Studies scholarship has documented the ways that World War II–era discourses on juvenile delinquency criminalized Mexican American youth and even painted certain aspects of youth culture—wearing zoot suits, gathering with Black youth at dances and pool halls—as deviant and anti-American.[5] In this literature, processes of racialized criminalization are most often examined through the disproportionate policing and incarceration of Mexican American youth, analyses of *People v. Zamora*, or the 1943 Zoot Suit Riots. During this same period, young Mexican-origin men were also being confined to Pacific Colony at higher rates than Mexican-origin women who were targeted more often than men throughout the 1930s. These high rates of confinement at Pacific Colony underscore a relatively understudied factor in the racialized criminalization of young Mexican-origin men: disability.

RACE AND DISABILITY IN THE PRODUCTION OF A HIERARCHY OF DELINQUENCY

Theories about the relationship between crime and mental deficiency were embedded in the workings of developing juvenile court systems and related state agencies in the early twentieth century. Although reformers began differentiating between types of crime and criminals in the mid-eighteenth century, it wasn't until the twentieth century that Progressive reformers began to focus on crime among youth, or what became known as juvenile delinquency.[6] Progressive reformers interested in delinquency among youth—or, as criminologist Anthony Platt called them, "child savers"—viewed their efforts in benevolent and humanitarian terms. They saw themselves as child advocates, removing children and youth from adult jails and prisons and placing them in different types of carceral settings purportedly designed to meet the needs of delinquent youth in more humanitarian and scientific ways.[7] Believing that some youths could be rehabilitated and saved from a future of crime, these reformers established a separate court system for juveniles in order to treat youthful offenders with scientific expertise.[8] These courts spurred the development of new and more specialized institutions and methods of social control with the intent to classify different types of criminals and implement treatments accordingly. In California this resulted in the expansion of juvenile courts, reform schools like the Whittier State School, and institutions like Pacific Colony where juvenile delinquents who were deemed "feebleminded" could be confined and treated.[9] These judicial apparatuses and institutions worked together to identify, apprehend, diagnose, manage, and deploy treatments upon delinquent youth.

In 1915, Fred C. Nelles, the superintendent of the Whittier State School, launched California researchers into prominence in the national conversation on juvenile delinquency when he established a Department of Research at his institution. Like many state institution administrators in California at the time, Nelles was inspired by the research on heredity and social ills that renowned eugenicists Charles Davenport and Harry Laughlin were conducting at the Eugenics Records Office (ERO) in Cold Springs Harbor, New York.[10] In an effort to emulate the eugenic research of the ERO and transform Whittier into more than just a youth "house of correction," Nelles founded the California Bureau of Juvenile Research (CBJR).[11] Often referred to as the "West Coast Representative of the ERO," the CBJR became an important site for the production of knowledge on the etiology of juvenile delinquency.[12] Using youths confined to Whittier and other California state institutions as nonconsenting subjects, researchers like Stanford psychologist Lewis M. Terman (and Terman's former graduate student J. Harold Williams) worked with the CBJR to conduct studies, collect data, and produce research on the causal relationship between mental defect and juvenile delinquency, thereby reifying connections between bad heredity and crime.[13] Some of this research was used to support the establishment of Pacific Colony, and researchers associated with the CBJR were enthusiastic proponents of institutionalization as an approach to dealing with certain youths apprehended by juvenile court authorities.

In 1916 the CBJR began publishing the *Journal of Delinquency*, a scholarly journal that circulated research on juvenile delinquency nationally. Articles published in the *Journal of Delinquency* document the ways that California researchers like Terman and Williams aligned with researchers in the relatively nascent field of juvenile delinquency in other parts of the nation in their reliance on disability—in the form of feeblemindedness and mental defect—to assert that some youths were born criminals. This biologization of crime established a hierarchy of delinquency whereby "normal" delinquent youth could be reformed and rehabilitated while "defective delinquents" required more severe intervention and punishment. This hierarchy of delinquency drew from existing stereotypes of immigrant youth and youth of color as "mentally deficient" to mark young Black and Mexican-origin men as pathologically criminal.

To be clear, the idea of crime as a manifestation of individual inherent defect or pathology was not new when the *Journal of Delinquency* began circulating in 1916. Anglo-American physicians and social scientists had been collecting crime data that purportedly illustrated the inherent criminality of immigrants and African Americans since at least the mid-nineteenth century.[14] In the late nineteenth century, the emergence of Social Darwinism supported deterministic views regarding crime and shaped thinking on what to do about supposed criminals.[15] American intellectuals were drawn to claims made by European criminologists such as Herbert Spencer and Cesare Lombroso about the biological origins of criminal behavior among poor people, and elaborated on the "intractability of human nature and the innate moral defects of lower classes."[16] American physicians in particular took up these theories, contributing to the increased medicalization of criminal behavior in the United States. Some American physicians like Benjamin Rush and Isaac Ray became leaders in nineteenth-century criminology, asserting that crime was the outcome of individual pathology and thus required bodily interventions.[17]

Research published in the *Journal of Delinquency* added a more scientific veneer to deterministic theories regarding crime, and while Lewis Terman's introduction to the inaugural 1916 issue claimed that the publication held "no pet theories to promulgate," a survey of the journal's articles indicates that theories of inherent criminality predominated, particularly in articles examining the relationship between intelligence and juvenile delinquency.[18] Articles published in the journal in the late 1910s and early 1920s clearly adopted a eugenic framework, drawing connections between individual pathology and crime and asserting that deviant behaviors were likely outward symptoms of mental deficiency. Terman praised this line of research in the first issue of the journal, remarking that this scholarship represented "epoch-making developments in individual psychology" that would "throw important light on the causes and prevention of delinquency."[19] This research informed the way that California state authorities across agencies approached certain youths accused of delinquency as well as state practices around punishment and prevention.

Theories about the exact biological origins of crime varied during the nineteenth and early twentieth centuries, and by the early 1920s the notion of criminality as a strict hereditary unit trait—a crime gene, for example—was discredited. Even the authors of one 1920 article on juvenile delinquency in California conceded that "the belief that crime and delinquency are inherited characteristics is not borne out by the most careful investigations," explaining that assessments of family histories "show no tendency to inherit criminality or delinquency."[20] While the *Journal of Delinquency* adhered to this shift away from strict theories of inheritance, the contributors upheld biological determinism by tying criminal behavior to intelligence and mental capacity, which *were* accepted as hereditary and were also tied to racial ideologies.[21] In other words, researchers conceded that criminal behaviors themselves were not inherited, but they asserted that certain conditions they deemed hereditary—"feeble-mindedness, psychopathic constitution, excitability, nomadism and weakened inhibitory mechanism with reference to several different forms of self-control"—were important causal factors related to crime.[22]

In order to fully understand the biological etiology of crime, the journal editors published research into these supposedly inherited characteristics, especially feeblemindedness. The research on feeblemindedness and delinquency among juveniles offered a convenient way to biologize criminal behavior and codified long-held beliefs about the relationship between crime and mental capacity: that crime was symptomatic of low intelligence and that people with low IQ scores were potential criminals.

Moreover, this research situated feeblemindedness as a lens through which to distinguish "normal" juvenile delinquents, whose behaviors could be either reformed or rationalized as youthful indiscretions and ignored, and "defective delinquents" whose criminal pathology posed a larger threat to society and thus required more invasive interventions.

The primacy of mental capacity as a factor in juvenile delinquency was highlighted from the outset in J. Harold Williams's article in the first issue of the *Journal of Delinquency*. Despite the fact that the main focus of Williams's piece was delinquency among "boys of superior intelligence," he began by proclaiming the importance of low intelligence in delinquent behavior, writing: "It cannot be over-emphasized that the average intelligence among our delinquent and criminal classes is considerably lower than in the general population." Williams explained that "delinquents [were] not, as a rule, merely ordinary children who [had] accidentally become victims of an environment which would similarly affect any person." Prefacing his study of delinquency among youth of "superior intelligence," Williams made clear to the reader that it was actually "low intelligence" that "account[ed] for the offenses committed" in most cases."[23] Williams conceded that youth of "normal" and even "superior mentality" engaged in delinquent behavior but, according to him, these youths were outliers and, in those cases, a more complex combination of heredity and environment were at root.

While environment was significant in Williams's theorizing on the cause of juvenile delinquency, he maintained that a youth's surroundings were more likely to contribute to delinquency if that young person had not "developed normally."[24] In other words, Williams's foray into this type of "nature versus nurture" debate acknowledged the role of social and structural factors (environment) in producing deviant conduct, but he ultimately emphasized mental capacity as the most important factor. Situating mental capacity as more important than environment had important policy consequences, particularly for youths labeled mentally deficient. Under this framing, efforts to ameliorate negative environmental factors were essentially futile in preventing the delinquent behavior of youths with low IQ scores. Because their delinquency was caused by biological defect, individual interventions as opposed to "environmental" adjustments were proposed as most impactful. In this way juvenile delinquency as a social problem was framed as a problem of individual pathology, and the solution rested on properly identifying youth with this particular condition (low intelligence) and imposing bodily interventions.

Studies performed by Williams, Terman, and other well-respected psychologists across the country on youth already labeled delinquent and confined in state institutions like Whittier worked to support the commonly repeated notion that low intelligence or feeblemindedness caused juvenile delinquency. These studies produced data indicating that a large portion of these delinquent youths had low IQ scores and that many were thus feebleminded. The diagnosis in these studies was established after the fact of delinquency. The analyses of this data in the articles published in the *Journal of Delinquency*, however, extrapolated the relationship between feeblemindedness and delinquency to predict future behavior and offer conclusions on the social implication of a low IQ score for any young person, regardless of their behavior. That is, not only were criminal and otherwise socially deviant acts figured as symptomatic of feeblemindedness, but a diagnosis of feeblemindedness flagged a young person as a potential future criminal.

In their 1917 article in the journal, prominent American psychologists Leland W. Crafts and Edgar A. Doll wrote that the "feeble-minded [were] undoubtedly more prone to commit crime than are the average normals," adding that "one of the most conspicuous evidences of the intellectual and social characteristics of feebleminded children is their habitual and often serious delinquency."[25] The psychologists also argued that inherent moral, physical, and intellectual "defects" led to delinquency, warning that "feeble-minded juveniles everywhere represent either actual or potential delinquents."[26] This line of thinking was adopted in California, and in 1920 researchers published an article in the *Journal of Delinquency* estimating that at least one-third of all youth labeled delinquent in California were feebleminded.[27]

Once researchers identified feeblemindedness as the main source of delinquent behavior among youth, they set out to add nuance to their theory on the psychological determinants of juvenile delinquency, publishing studies in the *Journal of Delinquency* on the impact of differing levels of intelligence or "mental grades" and the role that gender played in the expression of delinquency.[28] For example, in one of their studies on mental deficiency among juvenile delinquents, Crafts and Doll noted that it was "generally conceded that the majority of feeble-minded juvenile delinquents are moron."[29] By highlighting the "moron" diagnostic grade, the psychologists attempted to establish a particular association between "high grade mental defectives" and criminality. They asserted the "well established fact" that the different sexes were inclined to different types of crime.[30] A 1920 article clarified this point, asserting that for young girls delinquency was "confined almost entirely to one kind of offense [immorality] while for boys it include[d] almost every kind of waywardness."[31] In addition to proposing that certain grades of feeblemindedness were more closely tied to crime and qualifying delinquency along gendered lines, researchers of juvenile delinquency also established a relationship between intelligence and race that reified already existing notions about the inherent criminality of nonwhite populations in the country.

The idea that juvenile delinquency was caused by low intelligence came out of early twentieth-century reformers' concern over growing immigrant, working-class, and African American populations in U.S. cities. As historians of delinquency have demonstrated, Progressive reformers often blamed poverty and crime in urban centers on the behaviors of nonwhite (im)migrants and Black youth.[32] However, this theory of intelligence and delinquency was not applied evenly. Reformers addressed these populations differently. Some European immigrant youth were seen as redeemable and even potentially assimilable, while other groups of young people were viewed through a lens of fixed inferiority and inherent criminality.[33] Racism was embedded in the ways that reformers and researchers interpreted the behaviors of young people and how they decided who was redeemable and who was labeled a "defective delinquent." In Southern California, working-class Black and Mexican-origin youth were more likely to be seen as inferior, defective, and unredeemable, and thus more deserving of policing and confinement.

The *Journal of Delinquency* provided "evidence" for this practice of racialized criminalization through studies that underscored the notion that low intelligence, and therefore delinquency, were more concentrated among certain immigrant and racialized groups. In their two-part study of mental deficiency among juvenile delinquents published in the journal in 1917, Crafts and Doll declared that "nationality is of decided importance in this country" given that "a considerable proportion of our juvenile delinquents are foreigners or the children of foreigners."[34] Addressing

criminality among Black youth, they added that a considerable proportion were also "Negros" and that "in the Southwest many Mexicans and
Indians become inmates of reform schools."[35] To support this assertion,
Crafts and Doll cited the work of white social scientists who interpreted
the early twentieth-century wave of immigration through the eugenic
lens of "race suicide," including Jeremiah Jenks and W. Jett Lauck's 1913
book *The Immigration Problem* and Peter Roberts's 1912 book *The New
Immigration*, which claimed that "he (the son of the foreign-born) is
three times more criminal than the sons of the native-born."[36] This particular article highlights cross-disciplinary conversations between social
science researchers in producing this knowledge on race, intelligence, and
crime.

In the second part of their article, Crafts and Doll built on the previous assertion that crime was more prevalent among Black youth and the
sons of the "foreign-born" by citing preexisting studies on race and intelligence. The psychologists pointed to studies that purportedly documented
the lower "natural intelligence" of "the negro compared to the white."[37] In
their discussion of Mexican-origin youth, the psychologists cited Jenks
and Lauck's tome on the "problem" of immigration, which stated that "the
intelligence of Mexicans is decidedly less than average when taken as a
group."[38] Tying this claim more directly to Mexican American youth, Crafts
and Doll cited the work of Williams and Terman—who, in a 1914 psychological survey of young boys at the Whittier State School, concluded that
notwithstanding Mexicans' official classification as "white" (guaranteed
to them by the terms of the Treaty of Guadalupe Hidalgo), they should
be distinguished from Anglo-American whites "on account of intelligence
differences probably due to the intermingling of Indian blood."[39]

Lastly, Crafts and Doll called on a 1915 study of 150 delinquent boys by
Williams that "found racial differences in the proportion of mental defectives among juvenile delinquents; 6 per cent of the whites proved feebleminded, while 48 per cent of the colored, and 60 per cent of the Mexican
and Indian group were feeble-minded."[40] Using Williams and Terman's
research, Crafts and Doll concluded that there was a "serious racial factor in intelligence differences themselves." Indeed, low intelligence itself
became a constitutive component of racial difference. Moreover, the psychologists drew on this research to assert a causal relationship between

this racial distribution of intelligence scores and the high crime rate "casually observed" among Black and Mexican-origin youth.[41]

To be clear, the high crime rate among Black and Mexican-origin youth "casually observed" by researchers, their disproportionate confinement in state reform schools like Whittier, and their high rates of detention at juvenile hall were much more the result of overpolicing and active racialized criminalization on the part of juvenile court authorities than the outcome of inherent pathology.[42] Yet research published in the *Journal of Delinquency* consistently published studies asserting that Black and Mexican-origin youth were being confined because of their inherent propensity to commit crimes. Even noncriminal behaviors or status crimes like not attending school were analyzed with this racist and ableist lens. For example, in his 1918 article Willis W. Clark, a field worker at Whittier, gathered intelligence testing data on young men confined to Whittier and charged with truancy, which he characterized as "the kindergarten of crime."[43] His interpretation of the data supported a connection between feeblemindedness and delinquency among Black and Mexican-origin youth, finding that while one-fourth of white boys were feebleminded, half of the "colored and Mexican-Indian boys were definitely feebleminded."[44]

Extending his analysis into the homes of these boys, Clark described Black and Mexican-origin families as containing "a large amount of mental defect."[45] He found that only 10 percent of the white families were described as feebleminded, while "37 per cent of the Negroes, and 47.4 per cent of the Mexican-Indians were feebleminded."[46] Making clear what feeblemindedness among these families entailed, Clark described family members as exhibiting "unfavorable or unsocial traits or characteristics" such as "delinquency, alcoholism, excitability, sexual immorality, nomadism, tuberculosis, criminalism, and insanity."[47] Applying the framework laid out by Williams, Clark acknowledged that the material and social circumstances of the family were likely important factors in contributing to truancy rates among the confined boys he studied but ultimately concluded that "the factors of intelligence, school retardation, and heredity" were of "vital influence."[48]

The research published by the CBJR in the *Journal of Delinquency* proliferated a discourse of juvenile delinquency that combined ideologies of race and disability to establish a racial hierarchy of criminality. In the studies on California youth by Williams, Terman, and Clark, white youth appeared in the same juvenile correctional institutions as youth of color, presumably for engaging in the same behaviors, but somehow their deviance was different in both origin and consequence. That is, even if youth across racial categories engaged in the same types of deviant behaviors, the researchers argued that the etiology of their deviance was different and thus the boys should be treated differently. Deploying the results of racially biased intelligence tests, these California researchers claimed that the deviant behavior of Black and Mexican-origin youth was, in most cases, the result of mental defect resulting from general racial inferiority. The deviant behaviors of white youth, however, were seen as more complicated. Theirs were less about inherent defect and more about environmental factors—or perhaps merely a result of youthful rebellion. After all, these researchers understood that all youth acted out.

In his widely celebrated 1916 book on intelligence Terman wrote: "All of us in early childhood lacked moral responsibility. We are as rank egoists as any criminal. Respect for the feelings, property rights, or any other kind of rights of others had to be laboriously acquired under the whip of discipline. But by degrees we learned...." For Terman and his colleagues, the major determining factor in this learning process, aside from "the whip of discipline," was intelligence. "Without intelligence to generalize the particular," Terman wrote, "to foresee distant consequence of present acts, to weigh these foreseen consequences in the nice balance of imagination, morality cannot be learned."[49] In study after study, CBJR researchers circulated the notion that Black and Mexican-origin youth did not have the intellectual capacity to learn morality and that by nature their conduct leaned more toward the criminal. This became an integral part of the racialized criminalization of youth of color and how Mexican-origin youth, despite their legal designation as white, were relegated outside of whiteness. Moreover, because their delinquency was seen as the result of inherent mental defect, their cases required different types of state interventions. Police officers and juvenile court authorities could not simply let the rebellious behaviors of "defective delinquents" slide, and these youth were not suitable for placement in regular state reform schools. These young people were not seen as capable of reform and so they required confinement in a different type of institution. Moreover, the danger of their inheritable traits meant that they were reproductive as well as social threats.

The knowledge on juvenile delinquency produced by the CBJR played an important role in the establishment of Pacific Colony in Southern California in the mid-1910s. In fact, the 1917 legislative committee report on mental deficiency in California produced in support of the Pacific Colony bill included a piece titled "Feeble-Mindedness and Delinquency" by Williams, who at that time was the director of the CBJR. In that piece Williams informed the legislature that "a large proportion of delinquent children [were] feeble-minded," a condition he described as hereditary in nature.[50] According to Williams, building Pacific Colony would significantly reduce juvenile delinquency in the state, estimating that "at least one-third of juvenile delinquency in California can be prevented by the segregation, in their early years, of feeble-minded children."[51] Moreover, Williams asserted that Pacific Colony would offer a long-term benefit through reproductive constraint, making it so that these youth would "not contribute to the perpetuation of the defective delinquent class."[52]

The research printed and proliferated by the CBJR through the *Journal of Delinquency* represents the enshrinement of what sociologists Tukufu Zuberi and Eduardo Bonilla-Silva have called "white logic" and "white methods" with regard to juvenile delinquency in California.[53] Researchers embedded racism and white supremacy in their reasoning about the causes and consequences of juvenile delinquency, and shaped thinking around confinement and sterilization as solutions. They established a logic that tied low intelligence to crime—two constructs already used to constitute racial difference and social inferiority. As a result, determining deviance and defect, both in terms of intelligence level and social location, became a principal method of identifying current or potential delinquents who required state intervention. This logic and method shaped the way state social workers and juvenile court authorities in Southern California approached young people charged with acts of delinquency. Theories about race, crime, and disability circulated by the CBJR established a predictable path to Pacific Colony.

IMPLEMENTING THE RESEARCH: JUVENILE COURTS, STATE WORKERS, AND THE PATH TO PACIFIC COLONY

Research produced by the CBJR shaped the practices of social workers and psychologists employed by state welfare departments, public schools, and local juvenile court systems, most of whom were white upper- and middle-class women and men. In 1918 and 1919 the CBJR published instructions on how to appropriately and "reliably" evaluate and grade the homes and neighborhoods of youth charged with delinquent behavior in order to collect data and make determinations regarding appropriate intervention. According to researchers and social workers, family and neighborhood information was important in assessing delinquent behavior, and the instructions mirrored what CBJR fieldworkers did in their research on young people confined at Whittier as juvenile delinquents.

The method entailed assessing factors CBJR identified as pertinent and making rank determinations based on existing economic and racial hierarchies. For example, social workers reported the economic status of families as either "unskilled," "skilled," or "capitalist," granting higher positive value to families labeled "skilled" or "capitalist." Likewise, domestic spaces that reflected higher economic status and "good taste" were ranked higher than domestic spaces that were small or considered unkempt. The marital status of the parents and whether mothers were able to stay at home and supervise children were also seen as important factors when considering the cause of a child's delinquent behavior. Neighborhoods were similarly ranked; social workers examined the cleanliness of community areas and whether garbage and sewage were disposed of properly. They remarked on the quality of lighting in a neighborhood and whether the area was equipped with access to telephone, mail, railroads, or recreational facilities. Well-resourced neighborhoods afforded youth a better evaluation, while neglected neighborhoods resulted in poor evaluations. Social workers summarized their observations in five-hundred-word descriptions and assigned numeric scores.[54]

CBJR authorities and social workers saw this process of description and ranking as a form of objective assessment and an important means of collecting information on the environmental factors related to a young person's delinquent behavior. In effect, these reports established a spectrum of deviance and normalcy with regard to homes and neighborhoods that corresponded to proximity to white upper- and middle-class families and neighborhoods. They helped determine how similar or different these youth were to the social workers and researchers themselves. The more these youths deviated from the economic, familial, and community structures that these social workers inhabited and valued, the more deviant, delinquent, or potentially delinquent the youths became in the eyes of evaluators. Because most of the youths for which these assessments were being performed were from working-class backgrounds, this practice codified a notion that working-class neighborhoods were exactly the type of "bad environment" that could lead to delinquency for "normal" youths and exacerbate the criminal tendencies of "defective delinquents."

These reports were also useful in providing supplemental social data with which to interpret the results of intelligence tests. Specifically information on economic status, family history, homes, and neighborhoods was used to support a diagnosis of feeblemindedness when IQ scores were low and to support the same diagnosis when IQ scores were "borderline," "average" or even "normal." While psychologists believed in the ability of intelligence tests to measure mental capacity, they often relied on social data—information about an individual's family, home, or neighborhood—to make diagnoses. In this way negative family, home, or neighborhood reports coupled with a low IQ score or even just a suspicion of low mentality made the case for additional policing, detention, or institutionalization, while positive observations (coming from a "good" home or neighborhood) could help stave off these measures. As the instructions for one of the CBJR scales stated, the home and neighborhood were considered important factors in the moral development of children and "to be especially significant as regards children who eventually become public charges," asserting that "inferior" homes and neighborhoods were strongly "associated with and seem to breed social degeneracy."[55] The use of the metaphor of breeding was effective in the era of eugenics. According to the CBJR, not only was the reproduction of inferior humans breeding social degeneracy, but so were their physical spaces.

Originally devised to classify the conditions found in the home and neighborhood environments of boys confined to the Whittier State School, the scales were later used broadly to collect and classify additional social information about anyone that came into contact with a state worker. The scales largely reflected the imposition of white middle-class norms as valid standards for assessing the quality and value of the domestic and community spaces of people under state observation or care. As historians of public health in California have documented, state workers used methods of description and observation to establish standards of normalcy and

deviance in domestic and neighborhood spaces since at least the late nineteenth century.[56]

These standards consistently measured domestic and neighborhood spaces against white middle-class standards, marking the homes
and communities of working-class nonwhites not only as inferior but
also as hubs of disease, vice, and contagion. Moreover, the reports that
documented these observations often served as the basis for additional
reports, data collection, and overall knowledge production about both the
spaces and the people who lived there. This "scientific" data was then used
to justify health policy, state and medical intervention, or even neglect.
Likewise, the home and neighborhood scales published by the CBJR
reflected the consolidation of white middle-class domesticity and social
life as the normative ideal. Meanwhile, the homes and neighborhoods of
working-class people and people of color were figured not only as sites of
delinquency and diseases but also as sites that literally bred disability and
pathological criminality. Terman, in an article on feeblemindedness in
California schools published in an education journal, noted that research
on delinquency revealed several "nests of feeble-mindedness" throughout
the southern part of the state.[57] Moreover, because this information was
deemed valuable in the overall assessment of youth who came into contact
with juvenile authorities, state workers felt justified in invading the privacy of working-class communities in ways deemed not only unnecessary
but unimaginable for middle- and upper-class communities.[58]

The idea that certain households and neighborhoods bred delinquency
and disability was brought out in other state arenas, including in one
study on the origin, background, intelligence, and race of boys committed to Los Angeles welfare centers in the 1930s. In that study education
student Harry M. Perry asserted that certain neighborhoods produced an
inordinate amount of delinquency. Hollenbeck Heights, South Central,
and other neighborhoods with Mexican and African American populations were identified as producers of juvenile delinquency.[59] Perry wrote
that, in general, "the greatest number of delinquents come from those
families having the smallest incomes," highlighting connections between
poverty and crime.[60] What's more, the author highlighted "low mentality" as an "important contributory condition in cases of maladjustment,"
given that out of the 3,428 boys studied, 77.5 percent were given IQ scores

below 100.[61] Significantly, 77 percent of the young boys were transferred to welfare centers because of nonviolent crimes, including petty theft, truancy, and "incorrigibility."[62] Perry's study on boys committed to welfare centers not only repeated the connections between race, disability, class, and crime but also highlighted the types of low-level and vague offenses ("incorrigibility") for which working-class youth of color were being disproportionately punished.

By the late 1920s the CBJR had succeeded in making intelligence testing a standard component of processing youth brought to juvenile hall. In this "psychiatric approach to the problem of delinquency," child guidance clinics or mental hygiene clinics were instituted at juvenile hall, where a psychiatric social worker collaborated with probation officers to both administer intelligence tests and try to acquire additional information on the family, home, and neighborhood in order to make diagnoses and recommend interventions.[63] By the early 1940s the psychiatrists working for Los Angeles Juvenile Hall held psychiatric interviews with as many detained youth as possible, regardless of whether they were "known to the court" or even charged with an offense. Mildred Malm was among these psychiatrists and tested hundreds of youths like Raul, who appears at the outset of this chapter. By 1944, Los Angeles Juvenile Hall expanded to include an entire hospital division providing medical, dental, and nursing services as well as psychological and psychiatric exams. Psychological examiners who worked there not only administered exams but also wrote social histories, made recommendations, published reports, and gave public lectures on the youth that they processed. Often juvenile hall authorities sent social histories and "medical-psychiatric" reports directly to judges presiding over a young person's case before official hearings, thereby influencing case determinations.[64]

Given that juvenile courts were empowered by the legal doctrine of *parens patriae*, the practice of involving psychiatric information that was in part supplemented by social data on family and home life had serious consequences for youth and parents alike. *Parens patriae* gave the state control over a minor if their parents were deemed unfit. As a result, young people could be committed to state institutions if state agents determined it was in their best interest to be removed from inadequate environments or "immoral" parents.[65] Adopting methods used in research on juvenile delinquency, juvenile court judges approached their work in "medical-therapeutic terms."[66] If judges believed a "mentally deficient" youth was in an "immoral" environment, they could exercise their legal right to have that young person committed to a state institution. Indeed, the psychiatric branch of Los Angeles Juvenile Hall worked closely with the CBJR and Pacific Colony, and authorities that worked there even passed on requests for sterilization.[67] California state agencies worked in tandem, and their theories and practices resulted in a juvenile legal system where young men of color and Mexican-origin men in particular were more likely to be labeled feebleminded and sentenced to confinement at Pacific Colony. This was evident in Raul's experience and in the case files of many other young Mexican-origin men who were committed to the institution.

Fred Coronado was first subjected to intelligence testing at juvenile hall in 1947 when he was sixteen. Labeled mentally deficient by the psychiatrist there, Fred was committed to Pacific Colony a year and a half later when social workers determined that he "lack[ed] supervision" at home.[68] Alfredo Leon was picked up by police in the 1940s for riding in a stolen car when he was seventeen. Citing previous incidents with police, juvenile authorities required Alfredo to take psychological and psychiatric exams ordered by the court. Because he did not score well on these tests, Alfredo was labeled mentally deficient and sent to Pacific Colony.[69] In 1944, at fourteen, George Perez was caught with a group of friends in the midst of a "mini crime wave" that included petty theft and theft of an automobile.[70] The court ordered George to take psychological exams, and he was also labeled mentally deficient. The courts allowed George to remain in his home with his parents on a six-month probation period, but when he was apprehended for auto theft before the probation period was up, he was sent to Pacific Colony.[71] As the experiences of these three young Mexican American men illustrate, court-ordered intelligence tests at juvenile hall were directly related to institutional confinement. While results indicating mental deficiency did not always result in immediate confinement in an institution, low IQ scores marked them for more severe state intervention should they have any type of additional interaction with legal authorities. Thus, engaging in activities deemed criminal (truancy, running away, petty theft) came at a higher risk for youth diagnosed as mentally deficient because they could be sent to the institution.

Unlike sentencing in adult courts, young people committed to Pacific Colony were punished with confinement for an indeterminate amount of time and their freedom was placed in the hands of the clinicians at the institution. Some were released quickly, but others remained confined to the institution for most of their lives. This practice had been in place since Pacific Colony's opening but was legally codified in the mid- to late 1940s, when the juvenile courts expanded the use of the institution and its northern counterpart, the Sonoma State Home. A change in laws governing the practice of the California Youth Authority made it so that the courts could commit youth to either Pacific Colony or Sonoma for a ninety-day "observation period" if they were suspected of being a "defective or psychopathic delinquent." The Youth Authority was also empowered to commit youth labeled "defective or psychopathic" for an indeterminate amount of time without having to go back to court to process commitment.[72]

Legal changes mandated a minimum five-year probation period for these youth if they were ever paroled from the institution, which extended the amount of time that a person stayed under surveillance by the state. In addition to indefinite confinement and mandated parole periods, these youth were subjected to any treatments deemed necessary by institutional authorities, including sterilization. Case files from Pacific Colony indicate that this practice continued well into the 1950s and was used to confine young men for minor offenses. For example, in 1953 sixteen-year-old Antonio Guerrero was committed to Pacific Colony with a "minor delinquency history." The "outstanding feature" of his case was "a disorganized family constellation" and a mother who appeared to social workers as either "defective or else culturally subnormal" because she had children outside of marriage.[73]

In Southern California, where institutional authorities at reform schools and institutions for the feebleminded like Pacific Colony were given power and authority to both define and address juvenile delinquency, young Mexican-origin men were disproportionately identified as delinquent because of inherent mental deficiency. Racial theories of intelligence and delinquency shaped how authorities in the juvenile court system treated youth of color as well as how they were classified and diagnosed—whether they would be sent to a reform school or committed to an institution—and played a role in the type of treatment to which they were subjected. In this way, Progressive Era reformers and researchers believed they had discovered a new and scientifically grounded way to accurately "classify, sort, and segregate state wards along a continuum of normalcy to degeneracy."[74] In Southern California this often meant committing juvenile delinquents who were identified as feebleminded to Pacific Colony, where they could be further studied, diagnosed, treated, and sterilized.

"CRIMINAL TENDENCIES" AND "BAD RACIAL STOCK": THE REPRODUCTIVE CONSEQUENCES OF JUVENILE DELINQUENCY

Establishing feeblemindedness as an inheritable trait that caused criminal behavior, research on delinquency fueled eugenicists' assertions that the state needed to fund efforts to curtail the reproduction of the "unfit" for the benefit of society. In the beginning of the second issue of the *Journal of Delinquency*, J. Harold Williams asserted that "the perpetuation of feeblemindedness through the hereditary transmission of weakened stock means further increase in delinquency and crime."[75] Another article argued that "if feebleminded persons were prevented from producing children, juvenile delinquency would be reduced at least one-third and there would be reason to expect a proportionate decrease in crime and other social evils."[76] Acting on these assertions, the California Department of Institutions supported the sterilization of both women *and* men. In fact, one 1926 report published by the California Department of Institutions explained that institutional authorities advocated "sterilization of both sexes" as "common practice."[77]

As the studies published in the *Journal of Delinquency*, statements from institutional authorities, and historical research on juvenile courts suggest, Mexican-origin boys were viewed as a "criminally inclined group that needed to be dealt with harshly."[78] The problem of delinquency among Mexican-origin young men, however, was not just about crime; it was also cast as a reproductive issue that threatened the nation with racial degeneration. Crafts and Doll identified "low intelligence" among various non-Anglo racial groups as a pressing issue given "the mingling of the Caucasian nationalities as well as the presence of large numbers of Negros, Indians, Mexicans and Orientals in various sections of the country."[79] Their concern over the "mingling" of the races illustrates the overarching fear among early twentieth-century eugenicists of miscegenation and the potential "mongrelization" of the white race caused by Mexican reproduction.[80]

In his study of race and policing in Los Angeles during the first half of the twentieth century, historian Edward Escobar quoted Vanderbilt University economist Roy Garis, who stated that Mexicans in the Southwest were creating a race problem that would result in "the practical destruction, at least for centuries, of all that is worthwhile in our white civilization."[81] Significantly for Escobar's study and the research presented in this chapter, Garis supported his argument with studies establishing the inherent criminality of Mexicans. Even economists drew on assertions of inherent criminality in their arguments against Mexican immigration. When California's 1917 legislature established Pacific Colony, they legitimized confinement and sterilization as necessary approaches to deal with so-called feebleminded juvenile delinquents that were housed in juvenile reform schools across the state.[82] Over the course of more than two decades, juvenile court authorities worked with Pacific Colony staff to segregate, confine, and sterilize young working-class Mexican-origin men who in both the research and in the public mind came to symbolize delinquency and mental deficiency.

The construction of Mexican boys institutionalized at Pacific Colony as criminally defective and hailing from similarly defective and delinquent families is reflected repeatedly in the sterilization requests processed by Pacific Colony. A reading of the sterilization requests offers a better sense of how Pacific Colony clinicians actively biologized delinquency as part of the "bad racial stock" of Mexican-origin men to make a case for sterilization. The institution's officials often listed out the criminal offenses of Mexican-origin boys in their sterilization requests. For example, in the sterilization request for fifteen-year-old Miguel Lopez, who was admitted in April 1939, a clinician wrote that the boy was committed on the petition of a probation officer and that he was "an habitual truant, run-away and has been guilty of repeated burglary, shop-lifting, etc [sic]." These charges offered validity to the clinician's diagnostic description of Miguel: a "borderline case" with a "language difficulty and poor background." Moreover, the clinician that explained that Pacific Colony authorities were seeking permission to sterilize Miguel "on account of his history of delinquency."[83] Often written in shorthand and included in sometimes incoherent notes, the mentions of language difference and racial stock made sense to institutional authorities who had become well versed in the research published by the CBJR. Because previous research established a valid connection between race, crime, and intelligence, institutional authorities already knew how to build a convincing case for sterilization.

The categorization of petty crimes as symptomatic of mental deficiency is underscored by the sterilization requests as well. For example, Pacific Colony staff wrote in seventeen-year-old Rodrigo Quintanilla's sterilization request that he was committed on the petition of a probation officer after being arrested for stealing $87.75 worth of property from a home "with two other Mexican boys." This was the only comment documented in his sterilization request, which was processed by Pacific Colony authorities and approved by the California Department of Institutions two months after his admission to the institution.[84] In a different sterilization request, a clinician relied on reports from juvenile court authorities and educators to frame fourteen-year-old Antonio Duran as an inherent criminal. The clinician wrote that juvenile authorities apprehended the young boy on charges of burglary and petty theft after he "entered a residence and [had] taken several articles of small value." The clinician remarked that educators at Antonio's school described him as "high tempered, unreliable, an habitual truant and a bully" to other state workers.[85] Clinicians paired minor charges and descriptions by other state authorities with a diagnosis of feeblemindedness to increase their significance. In doing so, they situated what were largely nonviolent incidents as the early beginnings of a life of crime that might evolve into more dangerous acts by these boys. When placed alongside lower than "normal" IQ scores and diagnoses such as "borderline" and "moron," these seemingly minor criminal acts became seen as symptoms of mental deficiency and inherent pathology, rationalizing the need for sterilization.

To increase the specter of criminality, clinicians added racial descriptions of the boys, often commenting on their inferior "racial stock." The Pacific Colony official that authored Antonio's sterilization request, for example, described his parents as being "of low grade Mexican Mentality." In addition to listing eighteen-year-old Jose Leon's "various offenses," which included burglary, grand theft, and "incorrigibility," the clinician who authored his sterilization request also noted that Jose's parents were "native of Mexico," specifying that "they came from a racial stock of Mexicans and Indians."[86] This description fit neatly in line with earlier assertions that low intelligence was due to the "intermingling" of "Indian blood" underscoring notions of Mexicans as a largely racially mixed population. After commenting on Jose's racial background, the clinician wrote that the young man "should have the operation, taking into consideration his criminal tendencies." The Pacific Colony official that wrote a sterilization request for fourteen-year-old Saul Suarez—who was committed after having served a year in Whittier "on a charge of petty theft and burglary"— also made the claim that "his parents [were] low grade Mexicans."[87] In Antonio's, Jose's, and Saul's records Pacific Colony clinicians drew clear connections between the boys' criminality and their "racial stock" to create a heightened sense of biological inferiority. Mentioning the racial background of these boys was significant and shows that Pacific Colony authorities relied on an existing racial logic that assumed the intellectual inferiority of Mexicans and their inherent propensity toward crime to justify sterilizing young Mexican-origin men.

In addition to referencing Saul's bad "racial stock," the author of his record commented on the supposed low intelligence of his family, writing that eight of Saul's siblings were "said to be subnormal."[88] Characterizing the families of young Mexican-origin men as feebleminded or otherwise deviant also worked to legitimize requests for sterilization. In fifteen-year-old Francisco Mendoza's sterilization request, for example, a clinician wrote derisively about the boy's family.[89] After describing Francisco as a "behavior problem at home and in school," the clinician explained that the boy was committed after being "picked up by the Sheriff's office for entering a house and stealing jewelry and money." Following the description of his criminality, the clinician wrote that Francisco's "father deserted the family and it is reported that the mother's morals are questionable and that the boy would speak readily of the 'father we have now.'" In addition to suggesting that Francisco's mother was immoral, the clinician wrote that Francisco's paternal grandfather died of tuberculosis, evoking the notion of Mexicans as diseased. Selecting specific points to highlight about Francisco and his family, the clinician chose to paint a picture of questionable morals and disease—a family environment that was consistently tied to "defective delinquents" in research on juvenile delinquency.

In his sterilization request, eighteen-year-old David Morales's family was also disparaged by Pacific Colony officials. Like others, David was previously institutionalized at Whittier on a charge of petty theft and was transferred to Preston, where institutional authorities their decided he "was not a fit subject for Preston but should be confined in an institution for the feebleminded."[90] After describing David's institutional history, which suggested a pattern of criminality and incorrigibility, the author of David's sterilization request pointed out that David was one of twelve children and that his older brother was also institutionalized for mental deficiency. Considering David's history of criminality, family size, and the suggestion that other family members were also mentally deficient, Pacific Colony clinicians reasoned that David should be sterilized "on account of his low intelligence, criminal tendencies and poor family background."[91]

Clinician notes in the Pacific Colony sterilization requests highlighted the role that sterilization played in institutional authorities' plans to turn young Mexican-origin men into productive but not reproductive members of society. Fifteen-year-old Freddy Cortez, for example, was committed by a probation officer for stealing just after his father passed away. Within weeks after Freddy was admitted, the staff at the institution's clinical conference unanimously decided "he should be sterilized and placed on industrial parole after a period of training." That is, within weeks of admitting him, the medical staff at the institution decided that Freddy was only fit for a role in society limited to work as a low-wage laborer as opposed to a future that included being a parent. Luis Chavez and his sister were committed to Pacific Colony in 1929 when he just was nine years old, after his father was "killed in a brawl." Luis's mother had also passed away, but his record made no mention of how. In 1944, after thirteen years, institutional authorities requested permission from the Department of Institutions to sterilize Luis at the age of twenty-two. After having spent most of his life confined at Pacific Colony, clinicians decided that "following sterilization he would be suitable for consideration of an industrial parole placement."[92]

Assessing young men's potential to enter the industrial work force was a standard part of Pacific Colony procedure. Notes made by institutional authorities on index card files for other young Mexican-origin men point to the ways that clinicians viewed them as potential laborers. In one 1933 case a "Mexican" boy is described like this: "high moron level; manual in type; stable; trainable industrially." On the index card file for a different boy, a Pacific Colony staff member wrote that he was "good material for industrial parole after training. Detail to kitchen."[93] The ways that institutional authorities talked about all of these young Mexican-origin men shows how their reproduction was figured as a mere barrier to what state workers saw as their true potential: laborers in the industrial work force. Discussing them as work force "material" highlights in stark ways how Pacific Colony staff actively diminished the parenthood rights of young Mexican-origin men in favor of efforts to make them potentially productive citizens.

Upon release from Pacific Colony, many young Mexican-origin men did indeed enter the workforce. Willy Lopez, who was committed to Pacific Colony in 1942 at the age of twelve, was allowed a temporary leave in 1945 when he was finally able to return to school. Willy eventually joined the army and was ultimately discharged during his deployment in Germany in 1948. Juan Contreras, who was committed to Pacific Colony in 1940 at the age of eighteen, worked on the agriculture detail and lived in Cottage 15 during his three years at the institution. When he was finally released, Juan found employment on the railway and eventually moved north to work in the fig industry. He was not officially discharged until 1945. Frank Campos, who was committed when he was eleven, also lived in Cottage 15. He was granted leave from the institution after spending almost a decade at Pacific Colony. Frank found work at a defense plant and, after placing pressure on his social worker, was finally discharged a year and a half after his release. Positive remarks by social workers about Willy, Juan, and Frank illustrate the ways that Pacific Colony authorities not only valued the young men's labor contributions over their potential to have children but also point to the ways that institutional authorities tried to claim the success of self-sufficient former residents as their own.[94]

Although descriptions of the young Mexican-origin men sterilized at Pacific Colony were often brief, they were specifically chosen to fit a particular racialized medical narrative of Mexican deviance, defect, and threat in order to justify sterilization. The descriptions relied on a particu-

lar early twentieth-century racial understanding of intelligence and criminality as hereditary and conveyed the desire to constrain the reproduction
of certain feebleminded delinquents in order to preserve the racial health
of the nation and to combat crime. In addition to implementing the policies supported by the CBJR on the bodies of youth committed to the institution, Pacific Colony administrators used these young men as subjects in
research that replicated much of the thinking on race, intelligence, and
crime developed by researchers in the early part of the twentieth century.

YOUNG MEXICAN-ORIGIN MEN AND KNOWLEDGE
PRODUCTION AT PACIFIC COLONY

The CBJR's prolific research agenda gave California researchers national
prominence and local power over the lives and futures of youth deemed
defective and delinquent, but the research department closed in the late
1920s due to lack of state funding and the departure of researchers, fieldworkers, and staff. The nearly two decades of knowledge produced by the
bureau, however, helped codify connections between race, crime, and
disability, resulting in the targeted institutionalization of working-class
disabled youth and youth of color and the disproportionate institutionalization of Mexican-origin youth caught up in the juvenile court system. A
few years after opening in 1927, Pacific Colony itself started to fill the void
in research left by the closing of the CBJR, becoming an important site of
knowledge production on crime, race, and disability as well as the psychiatric and institutional techniques the state should use to address crime.

One of the ways institutional authorities proposed to transform or
rehabilitate purportedly "unproductive" and disabled populations was
by having them provide free labor for the institution and train them to
become laborers in low-wage service and care sectors upon release from
the institution. In this way Pacific Colony administrators, local communities, hospitals, and sanitariums profited from the labor of former residents
who became domestic workers and sanitarium or hospital attendants who
could be paid low wages because they were cast as low-skilled and defective. Young able-bodied Mexican-origin men at Pacific Colony provided
free and necessary labor for the institution while they were confined, but

they also became research subjects for studies by the superintendent, psychiatrists, and budding professionals in the fields of education, social work, and psychology. The knowledge produced by these studies not only added to the pathologizing research on crime and disability but also provided direct benefits to the researchers who gained professional praise and authority. This research buttressed existing dichotomous constructions of "defective" versus "normal" and "criminal" versus "innocent" while furthering the need for a professional class of helpers who benefited from these constructions both socially and economically.

During the early years of Pacific Colony's development, Norman Fenton, a psychologist from Ohio who worked at Whittier, played a fundamental role in establishing the institution. Once up and running, Fenton organized and led summer sessions on feeblemindedness for teachers and psychologists, often compelling residents of Pacific Colony to stand in front of his students for observation.[95] Fenton's courses were so popular that he eventually acquired a faculty position at Claremont Colleges, where he disseminated and expanded his research on residents confined at both Whittier and Pacific Colony. Fenton's position marked the beginning of a long-term relationship between Pacific Colony and Claremont Colleges. College students visited the institution, were allowed to observe residents in their lessons on different types of disability and, importantly, learned who to target for institutionalization. In the early 1940s, James A. Blaisell, president of the college, formed part of the Pacific Colony board of trustees, and by the end of the decade the institution was accredited for a yearlong training program for psychiatric residents. In this way Pacific Colony participated in what other scholars have described as a practice of increasing the prestige and jurisdiction of the helping professions.[96]

In addition to being used as live objects for class observations, some residents were kept in Pacific Colony longer than necessary because they were considered interesting research subjects. Felix Sanchez—who, like the young Mexican-origin men discussed earlier, was tested at juvenile hall after allegedly being involved in burglaries—was repeatedly described as not mentally deficient but was nevertheless committed to Pacific Colony. The Pacific Colony clinician who studied Felix noticed that he stuttered and thus found him to be a useful research subject and "interesting psychologically." As a result, the clinician ordered an x-ray of Felix's

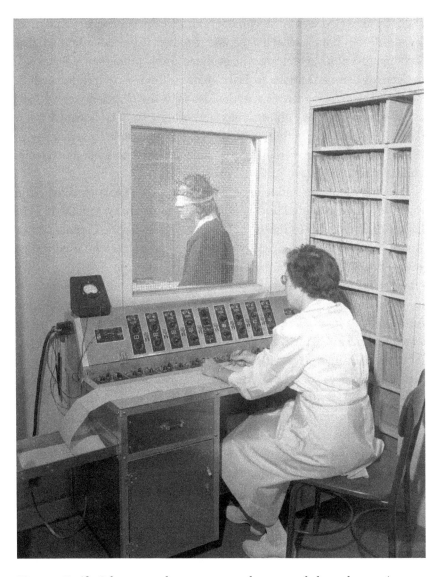

Figure 7. Pacific Colony nurse demonstrates an electroencephalograph on patient, 1950. *Los Angeles Times* Photographic Archives, Collection 1429, Library Special Collections, Charles E. Young Research Library, University of California–Los Angeles.

skull, an activated electroencephalogram, and a pneumoencephalogram. In addition to the physical exams, the clinician suggested administering sodium amytal (a barbiturate with sedative and hypnotic side effects) and anticonvulsive medications to Felix before interviewing him to see how the drugs would impact his speech. Although the clinician viewed Felix as an interesting test subject, Felix had other plans. He escaped a few days after being committed to Pacific Colony, and while he remained on escape for some time, Felix was eventually arrested on a narcotic charge and incarcerated.[97]

One 1950 study is emblematic of the ways that ideas established in the 1910s were repeated and confirmed in midcentury scholarship. In his social work master's thesis on Mexican boys in Pacific Colony, Arthur Palace wrote that of the twenty-one Mexican-origin boys he used for his study, sixteen had been committed to Pacific Colony as a result of a parole officer's recommendation, and three others were committed by referral from the California Youth Authority.[98] One boy had been recommended for placement in a boarding home, but that facility had no room and he was thus sent to Pacific Colony. The final young man was recommended for placement in a private institution but was not eligible for admission because he was Mexican.[99] All these young men were therefore committed to Pacific Colony through a juvenile justice agency, and none of the Mexican-origin male youths Palace observed had been committed by a parent. This was in stark contrast to the "Anglo-white" cases he observed, of which nine out of twenty-nine were committed by parental petitions.[100] This observation suggests that Mexican-origin male youths were likely removed from their families and committed at Pacific Colony against the wishes of their parents.

In addition to differences in routes of commitment, Palace made a telling conclusion regarding the distribution of diagnoses between the two groups. Focusing on boys diagnosed as "morons," Palace noted a decline in "Anglo-white" patients among the "moron" group and a "predominant distribution in the moron range" of the "Mexican-white" group.[101] This difference was even more significant when Palace divided the "moron" group into "high moron" residents, qualified with a higher-range IQ score between 60 and 69, and "low moron" residents, qualified with a lower-range IQ score between 50 and 59.[102] By separating the groups in this way,

Palace found that the Mexican-origin boys represented 47 percent of all of the "high-moron" cases and 35 percent of the "moron" group as a whole.[103]

The implication of Mexican boys having higher overall intelligence scores, Palace asserted, was that "anti-social behavior" and delinquency was a more important factor in their institutionalization. In other words, Mexican-origin boys committed more acts of delinquency than their white counterparts and thus required commitment at higher rates, even if their intelligence levels were relatively high. Palace made this argument based on his previous understanding of commitment practices at Pacific Colony, writing that institutionalization because of "intellectual impairment" was rare and more often the result of "emotional maladjustment manifested in asocial behavior."[104] Thus, instead of concluding that young Mexican-origin men faced racial bias within the legal system that resulted in higher rates of institutionalization, Palace concluded that mentally deficient Mexican-origin youths were more prone to delinquency and "emotional maladjustment" than white youths with similar IQ scores. This belief is highlighted in Palace's characterization of the Mexican boys he observed. He described them as more "aggressive," more likely to "act out," and more likely to engage in "anti-social" acts such as stealing, running away, and intoxication.[105] Palace wrote that many of the Mexican-origin boys committed acts of delinquency in concert with other youths, which he concluded was evidence of an inability to think independently.[106] Lastly, Palace asserted that the Mexican-origin boys represented more "congenital" types of delinquency, thereby reinforcing notions of racial hereditary defect.[107]

In addition to describing the "Mexican-white" boys at Pacific Colony as more prone to criminality despite their higher levels of intelligence, Palace depicted their family environment as a further source of pathology. Examining the family histories of both "Mexican-white" and "Anglo-white" groups, Palace found that while half of the Anglo-white boys had "good housing," only one out of twenty-one of the Mexican-origin boy's housing met that standard. He noted that the Mexican-white boys had "larger families," which (according to Palace) predisposed Mexican-origin boys to "a greater amount of parental incompetence."[108] Furthermore, Palace investigated the family history of delinquency for the two groups and found that the Mexican families had three times as many acts of delinquency than the white families.[109] Thus, he asserted that the need to commit Mexican-origin male youths to Pacific Colony did not merely stem from their propensity to commit delinquent acts, but was also brought on by "behavior problems, which developed in the family constellation."[110]

Well into the 1960s, Pacific Colony continued to be a site for research on disability and its connection to a host of other issues, and the people confined there were used to produce material published in lectures, master's theses, and journal articles. Much of this research continued to repeat notions about the inherent defect and criminality of working-class youth of color indicated by the disproportionate commitment of Mexican and Black youth to the institution. For example, an article published by George Tarjan, Pacific Colony medical director, in the *Pacific Sociology Review* in 1959 found that there were greater proportions of working-class Mexican American and Black youth in the institution than in the general population, especially among inmates with IQs higher than 50 and with a diagnosis of "familial" classification. Although the authors drew no conclusions, they proposed several hypotheses to explain this demographic pattern, including heredity, "cultural deprivation," and the tendency of "ethnic minorities and lower classes" to get in trouble with the law more often and thus require institutionalization.[111]

In addition to continuing to draw connections between race, crime, and disability that were reminiscent of research produced by the CBJR, this particular article also documents how justifications for the institutionalization of the disabled, the poor, and people of color were beginning to make a shift from rationales about defective heredity to cultural pathology.[112] The research conducted at Pacific Colony did more than confirm previous research on race, crime, and disability. It also worked to benefit the careers of many, including Dr. Tarjan, who served as the president of the American Association on Mental Deficiency, the American Academy of Child Psychiatry, and the American Psychiatric Association. In the early 1960s, after more than a decade at Pacific Colony, Dr. Tarjan gained national prominence as one of the architects of President John F. Kennedy's legislation regarding research, training, and services for people with intellectual disabilities.

This chapter highlights the historical connections between medical and penal notions of social deviance and the ways that racism and ableism converged in rationales for confinement and sterilization. Disability studies scholars have long established the need to broaden the analytical scope of incarceration to include the confinement of various "undesirable populations" in state institutions in order to examine state authorities' use of medical logic to expand the carceral state and effect population control.[113] While Pacific Colony was often cast as a more humane and rehabilitative form of confinement than the state's adult penal system, institutional confinement meant that psychologists made decisions regarding how long someone would be confined, what treatments they would be subjected to, and how long their parole period would be. Furthermore, being committed to Pacific Colony also meant that a person could be sterilized—a practice that was banned from the state's penal system. Situating Pacific Colony as part of the history of mass incarceration and highlighting the confinement and sterilization of Mexican-origin boys suggests a necessary broadening of analyses of incarceration as a Reproductive Justice issue. Recent scholarship by Reproductive Justice advocates correctly situate prisons as sites of "reproductive injustice" because people who are incarcerated face significant barriers to abortion, and pregnant people receive substandard reproductive care.[114]

Although that scholarship acknowledges the negative impact that the mass incarceration of men has on women and families in low-income communities and communities of color, the majority of the analyses focus on direct harms experienced by incarcerated women and pregnant people. Bringing young men of color into this particular history of sterilization challenges us to rethink the ways incarceration itself is a Reproductive Justice issue that is further exacerbated by lack of proper reproductive health care in the prison system. Imprisonment on its own is a form of sexual and reproductive oppression for young men who are locked away during the reproductive period. Moreover, the experiences of Mexican-origin youth at Pacific Colony underscore how reproductive injustices created by carceral practices are sustained by ideologies of inferior racial, intellectual, and economic capacity that impact both men and women's reproductive lives, albeit in different ways.

4 Riots, Refusals, and Other Defiant Acts

RESISTING CONFINEMENT AND STERILIZATION
AT PACIFIC COLONY

Shuffled between state institutions throughout her teenage years, Teresa Lago was painfully aware of the power state workers held over her body. Her life wasn't exactly easy before institutionalization. When Teresa was five, both of her parents, who were Mexican immigrants, died of pneumonia. Teresa was the youngest of six, and her siblings did what they could to stay afloat, but it was the Great Depression and they struggled economically. Despite these economic hardships, Teresa did well in school and mostly stayed out of trouble. Like a lot of teenagers, she started testing the limits of authority. In the mid-1940s, when she was sixteen, Teresa got caught stealing from a hotel. A juvenile court judge thought Teresa's behavior was out-of-bounds, and assessed her siblings' care as lacking, so he sentenced Teresa to confinement at a welfare facility. She earned her freedom on good behavior and moved to Los Angeles from the welfare facility to start anew.

A few months into her newfound freedom, Teresa learned she was pregnant, and a social worker had her confined to an institution for expectant mothers. This was a difficult time for Teresa. She was angry and depressed, and these feelings only worsened after her son was born. She tried to escape whenever she had the opportunity, but institutional authorities held her under constant surveillance. After the birth, state

Figure 8. Interior corridor in Hospital at Pacific Colony, Spadra, 192?. Courtesy of the California History Room, California State Library, Sacramento.

workers determined that Teresa's son could stay within the family. Instead of being put up for adoption or placed in foster care, they granted custody of the baby to Teresa's older sister. This was a small win, but Teresa felt overwhelmed by everything. The death of her parents, growing up in poverty, repeated institutionalization, experiencing pregnancy and birth in confinement, and the diminishment of her parental status—it was all too much for the nineteen-year-old to manage. Teresa was forced to stay at the home for expectant mothers even after giving birth, and a month later the staff worked with the courts to transfer Teresa to a state mental hospital. They described her as severely depressed, quickly "agitated", and thus requiring care at an institution for the mentally ill.[1]

Things got worse before they got better. At the state hospital, separated from her family and her newborn, Teresa withdrew even more from the world. Doctors described her as "almost catatonic" with "suicidal tendencies." Months later, when Teresa started improving, the hospital discharged her back to the courts, where the state's legal authorities decided that instead of reuniting with her son, Teresa should be confined to yet another institution. In the midst of her postpartum breakdown, a psychologist diagnosed Teresa with psychosis *and* mental deficiency, citing "sex promiscuity"—sex and reproduction outside of marriage—as evidence that she had low mental capacity. Although Teresa's psychosis had seemingly improved, a judge decided that her "mental deficiency" made her unfit for freedom and unfit to parent. With this diagnosis the judge had Teresa committed to Pacific Colony.

Teresa had already been through so much when she arrived at Pacific Colony at the age of twenty. In meetings with social service workers at the institution, she pleaded for release so that she could care for her son. Pacific Colony authorities had other plans. Uninterested in Teresa's wishes for her own life, clinicians at Pacific Colony focused their energies on trying to make her a compliant and productive "inmate." Teresa received no educational training because she was considered "too old" for school, and the clinical staff quickly determined that because of her "sex promiscuity," Teresa should be sterilized if she was ever going to be discharged. Teresa and her family had little say and no legal power regarding "treatment" or release. Measures for Teresa's progress and whether she deserved to be free from confinement were largely based on staff assessments of her behavior—whether she was acquiescent and performed well in her assigned work placements around the institution.

This was an arrangement that Teresa never accepted. Despite the overwhelming power state workers held in her life, Teresa remained unmanageable and she made known her discontent regarding confinement, forced labor, and sterilization. She incited chaos in her ward and repeatedly disrupted efforts to establish order and submission in Pacific Colony.

Teresa was unwilling to work for free, despite being placed on several different work assignments throughout the institution. On the day Pacific Colony staff scheduled her unwanted sterilization, Teresa caused a scene in the hospital building where hundreds of Mexican-origin women and men before her had been stripped of their reproductive capacity. Enraged, Teresa fought back, she resisted, and on the day of the surgery—despite years of state intervention into every aspect of her life—Teresa was successful and the operation was not performed.

In her early 1950's master's thesis on young women committed to Pacific Colony, social work student Margaret Frank narrated these details about Teresa's life and her defiant acts differently. According to Frank, Teresa's experiences, her reactions to hardship and pain, and her resolute defiance in the face of state authority were contributing factors to why she failed to be reformed. Teresa's insubordinate attitude, unwillingness to work, and her intense resistance to sterilization earned her the additional labels of a "cottage problem" and "completely uncooperative."[2] Like the psychiatrists, physicians, judges, and social workers before her, Frank analyzed Teresa's reactions to personal trauma and oppositional stance on state control over her bodily and reproductive freedom as additional evidence that she was indeed mentally, socially, and emotionally defective. Rejecting this reductive, pathologizing, and apathetic reading of Teresa's life, emotions, and actions, I contend that her rebellious acts were not evidence of individual defect. Instead, I read Teresa's actions—and the actions of the other Pacific Colony youth discussed in this chapter—as both symptomatic of invasive state power over the lives of people committed to public institutions and as defiant responses to that power.[3]

Teresa was not the first (and certainly not the last) to protest her sterilization—nor was she alone in refusing to cooperate with demands that she submit her body, emotions, and labor to institutional authorities. Young Mexican-origin women and men alongside their peers, families, and allies engaged multiple strategies in defiance of state power over their lives and bodies. Confined youth refused to cooperate with institutional authorities, caused chaos in their ward buildings, and orchestrated and executed escape plans. In defense of their institutionalized children, parents and family members refused to sign consent forms, sought out allies to help mitigate the overwhelming power of the juvenile court system, and even waged legal battles against the state. This chapter upends the pathologizing descriptions and interpretations Pacific Colony authorities and researchers made about the actions and behaviors of Mexican-origin youth confined to the institution. Countering the institutional framework of racialized defect and incompetence, this chapter narrates the disruptive and rebellious behaviors of institutionalized youth through a lens of agency. In these retellings, institutionalized Mexican-origin youth were not merely displaying symptoms of feeblemindedness, but they were reacting to the conditions they were forced to endure. Subverting the pathologizing narratives of researchers and state workers generates a deeper understanding of how invasive, pervasive, and violent state control was in this specific institutional setting. We also glean a sense of confined youths' defiance, resilience, and resourcefulness in (re)claiming bodily autonomy and how they mustered up and maintained dignity and humanity in a resolutely dehumanizing context.

As Teresa's experience illustrates, a diagnosis of mental deficiency or feeblemindedness offered state authorities significant legal power over a person's daily life and reproductive future. Connoting mental incompetence, this specific category of disability was effectively used by state authorities to diminish a person's rights and decision-making power.[4] Indeed, being committed to Pacific Colony involved a legal determination of incompetence and rendered individuals wards of the state. Thus institutionalization meant not only social segregation and a loss of freedom, but also a loss of bodily autonomy and minimal legal recourse. Decisions about the treatment, freedom, and future of confined youth were made by the same state authorities who deemed them pathologically deviant, burdensome, and unfit to reproduce. As disability theorists Nirmala Erevelles and Andrea Minear have described, individuals "located perilously at the interstices of race, class, gender, *and* disability" have historically been socially and legally constituted as "non-citizens and (no)bodies by the very social institutions (legal, educational, and rehabilitational) that [were purportedly] designed to protect, nurture, and empower them."[5]

Of course, as Teresa's story and the examples in this chapter document, Mexican-origin youth contested this legal and social process of dehumanization, although their acts of defiance may not always be recognized as such. In her "Sick Woman Theory," artist and disability theorist Johanna Hedva considers the modes of protest afforded to individuals deemed "sick" by society, including people who have been "historically pathologized, hospitalized, institutionalized, brutalized, rendered 'unmanageable,' and therefore made culturally illegitimate and politically invisible."[6] Removed from society and subjected to the total control of institutional authorities, people confined to Pacific Colony were intentionally rendered "politically invisible." Their legal status as wards of the court diminished the power their families had in their lives. And because of social and economic marginalization, many simply did not have access to the legal and social resources needed to mount a defense against the state. Moreover, as Hedva points out and as historians have demonstrated, traditional political institutions like state and federal courts have rarely been accessible or effective avenues for resistance for people deemed deviant, and traditional forms of protest like marching in the streets have not always been feasible options.[7]

Building on this literature, I consider the forms of protest available to Mexican-origin youth confined to Pacific Colony and to the families and allies that sought to intervene on their behalf in order to recover efforts to (re)assert their dignity and humanity. Reflecting on her own experience with chronic illness, Hedva asks, "How do you throw a brick through the window of a bank if you can't get out of bed?" In light of Hedva's work on disability and protest, I pose a similar question: How did Mexican-origin women and men protest institutional authority over their lives and bodies if they were rendered legally powerless, politically invisible, and constituted "non-citizens and (no)bodies" by the state? How did agency and resistance manifest in this context of extreme legal and physical constraint? What is documented here is a spectrum of defiant acts that were not recognized as protest, were often unsuccessful, and were sometimes met with violent punishments. These are the ways that institutionalized Mexican-origin youth defied institutional and state authorities and insisted on being more than just sterilized bodies that labored in and outside of the institution.

RIOTS, REFUSALS, AND EVERYDAY CHALLENGES TO INSTITUTIONAL AUTHORITY

In the summer of 1929 forty young people were transferred from the Sonoma State Home four hundred miles south to California's newly opened institution for the so-called feebleminded, Pacific Colony. These young people were not transferred for better care or to be closer to family but so they could provide free labor and "assist in the routine of the institution."[8] By the fall, several of the young women among this group were tired of confinement and tired of working for free. In clear expression of their discontent, a group of them led a riot. They shattered windows and broke out of their building, running over to the nearby boys' cottage to gather allies in their protest. On that day they made their anger known.

After quelling the riot and identifying the leaders, Dr. J. C. Johnson and his wife, who were in charge as superintendents and physicians, ordered punishments for the girls accused of instigating the uprising. The Johnsons had the girls' hair clipped and forced them to wear loose "orange mother hubbard gowns" while running heavy polishers over the institution's floors for hours. The Johnsons involved others in their punishments, compelling fellow residents to ignore and ostracize the girls. The point, according to the Johnsons, was to make the girls "feel as humiliated as possible" and to dissuade them (and their peers) from future defiance.[9] Legally entrusted with the care of these young people, Pacific Colony administrators chose ostracization and humiliation as ways to address what were certainly valid concerns regarding labor and freedom in the institution. Occurring just two years after Pacific Colony opened, this rebellion illustrates both how confined youth resisted and defied institutional authority and how authority figures relied on abusive tactics to discipline and manage those entrusted with their care. Residents of Pacific Colony recognized their confinement and the treatment they experienced as unjust and responded in ways that ranged from disruptive to destructive. Confined youth also realized that given the unequal power relationship between staff and residents, their behaviors had consequences. Nevertheless, many refused to comply with expectations regarding their labor and behavior and acted out individually and collectively.

One of the principal measures of success for Pacific Colony administrators was an orderly and productive resident population. Because diagnoses of feeblemindedness were so closely tied to juvenile delinquency, uncontrolled behavior, and poverty, treatment in the institution largely revolved around behavior management and vocational training. Staff held significant power over the daily lives of residents—deciding when, where, and how they slept, ate, and worked. Staff were also empowered to dole out punishments. More than disciplinarians, staff were also charged with documenting and assessing residents' behaviors, attitudes, and quality of work.[10] These assessments were then used to make decisions about parole or discharge from the institution. Thus, in very real ways, interactions between residents and staff, and staff assessments of resident behaviors, had significant consequences for the future of people confined to the institution. Young people at Pacific Colony were actively aware of the power staff had over their lives and often chose to remain cooperative, docile, and productive. Others, however, could not or would not comply with institutional expectations of behavior and labor. In doing so, they disrupted the work flow of the institution.

Young people had contentious relationships with institutional authorities who demanded their labor at Pacific Colony. In an ethnographic study of a specific group of youths confined to Pacific Colony described as predominantly "Negro and Mexican," anthropologist Robert Edgerton observed that many didn't "like to work" and would avoid doing their assigned jobs at the institution.[11] While his study examined youth during the early 1960s, Mexican-origin youth consistently refused to comply with labor demands throughout the institution's history. The 1929 riot was an early example. In 1950, when fifteen-year-old Ronaldo, the son of a migrant farm worker, was committed to Pacific Colony, he rejected demands for his labor. He "refused to work," "refused vocational training," and rebuffed his assigned work detail. Moreover, Ronaldo refused to "wear state clothes," declining to submit his labor and body to the institution. Similarly, Elena Verde, who was committed to Pacific Colony when she was fourteen following the death of her parents (who were Mexican immigrants), "failed to adjust" in her work assignment on the laundry detail.[12] In an assessment of her time at Pacific Colony, her adjustment was described as "only fair," in part because staff did not think Elena was a "good" or "efficient" worker. Despite the ways that researchers and institutional authorities assessed residents' refusals to work, when and how to work was one of the few decisions young people had control over. As described elsewhere in this book, unpaid resident labor was necessary in running the institution. Thus, when residents withheld their labor from laundry details, the kitchen, or nursery wards, their refusal obstructed the normal functioning of Pacific Colony.

Mexican-origin youth also proved disruptive and defiant in their behaviors toward institutional authorities. Many young people understood their confinement as a "cruel miscarriage of justice" and expressed their anger and frustration over being confined, controlled, and pathologized.[13] Confined youth acted out in various ways, including vandalizing and breaking hospital property, disobeying set rules of comportment, and sneaking out of their cottages after hours.[14] They stood up to institutional employees by disobeying direct orders, insulting and cursing at them, and even threatening to escape.[15] This behavior made their discontent tangible.

When Mexican-origin youth confined to Pacific Colony expressed anger, sadness, or frustration, they were often dismissed or pathologized as exhibiting "emotional disturbance." This was evident in the way authorities described Ronaldo and Elena.[16] Visibly distraught over being confined in the institution, Ronaldo suffered through "spells of crying." Yet this young boy's distress—an expected reaction to being separated from family—was described as "emotional instability." Compounded by his refusal to work, staff described Ronaldo as making a "poor adjustment" to Pacific Colony. Elena was also distraught over being in Pacific Colony. Some days, she acted out of anger, threw fits in her ward, screamed at residents and staff, and became violent. Other days, staff found Elena "uncommunicative and withdrawn."[17] By her second year in the institution, staff had labeled Elena "aggressive."[18] Whether loud and "aggressive" or quiet and "withdrawn," staff framed Elena's changing emotional states as tied principally to her disability label, unable or unwilling to consider these changes as responses to institutionalization. Elena refused to perform passivity and obedience and instead asserted her discontent and anger at being confined. Seemingly oblivious to the possibility that confinement at Pacific Colony might cause this series of emotional responses, institutional workers simply concluded that "authority was a problem to this girl."[19]

In addition to illustrating the ways that institutional authorities policed and pathologized the emotions of residents, these descriptions are indica-

tive of the ways that residents asserted their emotions regardless of the
consequences. Rosa Alvarez, a young working-class Mexican American
girl, also had a "problem" with authority at Pacific Colony. According to
her sterilization request, a psychologist described the fourteen-year-old as
"cooperative but only skin deep," suggesting that she was not completely
amenable to institutional authority.[20] As in the case of Elena, many youths
were willing to act out violently, and Rosa's request describes her as seem-
ing "set half-cocked to fight back." Young Mexican American boys were
also angry and engaged in fights with attendants and fellow residents.[21]
Jesus, the son of a Mexican ranch hand whose family faced extreme poverty, was committed at age twelve and "suspected of being a homosexual."
His experience in the institution was marked by "incorrigibility," frustration, and fights.[22]

Young people like Elena, Ronaldo, Rosa, and Jesus were strategic about
when to comply with staff orders and when it was worth risking punishment to transgress institutional control. Sometimes the disruptive behaviors of confined youth were spontaneous or immediate reactions to the
moment at hand. Other times, young Pacific Colony residents committed
"calculated violations": intentionally breaking hospital property, obstruct-
ing work routines, and sneaking away from their wards after hours.[23] These
intentional transgressions could offer youth immediate reprieve. Breaking
institutional property might release anger and exact revenge, refusing to
work might afford them some much needed rest, and sneaking away from
their wards might mean stealing leisure time with friends. While confined
youth undoubtedly recognized that misbehaving could result in punishment and negative reports from staff, they also wanted to make it clear
that they were not happy with their conditions in Pacific Colony.[24]

The practice of labeling the anger, frustration, and emotional out-
bursts of these youths as "emotional disturbance" or "emotional instability" worked to obscure the real impact of such traumas as the death of
a parent, extreme poverty, or being separated from family and confined
in a state institution at a young age. And still, the strong emotions and
disruptive behaviors detailed in the pathologizing descriptions of Pacific
Colony staff, clinicians, and researchers make apparent the deep pain
these youths carried from both past traumas and the crushing experience

of Pacific Colony. As one former resident described it, being in the institution made her feel "like an animal in a cage."[25]

When reflecting on their experiences of confinement, formerly institutionalized people offer alternate analyses of their violent and disruptive behaviors. One woman who was confined for several years in a different institution stated that she acted violently toward staff and residents and "started becoming a bully" because she was "sick and tired of people just beating me all the time" and decided: "I am not going to take this shit anymore."[26] On the other side of the country, a former resident of the Fernald State School in Massachusetts described "retreating into a fog of dissociation" to cope with the fear and anxiety of living in the institution. Other residents of Fernald described behaving violently in response to feeling violated by staff and other residents.[27] Heeding the reflections of people who experienced institutionalization firsthand, it is evident that obstructionist, disruptive, destructive, and even violent behaviors were some of the ways that confined youth reacted to and survived the conditions they were forced to endure. These reflections suggest that these youths tried to assert some semblance of control over their lives by making decisions about when, where, and how to cooperate.

Disruptive behaviors should certainly be considered assertions of agency in contexts of overwhelming constraint, but they could often have serious consequences. Uncooperative and rebellious inmates were intentionally humiliated and physically abused. Elena was often placed in restraint and seclusion in "the side rooms."[28] Solitary confinement for up to two weeks was a standard punishment in both Pacific Colony and Sonoma.[29] Jesus was repeatedly subjected to physical restraint.[30] These punishments did nothing to treat the supposed "mental defect" or "emotional disturbance" that psychiatrists, physicians, and other state workers claimed these young people were exhibiting and, instead, supported claims for continued confinement in Pacific Colony. In fact, these punishments likely inflicted great physical and emotional pain and psychological harm upon youths who were already struggling with complicated histories, pathologization, and institutional confinement. Moreover, these punishments exacerbated conditions that were already unbearable for many confined to Pacific Colony. In response, several Mexican-origin youths did their best to escape the institution completely.

AN EPIDEMIC OF ESCAPES

The white upper- and middle-class educators, psychiatrists, and social workers that advocated for Pacific Colony in the 1910s and 1920s argued that the institution would be a much-needed alternative to the state's prisons, jails, and juvenile reform schools. Guided by science and humanitarianism, these reformers asserted that the people they considered socially, mentally, and economically deficient would benefit through confinement at Pacific Colony. Instead of punishment, people labeled "feebleminded" would receive treatment, education, vocational training, and care. Through their work institutional authorities would prepare residents "for lives of usefulness, however obscure, for contentment, and good citizenship."[31]

According to advocates, Pacific Colony was a better financial investment for the state than other social supports such as cash or housing assistance, which helped people survive economic inequalities. In their view direct assistance merely perpetuated defect, while confinement at Pacific Colony might eliminate it through training and sterilization. In practice, the millions of dollars in state funds dedicated to Pacific Colony over two decades did little to improve the lives of the mostly working-class and disproportionately Mexican-origin inmates who lived in the institution. Moreover, confinement at Pacific Colony proved to be the opposite of education and care, and the institution was often a place where young people experienced neglect and violence.

To be clear, some inmates did experience the institution as a relief from poverty, violence, and ableism at home and in their communities. May Hatfield, for example, had a very unstable childhood and remarked that "in some ways it [Pacific Colony] was better than being outside."[32] Mary Franco experienced her time at Pacific Colony as somewhat of a refuge from the watchful eyes of her parents and older siblings.[33] The thirteen-year-old felt a greater sense of freedom being away from her strict household. However, Mary also experienced long-term physical and emotional harm from being sterilized there. A gynecologist who treated Mary after she was released from Pacific Colony said that the physician who performed the sterilization "butchered her" and she eventually had to undergo a full hysterectomy. When Mary was older, she became distraught over not being able to have children, and her marriage dissolved after her husband learned about the surgery. She had a long-term relationship but never remarried.

Indeed, for some youths who lost parents or whose parents or guardians were abusive, Pacific Colony was a better alternative than living on the streets. Others received much-needed medical care and treatment that their families might not have otherwise been able to access or afford. Unfortunately, that housing and medical care came at the expense of freedom, and although the institution provided safety from familial or community violence, many residents experienced violence from staff and fellow residents. Constant reports of escape over the years indicate that living conditions in the institution were intolerable to many. Perhaps one of the most pervasive and defiant acts of resistance to confinement in Pacific Colony and its peer institutions was escape. In her research into the case files of Whittier State School, California's leading juvenile reform school, historian Miroslava Chávez-García situates escapes as both "symbolic and real moments of individual and, sometimes, collective resistance."[34] I build on this work by highlighting Mexican-origin women's and men's escapes from Pacific Colony. Escaping the institution was one of the many ways they reacted to the violent conditions of confinement they endured, and one of the few options they had to regain complete authority over their lives.

Documented complaints regarding the "abuse of children" at Pacific Colony and the "unreasonable methods of discipline" appear in state archives as early as 1929, and restraint, solitary confinement, and humiliation were common forms of punishment at the institution.[35] Inmates and their families complained to social workers and even the governor about physical violence throughout the 1930s and 1940s.[36] Abuse was formally banned, but testimonies from former residents detail rampant use of violence. For example, the novelist Edward Bunker, who was committed to Pacific Colony by the Los Angeles Youth Authority for a ninety-day observation period as a teenager in the late 1940s, described the locked ward as "the most brutal place" he'd ever been.[37] Having lived in state boarding homes and juvenile reform schools throughout his childhood, Bunker had experienced several state institutional settings but wrote that staff at Pacific Colony could "get away with anything." According to Bunker, residents were forced to sit in silence on benches for hours in the dayroom.

Bunker also witnessed attendants organize fights between young men for their own entertainment.[38]

This claim is supported by a Pacific Colony attendant who in 1949 filed a complaint after witnessing colleagues "stimulating patients to fight and beating them themselves."[39] As punishment, attendants forced youths to "pull the block"—a heavy slab of concrete wrapped in wool with a harness attached to the body of an inmate. This punishment, nearly identical to the one given to the group of women that rioted in 1929, was doled out for hours a day and for days on end. One "Chicano from La Colonia in Watts" was forced to "pull the block" for thirty days as punishment for "getting high on phenobarbital." Bunker describes another cruel punishment devised by staff that involved hanging youths from overhead ventilation ducts by their wrists. Staff hung youths just above the floor so that if they didn't stand on the balls of their feet, all of their weight pulled on their arms and wrists, causing excruciating pain. In addition to these brutal punishments, Bunker received what he described as the most violent beating he'd ever experienced at the hands of several Pacific Colony staff.

Physical punishment and abuse was combined with emotional and medical abuse in the institutional setting. Martha was fourteen when her adoptive parents abandoned her. Shortly after, she was transferred from her initial placement in a foster home to Pacific Colony because of "several serious episodes of menorrhagia."[40] Reflecting on her four years at the institution, Martha stated: "Anytime you did something they [the staff] didn't like they'd threaten you with punishment like being locked up in a side room all alone. That's what they do, you know." In addition to isolation, the staff used sedatives and barbiturates to make residents more manageable. Martha recalled that staff would "drug me with narcotics, like amdol (amytal), then put me in a room all alone. How is a person going to live right when they're full of narcotics?"[41] As Martha's testimony reveals, punishments were not merely aimed at residents considered severe behavior problems or youths kept in the locked ward where Bunker was held. The physical, emotional, and medical abuse that residents experienced at Pacific Colony paralleled the experiences of people confined in other institutions across the country.[42]

In general, conditions of confinement proliferated abuse. The medical and social labels that degraded the humanity of Pacific Colony residents not only justified confinement but also forced them into vulnerable positions where they could be abused by staff and other residents. Because the people committed to Pacific Colony were labeled feebleminded, their complaints and concerns were easily dismissed. As Martha stated, being confined to Pacific Colony was "a rotten deal." As she put it: "I had my freedom taken away and was put behind bars like a criminal just because I didn't have a family and the State was tired of taking care of me." Martha recognized that she needed care, and it is clear based on her statement that at Pacific Colony she received the opposite.[43]

Residents of Pacific Colony who managed to avoid abuse and punishments nevertheless had to endure abysmal living conditions, including overcrowded facilities and sleeping arrangements and bad food. Fred, who was committed to Pacific Colony at the age of fourteen in 1942, stated that he frequently found sticks and rocks in the food, which he described as not "even fit for a dog to eat."[44] Testimonies from former Pacific Colony residents show that it never became the humanitarian, caring, and rehabilitative institution its founders described. As previous chapters have demonstrated, many working-class Mexican-origin youths were taken from their homes and labeled feebleminded in part because their living conditions did not meet white middle-class standards. In addition to IQ scores, psychiatrists and social workers used such details as impoverished and overcrowded living conditions, domestic violence, or drug use in Mexican-origin households as evidence of familial pathology and to establish a need to remove youth from the home. This removal presumed that living conditions at Pacific Colony were preferable to the ones in the young person's home, but this was rarely the case. Overcrowding was a constant in Pacific Colony through the 1930s and 1940s, and abuse seemed rampant.

Abysmal living conditions were not exclusive to Pacific Colony. Abusive practices and overcrowding pervaded practically all California state institutions, and in a 1946 message to the legislature governor Earl Warren recognized the "sordid" and "shocking conditions" in the state's institutions.[45] Warren had been aware of these conditions since at least the mid-1940s, and in December of 1946 the public was put on notice about the "sordid" ways that state authorities treated sick, impoverished, and disabled Californians. That year, the *San Francisco News* published a series of articles written by Al Ostrow with accompanying images that depicted not only overcrowded institutions and young people sleeping on floors in the hallway, but widespread neglect and lack of medical treatment in state institutions for the mentally ill and disabled.[46] Both the government and public response leaned toward reform and investment in the infrastructure and facilities of the institution, but little was done to address the immediate needs of the confined. Many young residents in Pacific Colony decided to take matters into their own hands and flee the institution in an attempt to live on their own terms away from the threat of abuse and the constant control of their lives and labor.

Both press and institutional records document escapes from Pacific Colony from the institution's opening to the middle of the century. Months after several young men were transported to a potential site for the institution to labor in building construction, five of them fled. A July 1921 article in the *Los Angeles Herald* reported on the escape of "Louis Maldonado, 16; Willard Williams, 16; John Hernandez, 21; Joe Rivera, 17; and Clarence Parker, 18."[47] In 1929 a sixteen-year-old Mexican American girl who was "troublesome and combative toward attendants" attempted to escape Pacific Colony multiple times.[48] Over the course of three decades, hundreds of youths escaped Pacific Colony, signaling Mexican-origin young people's unwillingness to remain confined. In fact, by 1943 the *Los Angeles Times* reported on what it called "an epidemic of escapes by juvenile prisoners" when inmates from various reform schools and institutions for the feebleminded managed to escape around the same time.[49] Indeed, residents escaped the institution at growing rates in the early 1940s. Institutional reports document twenty-nine escapes between 1939 and 1940; in 1941, 42 people escaped; in 1942, 78 were reported as "on escape"; and in 1943 a total of 125 people had escaped from the institution.[50] An analysis of reported escape figures published by Pacific Colony indicate that men escaped the institution at higher rates than women. However, both men and women found ways to flee and escaped the institution since its opening in the late 1920s.

Given the isolated location of Pacific Colony, the institution's connections with legal authorities, and the staff's capacity to wield punishments, decisions to escape were likely not taken lightly. Despite overcrowded conditions, residents knew that if they managed to escape, institutional

Table 3   Residents "on escape" from Pacific Colony, 1939–49

Year	Male	Female	Total
1939–40	16	13	29
1940–41	30	12	42
1941–42	61	17	78
1942–43	104	21	125
1943–44	70	31	101
1945	75	8	83
1946	53	50	103
1947	84	30	114
1948	69	49	118
1949	1	2	3

SOURCE: Author's compilation from Statistical Reports of the Department of Institutions of the State of California (Sacramento: California Department of Institution), 1939–49.

authorities would exert their power to locate and return them to Pacific Colony. Administrators often notified local law enforcement and juvenile authorities in the escaped individual's community of origin when someone managed to flee the institution. In addition to soliciting the help of law enforcement in apprehension efforts, institutional authorities published the names and other identifying information of escaped youths in the local newspaper. In 1930, for example, the *Los Angeles Times* published an article aimed at the City of Visalia asking for

> aid in the search for Felix Sanchez, 15 years of age, and Blanche Estrada, 14, who are said to have escaped from the Pacific Colony school at Spadra, last July, and who are thought to be living in this vicinity. Sanchez, although only a boy, is said to be a heavy user of marihuana, and is reported to be dangerous while under the influence of the narcotic. The girl is an epileptic, and authorities are anxious to locate her before she comes to some harm.[51]

As the *Los Angeles Times* piece illustrates, alongside identifying information, authorities also published information about the potential danger that escaped Mexican-origin youths posed to the community. Bits of information like being a supposed "heavy user of marihuana" played into already existing notions of Mexican-origin youth as drug addicts and criminals. Combined with the description of young Blanche as "an epileptic" who might be harmed if away from the institution, the short piece underscores the way that Pacific Colony existed at the intersection of medical and penal interventions: a place that confined dangerous youth as well as young people who needed medical care.

In the 1940s short two-sentence notices of escape were published under headlines framing the search for escaped youths in criminalizing and dehumanizing ways. In 1941, Antonio Encinas, Jose Ortiz, and Lino Villareal, all in their late teens, were named under a heading that read "Three Young Colony Fugitives Hunted."[52] Under this alarming headline, the piece stated simply that the young men escaped on a Saturday afternoon and were "still at large," according to San Dimas sheriff's deputies. A different piece published a year later declared that four escaped Mexican-origin teens were being "hunted by sheriff's deputies."[53] In their efforts to apprehend escaped youth, Pacific Colony administrators effectively collaborated with law enforcement and tried to involve the public. Moreover, describing young people as "fugitives" and "inmates" who were being "hunted" like animals by law enforcement communicated to the public that these youths were to be feared. In suggesting that they were potentially violent drug users, the articles made clear that the community would be unsafe if these youths were free. Establishing the need for apprehension and confinement, institutional authorities and law enforcement persuaded community members to assist in locating escapees, thereby increasing the likelihood that they would be returned to the institution.

Being returned to the institution was not the only consequence of absconding. Residents that were apprehended after an escape were punished in various ways, including isolation. Despite these consequences, young Mexican-origin women and men took the risk and successfully escaped on multiple occasions, often in groups, and in many cases colluding with other inmates of color. When sixteen-year-old Ralph escaped in September of 1949, for example, he took ten other residents with him.[54] In October 1930 two fifteen-year-old boys, William Martinez and Corinthian Green—who was described as "colored"—escaped Pacific Colony after being committed to the institution by Los Angeles juvenile authorities.[55] During another escape in 1942 a group of twenty-one young men between the ages of sixteen and twenty-one escaped from Cottage 15 after managing to restrain two staff members.[56] According to the *Los Angeles Times* report, the staff were "issuing the daily quota of tobacco to the older boys in the group" when one of them was "knocked unconscious with a chair" and the other "floored."[57] The youths took the keys from a staff member, unlocked the door, and climbed over the thirteen-foot steel wire fence to escape. The mass escape prompted the dispatch of "several carloads of deputy sheriffs," and staff searched the hills surrounding the institution.[58]

The next day, nine of the escaped youths were found along the Union Pacific Railroad and returned to the institution.[59] In a statement Carl E. Applegate, then deputy director of institutions, rationalized the escape by citing the institution's legal duty to house "ordinary mental defectives" with "delinquents who happen to be either defective or psychopathic types," which led to "occasional mishaps."[60] Applegate was effectively trying to blame escapes on the presence of a particular type of "mental defective," the ones who were criminally inclined. But escapes were a long-standing practice among confined youth; they were widespread and far from occasional. In 1946 another group of six youths managed to escape from the institution: "Florine Fry, 18; Trinidad Fuentes, 21; Rebecca Sivella, 20; Sam B. Teros, 17; Albino Ramirez, 17, and Frank Kratt, 17."[61] The fact that Pacific Colony residents frequently escaped in groups indicates that they not only wanted to live their own lives on the outside, but that they also wanted to help others get free. Moreover, according to the article on the 1946 group escape, this was Rebecca Sivella's second attempt at freedom from Pacific Colony.

As the newspapers describe, escapes were both pervasive and persistent—that is, many of the working-class Mexican-origin youths confined to Pacific Colony escaped the institution multiple times. Jesus, the young Mexican American boy mentioned previously, escaped from Pacific Colony on four separate occasions.[62] One Mexican American boy who was committed to Pacific Colony in 1945 when he was fifteen escaped the institution three times, each time taking a number of other patients with him: the first time with six, the second time with eight, and the third time with fifteen others.[63] Rosie, who was seventeen when she was committed in 1947, had several incident reports related to multiple escapes.[64] Sixteen-year-old Rafaela Aguilar, who was described as a "habitual run-away," actually managed to escape from three different institutions before being committed by a parole officer to Pacific Colony.[65]

Repeated escapes from different institutional settings reflected a persistent effort to be free, but they also signaled complete desperation. In 1941 seventeen-year-old George Vasquez was desperate to be home with his mother after being confined by juvenile authorities from the age of fourteen.[66] George was first committed to the Sonoma State Home in 1938 but, after managing to escape twice, was transferred to Pacific Colony. In August of 1941 he successfully escaped from Pacific Colony but was apprehended in April 1942 and sent to the Los Angeles "juvenile tank." In complete despair, George wrote a note to his mother, Juanita Vasquez, and then attempted suicide by hanging. The young people in the cells at juvenile hall alerted the guards, and George was taken to the jail hospital with "no serious injury." The injury of three years of confinement, however, was clear. He would rather die than return to Pacific Colony. George wrote to his mother: "I couldn't stand the torture of being locked up" and "I like to be home with you ... but they are going to send me back." The seventeen-year-old told police chief William Bright that he attempted suicide because he did not want to return to Pacific Colony. It's unclear if George was in fact returned to the institution, but Chief Bright had the boy confined to a padded cell because he remained suicidal. Unfortunately, George was not the only young person driven to suicide because of confinement. Benny Moreno and Edward Leiva died by suicide at the Whittier State School in 1939 and 1940 respectively.[67] These youths' experiences point to the considerable suffering that Mexican-origin youth endured in state institutions like Pacific Colony and Whittier—and the reasons why they took the risk to escape on multiple occasions.

Institutional authorities went out of their way to apprehend escaped youth, but their efforts were not always successful and escapes had differing outcomes. While many young people were quickly returned, others remained on escape for several months and even years. Joe Avila, for example, remained on escape for four-and-a-half years, and Ralph was on escape for eleven months.[68] During their time away from the institution, many young people returned home to their families, who did their best to hide escaped youth from state workers who might return them to the institution.[69] Other young people found work and figured out ways to make it on their own.[70] Ralph, for example, worked picking fruit in a farming community outside of Los Angeles during his eleven-month escape. He managed to avoid police for the most part until, on a visit to his family's house in the city, a Los Angeles police officer brutally apprehended him and returned him to Pacific Colony.[71]

John, who was committed to Pacific Colony when he was fourteen, escaped and managed to stay out for seven months. During that time he moved in with his sister and her husband in the San Fernando Valley.[72] His brother-in-law helped him get a job at the junk yard.[73] It wasn't until John was arrested by police "on a routine check-up" that he was sent back to the institution. Details in institutional reports about how these young Mexican American boys fared while on escape notably highlight their employment status and show that they largely stayed out of trouble. The reports on their experiences outside of the institution illustrate how police encounters carried increased consequences because of their history with Pacific Colony. While escaping Pacific Colony meant leaving the immediate confines of the institution, they were nevertheless marked by the diagnosis and record of institutionalization. Furthermore, as young Mexican American men, they were more susceptible to "routine check-ups" and apprehension despite their good behavior.

Returning to the institution meant a return to confinement, supervision, and punishment, but escapes also flagged Mexican-origin young people's reproductive capacity as particularly risky. Institutional authorities used escape attempts to further support the need to sterilize a young person. Fifteen-year-old Erica Sanchez, for example, was described as needing sterilization because she had "already tried to escape and is a menace to those with whom she comes in contact." Similarly, the clinical staff at Pacific Colony "unanimously agreed" that seventeen-year-old Beatrice Belen should be sterilized "without further delay on account of her history of running away," despite the fact that her father refused to consent to the operation. In his sterilization records a clinician describes twenty-year-old Frank Gomez as a "habitual run-away and a thief." Even though Frank's father refused to consent to his sterilization, clinical staff wrote: "As the boy is likely to escape from the institution and is a menace to society, we ask your authorization to sterilize him over and above the father's objection." In some cases it appears that an escape prompted the filing of a sterilization request. On February 12, 1940, Dr. Elizabeth Hoyte filed a sterilization request for fifteen-year-old Manuela Ramirez who, just the day before, had managed to escape Pacific Colony during a visit with her mother. Clinicians at the institution wanted to have sterilization approval for the young girl on file so that they could operate if or when she returned to the institution. In all of these cases young Mexican-origin women's and men's efforts to regain their freedom and their refusal to surrender to the confines of the institution were subsequently used as reasons why they required reproductive constraint.[74]

Escapes could be used to further justify sterilization, but they also posed a challenge to the bureaucratic and administrative processes of the institution. How could authorities monitor and manage absent bodies? Successful long-term escapes were especially problematic given that patients remained wards of the institution but could not be assessed. That this was a problem for institutional authorities is apparent in conference conversations regarding whether or not to discharge youth who were on escape for extended periods of time. In a clinical conference focusing on Joe, the young Mexican American man who was on escape for more than four years, the staff expressed frustration over both their inability to locate him and the uncertainty about whether to discharge him as "improved" or not.[75] In other cases long-term escapes did result in the parole and eventual discharge of some youths. According to institutional reports, six people were officially discharged from the institution while on escape in 1941 and in 1942 and twenty-three people were discharged after having escaped Pacific Colony.[76]

Even though Ralph was returned to Pacific Colony after being beaten by a Los Angeles police officer, he was subsequently released on parole for having made a "good adjustment" while out on escape. In Ralph's case, becoming economically self-sufficient and productive while on escape led to the administrative decision to allow him to stay out of the institution, although whether he was ever officially discharged is unclear. John was allowed to leave the institution after being returned by the police because his sister, brother-in-law, and his employer at the junk yard company intervened and promised to keep him out of trouble.[77] No doubt, severe overcrowding in Pacific Colony and proof of "good adjustments" contributed to decisions to allow some escaped youths to remain outside of the institution. Nevertheless, these examples illustrate how escapes posed bureaucratic challenges and could sometimes force the hand of institutional authorities to release or discharge young people.

While escapes did not lead to large-scale institutional or policy changes, in some cases escapes were a first step to achieving discharge. Furthermore, escapes were the most immediate way for young people to assert agency and bodily autonomy within a context of extreme physical control, abuse, and limited options. Escapes could also inspire hope and additional rebellious acts. Talking about escapes from the Fernald School in Massachusetts, former resident Charles Hatch remembered that boys in the institution shared stories about how they survived while on escape, "giving others courage" that they could make it on their own if they were free.[78] Far from being passive or docile in the face of institutional and legal authorities' attempts to discipline and control their bodies, youth confined to Pacific Colony took great risks to assert control over their lives and likely inspired others in the process.

PARENTS AND FAMILIES NAVIGATING INSTITUTIONAL POWER AND VIOLENCE

At the same time that young people were doing their best to survive and confront institutional authority, many parents were also doing what they could to have their children released and to prevent sterilization. As disability scholars Allison C. Carey and Lucy Gu have shown, the role parents have played in decisions regarding the institutionalization and treatment of their children is complicated, and parents have not always acted in ways that protect the safety and bodily integrity of youth.[79] The widely covered 1935 case of Ann Cooper Hewitt, whose mother had her declared mentally incompetent and sterilized in order to control her inheritance, exemplifies how some parents used medical diagnoses and state laws to control their children.[80] In her work on the Sonoma State Home, historian Wendy Kline has discussed the way parents used institutionalization and sterilization to control and punish their daughters for asserting sexual agency.[81] Mexican-origin families also relied on state institutions in efforts to police or punish their children's behavior. Aware of the frightening reputation that state institutions had, some parents used the threat of confinement in efforts to manage their children or warn them of what might happen if they misbehaved. In her pioneering oral histories with Mexican-origin women who grew up in Southern California during this period, historian Vicki Ruiz recorded one woman recalling the way her mother would threaten to send her to the Florence Crittenton Home—an institution for unwed mothers—if she became pregnant before marriage.[82]

In addition to relying on the threat of institutionalization to manage the behavior of their children, parents of physically or intellectually disabled children often chose institutionalization for their children. Parents made these decisions for many reasons. Some were influenced by pervasive ableism perpetuated by eugenics and wanted to avoid being associated with a disabled child or believed that a disabled child would cause social ostracization for the entire family.[83] Others chose institutionalization at the recommendation of a physician. Family doctors sometimes instructed parents to have disabled children committed for the same ableist reasons listed above. Other doctors recommended institutionalization for reasons related to medical care. Sometimes, even if parents rejected ableism, declined the advice of physicians, and wanted to provide for the medical care of disabled children in the home, this option was not always available to low-income parents who had to work outside of the home and faced a scarcity of medical support.

Regardless of the circumstances, parents often had more power in negotiating institutionalization, sterilization, and release than the young women and men who were subject to these interventions. However, that power was tempered by the authority vested in juvenile courts to diminish parental rights and render children wards of the state upon commitment to Pacific Colony. Once their children were declared wards of the state by legal authorities, decision-making power over treatments, sterilization, the length of confinement, and the terms of release was placed in the hands of institutional administrators and clinicians. Moreover, the fact that legal authorities collaborated with Pacific Colony officials added a considerable layer of coercion when parents were asked to do things like sign sterilization consent forms or return escaped youth to the institution. Parents were aware of the fact that legal consequences could extend to them, or their lack of cooperation could be used by institutional authorities to decrease contact with their child—for example, refusing to allow visits or approve release plans. Parents were also aware of the power that institutional authorities had over their children and often feared reporting abuse. In one 1944 letter from the governor's office to Dora Shaw Heffner, then director of the Department of Institutions, a state official wrote that a woman who refused to give her name called the governor to complain about conditions at the Sonoma State Home. She went to see her son there during Sunday visiting hours and found that he was in the hospital with a broken jaw. In addition to learning of her son's injuries, the woman reported abuse of other residents. Importantly, she refused to give her name because she feared that "her son would suffer reprisals."[84] In many cases parents and families were on the front line of negotiating release from the institution, and they made valiant efforts to prevent unwanted procedures like sterilization.

Parents often initiated paperwork to have their children committed to Pacific Colony, but records related to commitment and descriptions contained in research on individuals committed to the institution suggest that state workers including parole officers, social workers, and court judges played a frequent and important role in these processes for Mexican-origin youth. The details of each individual case is different, but many suggest that decisions to file paperwork were made under court order or coercion, or under the strong suggestion of a state official. What's more, many parents later expressed regret in their decision to sign commitment papers and subsequently fought to have their children released. George Ramirez's parents filed paperwork to have their son committed to Pacific Colony in 1945 when George was fifteen. They did so at the behest and with the help of juvenile court authorities who asserted that this was a solution to the boy's rebellious behavior. They went along with the recommendation, believing that institutionalization would teach the fifteen-year-old that his actions had consequences and a period of confinement would help him reform.

However, when they were ready for George to return from this punishment, his parents were met with resistance from Pacific Colony administrators. The parents sent a number of letters requesting their son's release, and when that didn't work, they "engaged an attorney in an attempt to secure his discharge."[85] Having the upper hand, Pacific Colony clinicians responded to the parents' request by making the boy's release contingent on the parents having "concrete plan of supervision for George which included a job."[86] Pacific Colony administrators were legally empowered by the state to decide the terms of release, leaving George's parents with the responsibility of financing legal procedures, acquiring employment, and proving to clinicians that they could appropriately supervise their son. The presence of a lawyer likely increased pressure on Pacific Colony administrators to consider release for George, but in the end he was only reunited with his parents once staff approved their plan for care.

Similarly, after Joe's mother facilitated her son's commitment to Pacific Colony in 1945, she regretted the decision and attempted to have him released. She made six formal requests to have him placed on leave and eventually acquired the assistance of an attorney. Like in George's case, she had to submit a plan for supervision and promised to have Joe work in his uncle's tortilla factory.[87] Likewise, Sam, who was seventeen when he was admitted to Pacific Colony in 1946, was committed under an application initiated by his parents. His mother visited him frequently, and after eight months she requested he be discharged. She repeated the request at least three times and in her last letter indicated that she had a job for Sam with his father.[88] It was only after three requests and assurances that the boy would be employed that Pacific Colony administrators agreed to release her son. As these examples reveal, the role parents played in the institutionalization and release of their children was complicated. While they were complicit in the commitment process, the context of judges, police officers, and doctors directing them to initiate paperwork indicates that they, at the very least, faced pressure to choose institutionalization for their children. It is unclear whether these parents were fully informed about the legal ramifications of institutionalizing their children, or if they understood the treatment their children would face in Pacific Colony. If they were unaware that institutionalization meant giving up their legal rights, then their role in the commitment process was marked by deception. What is clear is that parents made significant efforts to get their children out of the institution, requesting discharge and indefinite leaves of absence, and even contracting attorneys for legal assistance.

The role of families and guardians in consenting to sterilization at Pacific Colony is also complicated. As wards of the state, people committed to Pacific Colony were denied decision-making power over their own treatment and lives. Institutional authorities had the legal right to make decisions about sterilization. Effectively stripped of reproductive and bodily autonomy, the institutionalized were rarely, if ever, asked whether they wanted to be sterilized. This, of course, does not mean that they did not assert themselves into the decision-making process. Some, like Teresa, attempted to prevent the sterilization in the moment. A very small number of sterilization requests indicate that some young Mexican-origin women desired the operation and were eager to facilitate the process, likely in an effort gain release from the institution.[89] Residents of Pacific Colony understood that sterilization was in most cases required if a person was going to be paroled or discharged. Because residents were not formally asked to approve of their own sterilization, they relied on family members and legal guardians to try to prevent the operation. As legally appointed consenters, parents, family members, and legal guardians were the ones primarily involved in decisions regarding consent for sterilization and thus became the figures whose efforts to resist sterilization were most visible in institutional and legal archives.

Under the state's eugenic sterilization law, medical superintendents had full authority to sterilize individuals committed to their institutions, and thus parental consent was not a legal requirement. As a means to protect institutional authorities and the state's sterilization law, however, the California Department of Institutions implemented a process of obtaining signed consent forms from parents and guardians.[90] As eugenicists Paul Popenoe and E. S. Gosney remarked in their 1928 study of sterilization in California, "the primary purpose of this policy was to protect the law by avoiding the possibility of litigation."[91] In other words, in this context consent was not meant to ensure informed approval for the surgery from an individual or an individual's legal guardian. Instead, it was to protect institutional authorities and the state's eugenic sterilization law by obtaining supporting documentation for sterilization.

As a result of this practice, signed consent forms accompanied a majority (about 95 percent) of sterilization requests processed by Pacific Colony. Studies of consent have traditionally understood the existence of signed consent forms as evidence of parental complicity with institutional decisions regarding sterilization and in some cases the consent forms do reflect approval.[92] However, given the state's acquired legal status over their children and the fact that officials at Pacific Colony often required sterilization before release, the existence of signed consent forms should not be correlated to evidence of freely given permission for the operation. Institutional authorities used consent to sterilization as a barrier to contact with residents—if parents or guardians wanted to see their children or have them released, they had to consent to sterilization first.[93] In his study of Pacific Colony, Edgerton wrote that the letter sent to parents or guardians asking for their consent to sterilization stated "*inter alia,* that sterilization would 'permit parole, leave of absence, and visits with less fear of undesirable complications.'"[94] Thus he wrote that sterilization was performed "unless there was a profoundly negative reaction on the part of a relative or guardian." In addition to making sterilization a necessary condition for contact and release, many sterilization consent forms contain witness signatures from parole officers, judges, and other state authorities, which suggests a level of legal coercion.[95] Some consent forms used to process sterilization requests were unclear about the purpose of the request. For example, one version of the consent forms read that the signee was approving "sterilization or any other condition requiring surgical operation."[96] Moreover, language barriers, literacy, and the existence of blanket consent forms that did not specifically mention sterilization call into question the existence of full consent even if a signature appeared on a consent form.

When parents refused to add their signature to consent forms, medical superintendents simply forwarded relevant details to the Department of Institutions to approve the sterilization above and beyond the parents' wishes. In all of the Pacific Colony sterilization requests I reviewed, the director of the Department of Institutions always sided with the superintendent in approving the operation. Parents who refused to sign consent forms and who voiced their objection to the sterilization were accused of ignorance about what was best for their children, were described as uncooperative, and in many cases were labeled mentally deficient themselves.[97] In letters written by Pacific Colony clinicians to the director of the Department of Institutions, they described nonconsenting parents as "subnormal," incapable of understanding their child's deficiencies, and summarily unqualified to make decisions about the reproductive futures of their children.[98]

Legally and in practice both parents and their institutionalized children were rarely regarded as full agents capable of making decisions about confinement or sterilization. According to institutional authorities, a parent's decision about sterilization was only valid if it could be used to ensure the operation would be done without the fear of liability. By diminishing parents' decision-making power over where their children lived, how they were treated, and whether they would leave the institution with their reproductive capacity intact, Pacific Colony authorities replicated oppressive practices prevalent in other government contexts, including juvenile court systems and federal Indian boarding schools.[99] They reflect the antecedents of what legal scholar Dorothy Roberts has described as punitive child welfare policy that systematically separates Black children from their parents, largely based on racist stereotypes of Black motherhood.[100]

Despite the legal power of institutional authorities and the coercive context of consent practices, the parents of Mexican-origin youth committed to Pacific Colony vocally and repeatedly refused to consent to sterilization. In 1936, Adriana Lopez was committed on the petition of a parole officer after she was found to be both "guilty of theft" and "a decided sex problem."[101] When her mother was approached about consenting to Adriana's sterilization in 1938, she "persistently refused to give her consent." Parents also objected outright to the sterilization of their sons. In 1938, for example, institutional authorities sought written consent for the sterilization of fourteen-year-old Gerardo Sosa, who was committed on petition of a parole officer on charges of "petty theft and burglary." Gerardo's records reveal that his father refused to consent to the operation on three separate occasions. In both Adriana's and Gerardo's cases the medical superintendent described the defiant parents as "low grade Mexican[s]," while pointing to their deviant behavior and the "bad reputation" of the patient and families as reasons why the Department of Institutions should authorize the sterilization "over and above" the parents' refusal. Despite the fact that the last word on sterilization remained in the hands of the state, the cases of Adriana and Gerardo reveal that many Mexican-origin parents refused to sign off on the sterilization of their daughters and sons and did so explicitly and repeatedly.[102]

GATHERING ALLIES IN THE STRUGGLE
AGAINST STERILIZATION

In the face of considerable institutional power and the erosion of parental rights, families shored up support from community allies who might be able to exert influence in matters of state-mandated sterilization and confinement. Some parents asked religious leaders to intervene on their behalf. For example, sixteen-year-old George Cortez's father flatly objected to his son's sterilization "on a religious basis."[103] When Pacific Colony staff insisted on performing the surgery, George's father enlisted the family priest to help prevent the sterilization. In these cases religious leaders wrote letters to Pacific Colony administrators reiterating the parents' stance against the operation, asserting the desire to preserve their children's reproductive capacity, and in some cases requesting that their children be released from the institution. In the early 1940s, Bernard Perez, the "spiritual advisor" of a family whose daughter was in Pacific Colony, wrote to Pacific Colony surgeon Dr. Elizabeth Hoyte stating that the young woman's mother "did not want her daughter to be sterilized and asked that [institutional authorities] parole the girl without sterilization."

Fifteen-year-old Marco Mendoza's father called on the family priest to help prevent sterilization. In reference to Marco's case, a Pacific Colony clinician wrote: "We received a refusal through the priest, the refusal being on a religious basis." In all of the cases I reviewed, letters from religious authorities did little to prevent sterilization, and clinicians sometimes wrote dismissively about the religiosity of Mexican-origin families. In these cases, Pacific Colony officials used the religious beliefs of parents as evidence of cultural backwardness and their inability to understand science or make rational decisions about their children's medical condition and needs. Faith certainly informed parents' positions on sterilization, but the letters penned to Pacific Colony administrators reflect more than just religious beliefs about reproduction. These letters document one way that parents tried to leverage the power of respected community leaders in their struggles with state authorities over their children.[104]

Religion surely played a role in parents' views on sterilization, but many simply did not want their children to be sterilized and saw institutional authorities' insistence on the operation as a serious escalation of power.

When parents realized that their children could be sterilized against their wishes, parents involved officials they believed might have considerable sway with Pacific Colony administrators. In some cases parents called on the Los Angeles Mexican Consulate for support. Like religious leaders, consular officials wrote letters on behalf of parents, formalizing demands that the state abstain from sterilizing a family member. These letters offered official backing from a respected government entity. In addition to writing letters of protest, the consulate also offered families legal resources.[105] While consular regulations officially forbade granting assistance to U.S. citizens, this directive was difficult to enforce in practice. As historian Francisco E. Balderrama has noted in his study of the Los Angeles consulate, consular officials and Mexican-origin residents of Los Angeles did not systematically draw distinctions between Mexican and Mexican American citizenship because cultural, linguistic, and familial ties were so strong across citizenship status.[106] Furthermore, dual citizenship—the result of birthright or jus soli citizenship from the United States and jus sanguinis citizenship from Mexico—allowed the consulate to intervene in some issues involving Mexican Americans.[107] Thus the Mexican consulate became an important asset for Mexican-origin families in matters of discrimination in Southern California.

Assistance from the Los Angeles consulate figured prominently in a number of Mexican-origin parents' attempts to prevent sterilization. In the case of one young Mexican American girl, for instance, Pacific Colony officials wrote: "The Mexican consul in Los Angeles has written to us verifying the parents' objection to sterilization and stating that the consul had taken the liberty of informing the mother that such operation would not take place without her consent."[108] At least once before involving consular officials, this young girl's parents plainly informed Pacific Colony administration that they did not want their daughter to be sterilized. Presumably, Pacific Colony staff made clear that they intended to operate on the girl regardless, and thus the parents approached the Mexican consulate for assistance. Consular officials wrote to Pacific Colony administrators to buttress the parents' objection and put institutional authorities on notice that they were monitoring the case. Unfortunately the consul did not have the legal authority to prevent sterilizations. Despite the letter reiterating the parents' desire to preserve their daughter's reproductive capacity, and despite informing the mother that her decision would be respected, the California Department of Institutions approved the sterilization without consent.

Miguel Hernandez's parents also acquired assistance from the Mexican consulate to prevent the sterilization of their thirteen-year-old son, who was committed to Pacific Colony in June of 1949. When officials at the institution refused to respect Miguel's parents' decision and disregarded attempts to intervene by consular officials, Raymond E. Young, consul of Mexican Affairs, went beyond the institution. Finding Pacific Colony authorities unrelenting in their effort to sterilize the thirteen-year-old, Young wrote a letter to California governor Earl Warren declaring malfeasance. Young's efforts on behalf of the Hernandez family resulted in an investigation of Miguel's case and prompted an explanation from Pacific Colony superintendent and medical director George Tarjan. In his letter to the governor, Tarjan described Miguel as a case of "mental deficiency, moron grade" and explained that the boy "came to the attention of the juvenile authorities because he used profane and indecent language in the presence of women on a public street and because he had maliciously thrown rocks at women walking on the street." After summarizing the accusations made against Miguel, Tarjan highlighted the fact that his parents were Mexican citizens, that his father worked as a fruit picker, and that "neither of the parents [spoke] English." Tarjan prefaced the family's assertion that Miguel was being "mistreated by his placement at Pacific Colony" with the observation that the boy's parents did "not seem to acknowledge the boy's limitation."

By bringing up citizenship status, the language abilities of Miguel's parents, and their supposed lack of attention to "the boy's limitation," Tarjan worked to tacitly discredit the parents' allegations of mistreatment. Tarjan included a detail that was completely irrelevant to the matter at hand—an allegation by a probation officer that two of Miguel's older brothers fled to "Old Mexico . . . in order to avoid the draft." While Tarjan acknowledged correspondence with the Mexican consulate regarding the parents' refusal to consent to sterilization, the Pacific Colony superintendent dedicated the majority of his report to the governor to discrediting the family and weakening their claims of mistreatment. The result of the investigation and whether Miguel was in fact sterilized are unknown. However, it is evident that Miguel's parents sought the assistance of the Mexican consulate in preventing the sterilization of their son and escalated their claims of malfeasance to the governor's office.[109]

In 1935 the Mexican consulate also interceded on behalf of Maria Tellez. As the "Informe de Proteccion" on her case details, Maria's father called juvenile authorities for assistance when the two had a disagreement. Upon being detained, Maria was subjected to mental and physical exams that ultimately led juvenile officials to deem her in need of institutionalization and sterilization. This intervention by legal officials went far beyond what Maria's father expected, however, and when he realized his legal authority as a parent was being disregarded, he issued a complaint with the Los Angeles Mexican Consulate. The consulate took up the case, proposing to take whatever measures necessary to address a decision they recognized as thoroughly unjust.[110]

> Esta niña tuvo ciertas dificultades con su padre, Señor Alberto Tellez, quien se vio obligado a pedir un consejo de las autoridades juveniles. Estas se tomaron la atribución de arrestar a la niña Tellez y después de someterla a ciertos exámenes físicos y mentales la condenaron a ser esterilizada. El señor Tellez se quejó con el Consulado y desde luego se tomaron las medidas necesarias para evitar que se lleve a cabo tan injusta decisión y se interpuso con la ayuda del Abogado Consultor, señor John Oliver, un amparo en la Suprema Corte de Justicia del Estado.

> This young girl had certain difficulties with her father, Mr. Alberto Tellez, who felt obligated to seek advice from the Juvenile authorities. These authorities took it upon themselves to arrest the young Tellez girl and after subjecting her to certain physical and mental exams condemned her to be sterilized. Mr. Tellez complained to the Consulate and since then they took the measures necessary to prevent such an unjust decision with the help of the consular lawyer, Mr. John Oliver, filed a claim in the State's Supreme Court.

In an effort to prevent Maria's sterilization, the Mexican consulate appointed consular attorney John Oliver to the case and filed a suit with the courts.[111] Maria's father sought to assert his parental rights and prevent his daughter's sterilization. Not only does Maria's case illustrate the ways that parents and the Mexican consulate worked together to prevent sterilization. It also makes clear that all parties involved viewed the actions of juvenile authorities and Pacific Colony administrators as unjust. The outcome of Maria's case is unknown, but other court documents indicate that her father wasn't the only parent to use the courts to try and protect the reproductive autonomy of their child.

GARCIA V. STATE DEPARTMENT OF INSTITUTIONS: ASSERTING REPRODUCTIVE AUTONOMY

On Monday, December 18, 1939, a few days before Christmas, Sara Rosas Garcia, a working-class single mother of nine, filed a writ of prohibition to prevent the institutionalization and sterilization of her eighteen-year-old daughter, Andrea. A Los Angeles probation officer petitioned the courts to have Andrea committed to Pacific Colony, and Sara knew that the primary purpose of commitment was to have her daughter forcibly sterilized. Desperate to help her daughter, Sara obtained legal aid from the Mexican consulate, and consular attorney David C. Marcus filed a writ of prohibition on her behalf.[112] In the filing, Marcus made Sara's position regarding both institutionalization and sterilization clear: either action by the state would be unjust, "against [their] wishes and desires"—and, if performed, would be done "without their permission or consent."[113]

In addition to expressing opposition to Andrea's commitment and sterilization, Marcus waged a strong legal argument against sterilization grounded in the eighteen-year-old's constitutional rights as an American citizen. Attacking the validity of California's sterilization law head-on, Marcus asserted that the state's practice of eugenic sterilization was a contravention of the Fourteenth Amendment because it violated Andrea's inalienable right to life, liberty, and the pursuit of happiness. Because the sterilization law was only applied to people committed to state institutions, Marcus argued that it also violated the equal protection clause. Lastly, in the writ of prohibition, Marcus challenged the authority of institutional officials to make decisions about sterilization. He wrote that, because institutional administrators and clinicians were not part of the state's judicial body, and because they did not provide a formal notice and appeals process vetted by the state's judicial body, sterilizations ordered by institutional authorities violated a person's right to due process.[114]

Following his legal criticism of the state's sterilization practices more broadly, Marcus stressed the importance of the petition for Andrea in particular. This was a matter of Andrea's "God given right of procreation." If the operation took place, there would be no remedy, causing Andrea and her mother "great and irreparable damage."[115] Marcus described the state's sterilization statute as representing a grave excess in the "police power of the state."

The writ of probation Marcus filed on behalf of Sara and Andrea Garcia situated a person's right to parenthood within a broader set of constitutional rights that the state's legal body was beholden to uphold. Marcus's argument asserted that California's sterilization statute represented overreach of state power by diminishing equal protection, due process, and interfering in an individual's right to bodily autonomy. Despite this persuasive analysis, the writ of prohibition was denied in a two-to-one decision the same day it was filed. Accepting and upholding Marcus's petition would mean acknowledging California officials' complicity in creating a class of citizens whose constitutional rights—and bodies—were consistently violated. Writing the dissenting opinion, Judge White agreed with parts of Marcus's argument. White asserted that, because the sterilization order deprived a person of the right of procreation, it merited judicial consideration beyond the administrative arena of the California Department of Institutions. Highlighting the severity of this practice, White wrote: "To clothe legislative agencies with this plenary power, withholding as it does any opportunity for a hearing or any opportunity for recourse to the courts, to my mind partakes of the essence of slavery and outrages constitutional guarantees." White's reference to slavery was incisive on multiple fronts. Indeed, upon being committed to Pacific Colony, Andrea's body and future became subject to the decisions of the institution as a ward of the state. Furthermore, the ableist logics used to justify slavery—arguments about the racial inferiority of Africans; their social, political, and mental incompetence; and the profits to be extricated from managing their reproduction—were the premise upon which many Mexican-origin youths like Andrea were categorized as mentally deficient, confined, forced to work for free in the institution, and subject to reproductive constraint.[116]

Despite their efforts and Judge White's harsh dissent, Andrea was committed to Pacific Colony four months later, in April of 1941. They placed her in Cottage 16 and likely had her join a work detail. That same year, Pacific Colony authorities processed paperwork to have her sterilized. The request was accompanied by a consent form signed by her mother with witness signatures from Elizabeth Buckley from the Los Angeles Police Department and Ida Lawson Valley, the director of attendance of the Los Angeles City Schools. The writ of prohibition and the legal case that the Garcias brought against the state are not mentioned in any of the paperwork related to the sterilization request, and institutional documents related to Andrea's case completely omit the valiant effort made to prevent the operation.[117] Despite the loss in court, Andrea remained defiant. Ultimately, Andrea was not sterilized. She also escaped Pacific Colony, managed to evade return, and in early 1944 she was officially discharged while still out on escape.[118]

Traditional political institutions like the courts have rarely proven effective or accessible to working-class, racialized, or otherwise marginalized people.[119] Indeed, Sara and Andrea Garcia's efforts illustrate how the state's legal system failed to protect Andrea and diminished Sara's parental authority. Andrea's experience reveals the ways that constitutional rights such as equal protection before the law, due process, and access to life and liberty are easily revoked under allegations of incompetence. People rendered "non-citizens and (no)bodies" by the state through processes of racialized, gendered, and ableist labeling seemingly have no rights, and a legal system that doles out rights based on notions of competency, dependency, and deservingness cannot offer equal protection to all bodies. Reading the Garcia case as a failure, though, would be a further injustice. The case speaks to the struggles that Mexican-origin youth waged to confront pathologization, institutional confinement, and reproductive constraint—and should be read as such. It is part of a long history of resistance to reproductive oppression. That is, while racist and ableist logics justified institutionalization and sterilization and effectively stripped working-class Mexican-origin youth of bodily and reproductive autonomy, these youths and their families found ways to minimize, evade, and resist violent state interventions. Sometimes subtle and other times riotous, their actions illustrate how policies meant to manage and oppress nonconforming people elicited a broad range of responses that constitute a spectrum of defiance.

Decades after Sara Garcia's legal effort to prevent Pacific Colony officials from sterilizing Andrea, other legal cases proved triumphant in establishing reproductive autonomy as protected by the constitution. U.S. Supreme Court cases like *Griswold v. Connecticut* (1965) and *Roe v. Wade* (1973) ruled that the constitution protected the right to liberty and privacy in matters of birth control and abortion respectively. But not all reproductive bodies seem to be covered by the U.S. Constitution. In the conclusion I revisit another legal battle against sterilization abuse waged by Mexican-origin women in Southern California—*Madrigal v. Quilligan* (1975). Discussing this 1970s antisterilization abuse case in light of Andrea Garcia's experience offers important insights on why Reproductive Justice activists and scholars insist on an organizing and analytical framework based on principles of human rights and justice as opposed to the U.S. Constitution.

Conclusion

In the quote that opens this book an unnamed survivor of institutionalization at Pacific Colony questions why California state workers sterilized her
without permission and without explanation. "The sterilization wasn't for
punishment, was it? Was it because there was something wrong with my
mind?"[1] Her questioning outlines a key point that I have tried to elaborate
throughout the book: that state practices of confinement and sterilization at Pacific Colony rested on a coalescence of racist and ableist logics
that were bolstered through alternating and evolving discourses of punishment, treatment, and care. When early twentieth-century experts in
psychology, education, social work, and juvenile delinquency lobbied the
California legislature to establish Pacific Colony, they argued that institutionalization and sterilization were the most humanitarian and scientific
approaches to dealing with what they saw as the social and economic consequences of mental defect and inferiority.

Relying on eugenic science on intelligence ranking and testing, this
consortium of experts asserted that people with low intelligence—namely
people labeled "feebleminded"—were sowing social and economic discord
in the form of poverty, immorality, and crime. To contain this threat, state
authorities wielded their power across agencies to identify, label, insti-

tutionalize, and sterilize people deemed mentally defective, economically burdensome, sexuality delinquent, and criminally inclined. By and large young working-class, disabled, and nonwhite Californians were sentenced to confinement at Pacific Colony based on the argument that they represented a social menace *and* that the institution was the only place they could receive appropriate care and treatment. They were forcibly sterilized on the basis that their supposed mental defect was hereditary *and* on the basis that they were incapable and undeserving of parenthood. Since its doors opened in 1927 and into the early 1950s, Pacific Colony clinicians and collaborators from other state agencies insisted that treatment and care for the disabled, the impoverished, and for youth of color should be delivered in the form of segregation, confinement, and reproductive constraint.

Pacific Colony was an exemplar in state efforts at population control and is illustrative of the ways that large social problems have been biologized and addressed at the expense of already marginalized populations. By centering the experiences of young working-class Mexican-origin women and men, this book highlights the convergence of ideologies of race, disability, gender, and class in science on intelligence that rationalized an expansive matrix of reproductive oppression. As my research details, this matrix extended beyond sterilization to include the efforts state authorities made in policing and pathologizing working-class youth and families of color, particularly through their methods of identifying and categorizing disability. Part of this matrix included the systematic legal and practical stripping of bodily and reproductive autonomy that people experienced at Pacific Colony through commitment and unwanted reproductive surgeries.

The legal process of commitment extended this matrix of reproductive oppression to the parents of youth whose decision-making authority regarding the treatment, freedom, and reproductive capacity of their children was diminished, denigrated, and disregarded. Keeping the three pillars of Reproductive Justice in mind, the book highlights how youth committed to Pacific Colony and their parents and family members were stripped of both the right to have children and the right to raise one's children in safe environments.[2] This history represents part of a larger history of disability oppression that underscores a persistent assumption that no one would want to birth a disabled child and that any "good future" depends on the prevention and elimination of bodies labeled "defective."[3] These state practices supported and legitimized medical, cultural, political, and economic understandings of disability as both undesirable and a social threat.

As the book lays out, Pacific Colony was an exemplar but it was not necessarily unique. The institution reflected a reorganization and reboot of the long-standing role of racism and ableism in arguments for confinement and reproductive constraint in the United States. In many ways science on intelligence, mental defect, and the label of feeblemindedness, in particular, reified already existing social inequalities grounded in racism, ableism, and classism, representing an entrenchment of white supremacy in the early twentieth century. Sociologist Ruha Benjamin's necessary work on the social dimensions of science, technology, and medicine is particularly instructive here. As a medical diagnosis that combined social location and supposed mental capacity, "feeblemindedness" became a "conduit" through which previous forms of discrimination and inequality were upgraded and legitimized.[4] Constructing narratives of "economic incompetence" and social threat, researchers drew on already existing ideologies of race, disability, gender, and class to both make the label of feeblemindedness "matter" and to make confinement and reproductive constraint legitimate social policy. All told, this history of Pacific Colony highlights the deep-seated intersection of racial, reproductive, and disability oppression.

In the early 1950s the institution underwent a name change—from Pacific Colony to Pacific State Hospital—as part of a statewide administrative shift away from large-scale confinement and sterilization. Indeed, sterilizations fell drastically. Between 1929 and July 1951, Pacific Colony reported a total of 1,836 sterilizations split relatively evenly between both men and women (947 women, 889 men). Between July 1951 and July 1961, Pacific State Hospital reported 28 sterilizations, all performed on women committed to the institution.[5] More research is needed to produce a full account of this drastic decline in sterilizations, but one major factor was a change in the state's sterilization law that made it more difficult to process sterilizations and opened institutional authorities up to litigation. Although the 1950s saw a decline in sterilizations in state institutions and a general reconsideration of mass institutionalization, ableism, racism, and classism remained. As Benjamin highlights in her insights on science and medicine, arguments regarding social inequality, race, disability, and reproductive oppression frequently undergo updating, reboots, and often get dispersed in other fields of knowledge and power centers.

Labels like "feebleminded" were upgraded to seemingly less derogatory terms like "mental retardation" and testing criteria for labeling and categorization underwent several updates. In the 1950s and 1960s mental health professionals began moving away from theories of strict hereditary defect and toward theories of social and cultural deprivation. These theories were less explicit in their eugenic underpinnings but were nevertheless informed by racism and ableism. They maintained the notion that poverty, crime, and violence were the outcomes of defect and deficit in the families, communities, and cultures of low-income and often urban people of color.[6] These updated theories influenced social policy in ways that were reminiscent of the first half of the twentieth century. By midcentury states began funding policies and programs that targeted the supposed social, cultural, and environmental deprivation of individuals as opposed to structural forces that create inequalities.[7] Funding for mass confinement shifted from state institutions to the expansion of prisons, which usurped the role of asylums and state hospitals in practices of punishment and treatment aimed at poor people, the disabled, and people of color.[8]

Although eugenic sterilizations slowed inside California state institutions, the idea that some people needed to be forcibly sterilized remained. As anthropologist Adelaida R. Del Castillo pointed out in her classic piece on Mexican-origin women's experiences of sterilization, a 1960s Gallup poll showed that 20 percent of the public were in favor of sterilizing welfare recipients.[9] In their research on sterilization abuse in Southern California during the 1960s and 1970s, Elena Gutiérrez and Virginia Espino highlighted the widespread belief among doctors in public-serving hospitals that it was their social "responsibility" to encourage and in many cases coerce low-income women—who they saw as economic burdens and irresponsible breeders—into unwanted sterilizations.[10] In the 1970s increased funding for family planning at the federal level coalesced with concerns about overpopulation, welfare dependency, and physician bias and thousands of low-income Women of Color experienced sterilization abuse in public hospitals and in Indian Health Services facilities across the country.[11]

Physicians were not the only authority figures that continued to impose sterilizations. Reminiscent of the Pacific Colony practice of requiring sterilization before discharge or parole, judges in California in the 1960s coerced both women and men into agreeing to sterilizations in exchange for probation or lesser charges.[12] Eugenic sterilizations continued in North Carolina, where social workers targeted working-class Black women on welfare in their recommendations to the state's Eugenics Board well into the early 1970s.[13] Although these sterilizations did not occur in state institutions and were not explicitly about disability, they nevertheless relied on and perpetuated the notion that some people are simply "unfit" to reproduce and that authority figures (physicians, social workers, judges) were justified in violating certain people's reproductive autonomy. Some clinicians and public health workers even believed it was their responsibility to manage the reproductive capacity of low-income women and Women of Color to curb poverty and overpopulation.[14] Notions of fitness for parenthood continued to be correlated to race, poverty, and crime. Thus racism, ableism, and classism remained rampant in mental health, medical, and legal realms after the 1950s, fueling a reconfigured matrix of reproductive oppression that dispersed practices of confinement and reproductive constraint into other realms and under different names.

Unfortunately, racism and ableism continue to converge today in harmful ways through state systems that are meant to provide care, treatment, and protection. As one formerly institutionalized person stated in the 1970s: "We are not out of the dark ages yet."[15] Scholars have documented the persistent ways that youth of color with disability labels continue to experience high rates of segregation and criminalization in school and confinement in medical and carceral settings.[16] Recent reporting shows that youth with disabilities continue to endure physical violence in the form of restraint and seclusion.[17] Within months of writing this, Florida police sent a six-year-old Black girl to a mental health facility because educators and legal authorities assessed her behavior to be "out of control."[18] Weeks ago, Judge Mary Ellen Brennan of Oakland County, Michigan, removed a fifteen-year-old Black girl with a disability from her mother and placed her in a juvenile detention facility referred to as a "treatment program" because she didn't complete her online homework during a pandemic. In her remarks the judge asserted that the girl was a "threat to (the) community" and even a threat to her mother, despite the fact that her mother was desperately trying to have her daughter released. Brennan ordered this course of "treatment" for the fifteen-year-old in the midst of a global pandemic that made carceral settings like juvenile detention centers hotspots for a deadly virus. In the face of the girl's and her mother's clear distress over the situation, Brennan stated that she thought the girl was "blooming" in the detention center and was "exactly where she needed to be."[19] As these recent cases illustrate, educational and legal authorities continue to use language of care and treatment to both punish and incarcerate youth with disability labels and justify dismissing and diminishing parental authority.

These practices also persist in the ways that the federal government justifies violent policies aimed at immigrant youth and families—particularly youth confinement and family separation. In 2017 the Trump administration began separating migrant children from their parents and placing them in confinement in an effort to punish immigrant families for seeking entry into the country and deter future migrants.[20] Federal authorities described this practice as the logical consequences of breaking the law but also as a humanitarian act. In his defense of family separation Alex Azar, secretary of Health and Human Services, asserted that separating migrant children from their parents and confining them in horrid conditions was "one of the great acts of American generosity and charity." Azar added that the U.S. government was effectively "saving kids" from parents who were irresponsibly "smuggling" their children into the country. Azar added justification to the separations by describing the immigrant parents as largely criminal and "demonstrably unfit."[21] Aimed at mostly Central American and Mexican immigrant families, these descriptions echo rationales used to remove Mexican-origin youth from their parents and confine them to Pacific Colony and represent the ways that these ideas remain as powerful dog whistles in today's political context.[22]

Far from the "compassionate environments" providing access to health care and education that Azar described, facilities used to confine migrant youth are described by the youth themselves and reporters as cramped, unsanitary, and rife with neglect.[23] In 2019 the American Medical

Association wrote a letter expressing concern over conditions in detention centers to the U.S. House of Representatives Committee on Oversight
and Reform as part of a set of hearings titled "Kids in Cages: Inhumane
Treatment at the Border."[24] Moreover, in some facilities private contrac-
tors collaborated with mental health professionals to manage confined
youth in abusive ways. In one facility a psychiatrist who had no board certification prescribed powerful psychotropic drugs to immigrant children
without parental consent.[25] In another facility a teenage asylum-seeker
from Honduras assumed the disclosures he made to a clinician in gov-
ernment-ordered therapy sessions would be private. Yet the sessions were
used in Immigration and Customs Enforcement (ICE) filings to argue
that the young man should remain incarcerated and should ultimately
be deported. As others have pointed out, the family separation policy is
the most recent iteration of a long U.S. government tradition of violently
separating families deemed unfit and undeserving of inclusion in the body
politic.[26] The way that this government policy was enacted and justified
reflects a present-day example of how youths and parents deemed unfit
and undeserving are continually subjected to confinement, medical violence, and constructed as outside of the bounds of parental rights, patient-
doctor confidentiality, and bodily autonomy.

Sterilization abuse continues in legal and carceral settings under rationales grounded in biologized understandings of poverty and criminality.
Between 2006 and 2010 more than one hundred women were illegally
sterilized in a California prison.[27] In 2017 a Tennessee judge suggested
sterilization in exchange for a lesser sentence.[28] In both cases the physicians and legal authorities involved implied that sterilization was an
appropriate state-sponsored sanction for irresponsible and dependent
breeders. Furthermore, in the California case the physician suggested that
sterilization benefited the public writ large by saving the state money in
the future welfare costs of "unwanted children." Even today, physicians
and legal authorities continue to rely on core tenets of eugenics to justify
violating the reproductive and bodily autonomy of already marginalized
people. Most recently, in September of 2020 the organizations Project
South, Georgia Detention Watch, Georgia Latino Alliance for Human
Rights, and South Georgia Immigrant Support Network filed a complaint
on behalf of immigrants detained at the Irwin County Detention Center

wherein five women describe undergoing unwanted hysterectomies while in detention.[29] While details about what these women went through are only just being reported, their experiences are a testament to how toxic and violent impulses to make reproductive decisions on behalf of marginalized groups remain deeply rooted, and how conditions of confinement make these individuals even more vulnerable to medical abuse.

At the same time that we can trace the persistent and intersecting practices of disability, racial, and reproductive oppression, we can also track equally unwavering and multifaceted responses. Based on their experiences, communities of color grew increasingly aware of the ways that mental health and legal authorities collaborated to construct people of color as pathologically criminal and subjected them to invasive treatments and punishment. In the 1970s, when the Black Panthers caught wind of a proposed violence center at UCLA that would study the psychological origins of crime, they organized successfully to prevent it. In this effort they built an impressive coalition with the western region of the NAACP, the National Organization for Women, the Mexican American Political Association, the Committee Opposing Psychiatric Abuse of Prisoners, the United Farmworkers Organizing Committee, and the California Prisoners' Union. In their arguments against the violence center this coalition rightly asserted that researchers would likely produce knowledge that effectively biologized violence as inherent among already marginalized groups. Instead of looking for the source of violence in biology, the coalition highlighted the social and economic components of crime. They pointed out that the center would likely subject already marginalized communities to surveillance, incarceration, and unwanted medical procedures.[30]

People with disabilities have played an active role in contesting the ways that medical and state authorities wielded pathologization, confinement, and unwanted medical procedures during the same period. People who experienced confinement in state institutions mobilized the deinstitutionalization movement through self-advocacy. People with disabilities took over leadership positions in organizations that began as parent-led efforts to reform institutions to assert their value and humanity and demand rights in all sectors of life.[31] Disabled people of color like Roland Johnson have organized and shared stores on their own terms, asserting that disabled people should be in control of their own lives.[32]

Speaking about their experiences, disability rights activists critiqued the ways that states implemented treatment and segregation, challenging medical, political, and social culture around disability. Clinicians and mental health professionals also began questioning the legitimacy of disability labels, recognizing the great harm that the labels justified.[33] Deinstitutionalization was a huge grassroots undertaking, and between 1977 and 2015 the number of people with intellectual disability labels living in institutions decreased by 80 percent.[34] As sociologist Liat Ben-Moshe has detailed, deinstitutionalization was a largely successful effort at massive decarceration and thus offers important lessons for the contemporary prison abolition movement.

Discriminatory and abusive experiences with social workers, welfare agents, and physicians in public hospitals during the 1960s and 1970s also informed Chicana feminist ideologies and organizing in Southern California. Chicana feminists recognized that their everyday struggles stemmed from systemic racial and economic oppression that targeted their bodies and livelihood.[35] Organizers like Alicia Escalante, who founded the Chicano Welfare Rights Organization in 1967, confronted the racist practices of the Los Angeles Welfare Department in particular. Not only did she highlight the ways that impoverished women and single mothers were cast as undeserving burdens on the system, but she also articulated a critique of state administrators and welfare workers—most of whom were white professionals—who profited socially and economically from the poverty of Chicano families.[36] As an advocate for low-income women, Escalante was one of the first to learn about sterilization abuse at the Los Angeles County–USC Medical Center.[37]

In the 1970s and 1980s Chicana feminists understood sterilization abuse as an outcome of eugenics and as embodied manifestations of intersecting systems of oppression.[38] Experiences of sterilization, confinement, and marginalization provided the context in which Chicana feminists formulated their political consciousness and informed the decisions that they made about which state apparatuses and interventions they would seek to challenge and transform. Thus, when it became clear that Mexican-origin women were being coercively sterilized at the Los Angeles County–USC Medical Center, Chicana feminists not only filed a legal suit but also embarked on a massive campaign to educate the public on the gendered, racial, and class underpinnings of sterilization abuse. In *Madrigal v. Quilligan* (1975) a group of Mexican-origin women filed a class-action lawsuit asserting that their civil and constitutional rights to bear children were violated when they were forcibly sterilized by obstetricians at the USC Medical Center. Like the argument in the 1939 Garcia suit discussed in chapter 4, *Madrigal v. Quilligan* was a solid and compelling case in which Mexican-origin women asserted their right to bodily and reproductive autonomy. Yet, also like the Garcia case, the courts ruled against the women.

Although the women did not win the lawsuit, they made significant change in public opinion on sterilization abuse and challenged California practices of sterilization.[39] The cases of *Garcia v. State Dept. of Institutions* and *Madrigal v. Quilligan* highlight the persistent violence that Mexican-origin women and their families have endured at the hands of state authorities. However, the cases also represent a long history of Chicana feminist analysis of the intersections of race, class, gender, and reproductive oppression as well as their resistance to these intersecting systems of oppression. Including *Garcia v. State Dept. of Institutions* in this legal analysis of Chicana feminist resistance to reproductive oppression adds an often neglected component—disability and ableism.

When a group of Women of Color came together to create the Reproductive Justice framework in the 1990s, they insisted on remembering histories of eugenics, sterilization abuse, and the multiple ways that population-control efforts diminished the dignity, safety, and autonomy of women, families, and communities. These women insisted on analyzing and exposing the ways that state agencies devised and implemented harmful policies under the guise of treatment, care, and access. In doing so, they established a framework that drew on both the similarities and differences across their collective experiences to wage incisive critiques of systems of reproductive oppression in the United States. Recognizing that legal battles that grounded arguments in equal access to constitutional rights—like *Garcia v. State Dept. of Institutions* and *Madrigal v. Quilligan*—and liberal principles like "privacy" and "choice" rarely resulted in justice for marginalized people, Reproductive Justice founders grounded their values and claims in a human rights framework. They thus expanded both the scope and demands involved in achieving reproductive freedom, establishing a broad-based, inclusive, and intersectional frame-work for organizing and analysis.[40] As Dorothy Roberts has written: "RJ [Reproductive Justice] is a model not just for women of color, nor just for achieving reproductive freedom. RJ is a model for organizing for human equality and well-being."[41]

Today, organizers and thinkers in Reproductive Justice and Disability Justice movements in the United States converge in their critiques of reproductive oppression and other related forms of state violence. Both maintain that the state is never justified in wielding violence or (re)estab-lishing, (re)organizing, and maintaining social inequality based on bodily difference. Both honor and uphold the inherent value of all humans and their right to dignity and bodily autonomy. Both demand that govern-ment play a radically different role in the lives of people. Not only should government abstain from creating and upholding inequality and violence, but these movements assert that it is the role of government to create the conditions for all people, families, and communities to flourish. In other words, the Reproductive Justice and Disability Justice movements argue that everyone has the "human right to make personal decisions about one's life" and that it is "the obligation of government and society to ensure the conditions are suitable for implementing one's decisions."[42]

To be clear, this vision is not new. Reflecting on her experience of institutionalization, Patty asserted that people "have to learn that we are human, too."[43] Similarly, when talking about how he thought the state should change their approach to people with disability labels, Ed, who experienced institutionalization, stated: "Let's give them all the chances possible. Teach them to make choices. There is no need for things like peo-ple being overdrugged. We have to give people maximum chances."[44] These early insights are at the core of widespread and growing Reproductive and Disability Justice movements.

Writing this conclusion in the midst of a global pandemic, it is easy to see how ableism and racism continue to perpetuate expansive reproduc-tive oppression. However, this moment is also brimming with examples of the way people are applying, developing, and acting on Reproductive and Disability Justice insights particularly in the movement to abolish the prison industrial complex and end state violence. Not only do scholars continue to insist on disability and reproductive oppression as important analytics in understanding carceral logics, but young people are taking up these analyses in both their thinking and approach to organizing.[45] For example, in *Teen Vogue*, a relatively mainstream publication aimed at a young audience, journalist Tyra Bosnic offered important nuance for current conversations about rerouting police funding into mental health. Citing her personal experience and interviewing experts on the subject, Bosnic points out the ways that mental health systems can mirror practices of criminalization and incarceration—a point that this book supports.[46] In another piece, reporter Cecilia Nowell writes about the ways that tear gas wielded against racial justice activists during summer of 2020 protests for Black Lives caused bodily harm to people who menstruate and miscarriages among pregnant people.[47] If these two pieces are any indication, it's clear that, as founder and scholar of the Reproductive Justice framework Loretta Ross has written, "young people are on the front lines of this struggle."[48] Young thinkers and organizers are drawing connections, questioning single-issue causes, and rejecting single-issue solutions. They are on the vanguard of social justice movements today, and with their light we might be ushered out of the dark ages.

Appendix

Tables 4 and 5 provide the raw data used to create Figures 2 and 6, which appear in chapters 1 and 3, respectively. Table 6 includes an accounting of all of the racial descriptors used to label people committed to Pacific Colony between 1927 and 1947.

Table 4   Spanish-surnamed patient requests processed by Pacific Colony, 1928–51

Year	Spanish-surname sterilization requests	Non-Spanish- surname sterilization requests	Total	Spanish-surname as a percentage of total (%)
1928	3	8	11	27.3
1929	12	21	33	36.4
1930	28	118	146	19.2
1931	18	63	81	22.2
1932	14	37	51	27.5
1933	21	99	120	17.5
1934	21	133	154	13.6
1935	27	65	92	29.3
1936	28	93	121	23.1
1937	27	64	91	29.7
1938	19	59	78	24.4
1939	25	47	72	34.7
1940	48	89	137	35.0
1941	61	136	197	31.0
1942	30	73	103	29.1
1943	27	45	72	37.5
1944	23	47	70	32.9
1945	20	65	85	23.5
1946	17	58	75	22.7
1947	15	62	77	19.5
1948	11	41	52	21.2
1949	16	57	73	21.9
1950	12	34	46	26.1
1951	10	43	53	18.9
Total	533	1,557	2,090	25.5

SOURCE: Author's compilation from "Sterilization Records," Department of Institutions, Department of Mental Hygiene, California State Archives.

Table 5 Admissions to Pacific Colony by Mexican-origin and sex, 1927–47

Year	Male	Female	Total
1927	4	4	8
1928	6	6	12
1929	19	23	42
1930	16	16	32
1931	8	17	25
1932	8	29	37
1933	13	17	30
1934	8	16	24
1935	13	15	28
1936	10	23	33
1937	8	17	25
1938	7	13	20
1939	14	18	32
1940	76	50	128
1941	56	43	99
1942	39	29	68
1943	33	31	64
1944	22	20	42
1945	40	18	58
1946	43	23	66
1947	20	11	31

SOURCE: Author's compilation from Patient Synopsis, 1927–47, Department of Developmental Services, Lanterman Development Center, C01882, California State Archives.

Table 6   Racial descriptors used to label
individuals admitted to Pacific Colony,
1927–47

Racial descriptors	Number of individuals
White	2,885
Mexican	907
Black	190
Italian	48
Jewish	46
Indian	30
Japanese	25
Chinese	4
Spanish	4
Armenian	4
Greek	4
Filipino	3
Puerto Rican	2
Mexican Black	1
Korean Mexican	1
Hawaii	1
Creole	1
Russian	1
Slav	1
Polish English	1
Hungarian	1
Syrian	1
Gypsy	1
Portuguese	1
German	1
French	1

SOURCE: Author's compilation from Patient
Synopsis, 1927–47, Department of
Developmental Services, Lanterman
Development Center, C01882, California State
Archives.

Notes

INTRODUCTION

Epigraphs: The first quotation is from G. Sabagh and Robert B. Edgerton, "Sterilized Mental Defectives Look at Eugenic Sterilization," *Eugenics Quarterly* 9, no. 4 (December 4, 1962): 220. The only other description given for this person is that they identify as a woman. The second quotation is also in Sabagh and Edgerton, "Sterilized Mental Defectives Look at Eugenic Sterilization," 221. The only other description given for this person is that they identify as a man.

1. Wendy Kline, *Building a Better Race: Gender, Sexuality, and Eugenics from the Turn of the Century to the Baby Boom* (Oakland: University of California Press, 2005); Natalie Lira and Alexandra Minna Stern, "Mexican Americans and Eugenic Sterilization: Resisting Reproductive Justice in California, 1920–1950," *Aztlán: A Journal of Chicano Studies* 39, no. 2 (Fall 2014): 9–34; Alex Wellerstein, "States of Eugenics: Institutions and Practices of Compulsory Sterilization in California," in *Reframing Rights: Bioconstitutionalizm in the Genetic Age*, ed. Sheila Jasanoff (Cambridge, MA: MIT Press, 2011), 29–58; Alexandra Minna Stern, *Eugenic Nation: Faults and Frontiers of Better Breeding in Modern America* (Berkeley: University of California Press, 2005); and Miroslava Chávez-García, *States of Delinquency: Race and Science in the Making of California's Juvenile Justice System*, 1st edition (Oakland: University of California Press, 2012), 143–50.

2. James W. Trent, *Inventing the Feeble Mind: A History of Mental Retardation in the United States* (Oakland: University of California Press, 1995); Stephen

T. Murphy, *Voices of Pineland: Eugenics, Social Reform, and the Legacy of Feeble-mindedness in Maine* (Charlotte, NC: Information Age Publishing, 2011); Michael D'Antonio, *State Boys Rebellion* (New York: Simon & Schuster, 2005); Steven Noll, *Feeble-Minded in Our Midst: Institutions for the Mentally Retarded in the South, 1900–1940* (Chapel Hill: University of North Carolina Press, 1995); and Gregory Michael Dorr, *Segregation's Science: Eugenics and Society in Virginia*, 1st edition (Charlottesville: University of Virginia Press, 2008).

3. According to the 1910 and 1930 census, the Mexican-origin population did not exceed 6.5 percent. See U.S. Census Bureau (1910) and U.S. Census Bureau (1930).

4. Nicole L. Novak et al., "Disproportionate Sterilization of Latinos under California's Eugenic Sterilization Program, 1920–1945," *American Journal of Public Health* 108, no. 5 (May 2018): 611–13.

5. To be clear, this was not the only medical rational used to justify institutionalization and sterilization. During the early twentieth century, "mental illness" was often cited as a reason for sterilization, and epilepsy was also a diagnosis that could lead to both confinement and sterilization. Later in the century, in places like North Carolina, "economic fitness" predominated in justifications for sterilization but "feeblemindedness" remained as a medical rationale. Thus my point is that "feeblemindedness" or "mental defect" was one of the most consistent and widely used *medical* diagnosis used to justify eugenic sterilization and was of course the principal way that people were legally committed to institutions for the so-called feebleminded throughout the first half of the twentieth century. For more on the notion of feeblemindedness, see Trent, *Inventing the Feeble Mind*; Dorr, *Segregation's Science*; Karin Lorene Zipf, *Bad Girls at Samarcand: Sexuality and Sterilization in a Southern Juvenile Reformatory* (Baton Rouge: Louisiana State University Press, 2016); Allison C. Carey, *On the Margins of Citizenship: Intellectual Disability and Civil Rights in Twentieth-Century America* (Philadelphia: Temple University Press, 2010); Murphy, *Voices of Pineland*; Michael Rembis, *Defining Deviance: Sex, Science, and Delinquent Girls, 1890–1960* (Urbana: University of Illinois Press, 2013); Kline, *Building a Better Race*; Paul A. Lombardo, *Three Generations, No Imbeciles: Eugenics, the Supreme Court, and Buck v. Bell*, 1st edition (Baltimore, MD: Johns Hopkins University Press, 2010); Mark Rapley, *The Social Construction of Intellectual Disability*, 1st edition (New York: Cambridge University Press, 2004); Noll, *Feeble-Minded in Our Midst*; and Molly Ladd-Taylor, "The 'Sociological Advantages' of Sterilization: Fiscal Policies and Feebleminded Women in Interwar Minnesota," in *Mental Retardation in America: A Historical Reader*, ed. Steven Noll and James W. Trent (New York: New York University Press, 2004), 281–99. Disability labels that seemingly represent the mental capacity of individuals continue to be used as reasons why young people should be segregated in schools, subjected to confinement, and sterilized. See Alison Kafer, *Feminist, Queer, Crip*, 1st edition (Bloomington: Indiana University Press, 2013);

Nirmala Erevelles and Andrea Minear, "Unspeakable Offenses: Untangling Race and Disability in Discourses of Intersectionality," *Journal of Literary & Cultural Disability Studies* 4, no. 2 (2010): 127–45; and Subini Ancy Annamma, *The Pedagogy of Pathologization: Dis/Abled Girls of Color in the School-Prison Nexus* (New York: Routledge, 2018).

6. Trent, *Inventing the Feeble Mind*; Carey, *On the Margins of Citizenship*; Kline, *Building a Better Race*; and Rapley, *Social Construction of Intellectual Disability*.

7. Lewis M. Terman, *The Measurement of Intelligence: An Explanation of and Complete Guide for the Use of the Stanford Revision and Extension of the Binet-Simon Intelligence Scale* (Cambridge, MA: Riverside Press, 1916).

8. Terman, *Measurement of Intelligence*, 3–21.

9. For more on intelligence testing, see Paul D. Chapman, *Schools as Sorters: Lewis M. Terman, Applied Psychology, and the Intelligence Testing Movement, 1890–1930* (New York: New York University Press, 1988); and Gilbert G. Gonzalez, *Chicano Education in the Era of Segregation* (Austin: University of North Texas Press, 2013).

10. Rapley, *Social Construction of Intellectual Disability*, 31.

11. Rapley, *Social Construction of Intellectual Disability*, 27, 42. Rapley argues that mental deficiency is a "hypothetical construct"—that is, instead of being a concrete thing, it is an "idea, or historically contingent *way of talking* about people who appear in need of assistance and who are not very good at IQ tests" (emphasis in original).

12. Rapley, *Social Construction of Intellectual Disability*, 49. When talking about "competence" in particular, Rapley points out that it is not an inherent trait but an "inter-subjectively accomplished, practical performance"—that is, "competence" is not something that can be found within the individual, but a performance made available for evaluation in specific social relations (56).

13. This work builds on a rich body of scholarship that documents how reformers and researchers drew on science and public health to reify inequality and hierarchies of difference in the late nineteenth and into the twentieth centuries. Some examples include Julian B. Carter, *The Heart of Whiteness: Normal Sexuality and Race in America, 1880–1940* (Durham, NC: Duke University Press Books, 2007); Mary E. Odem, *Delinquent Daughters: Protecting and Policing Adolescent Female Sexuality in the United States, 1885–1920*, 2nd edition (Chapel Hill: University of North Carolina Press, 1995); Natalia Molina, *Fit to Be Citizens?: Public Health and Race in Los Angeles, 1897–1939* (Berkeley: University of California Press, 2006); Chávez-García, *States of Delinquency*; Dorr, *Segregation's Science*; Rembis, *Defining Deviance*; and Nayan Shah, *Contagious Divides: Epidemics and Race in San Francisco's Chinatown* (Berkeley: University of California Press, 2001).

14. Douglas C. Baynton, "Disability and the Justification of Inequality in American History," in *The Disability Studies Reader*, 4th edition, ed. Lennard J. Davis

(New York: Routledge, 2013), 18–19; Rapley, *Social Construction of Intellectual Disability*, 14; and Rembis, *Defining Deviance*.

15. Carey, *On the Margins of Citizenship*; and Trent, *Inventing the Feeble Mind*.

16. Rapley, *Social Construction of Intellectual Disability*, 15; Carey, *On the Margins of Citizenship*; Liat Ben-Moshe, Allison C. Carey, and Chris Chapman, "Reconsidering Confinement: Interlocking Locations and Logics of Incarceration," in *Disability Incarcerated: Imprisonment and Disability in the United States and Canada*, ed. Liat Ben-Moshe, Chris Chapman, and Allison C. Carey (London: Palgrave Macmillan, 2014); and Trent, *Inventing the Feeble Mind*.

17. Scholarship in Critical Disability Studies is integral to my analysis in this book. Particularly the following scholars: Julie Avril Minich, "Enabling Whom? Critical Disability Studies Now," *Lateral: Journal of the Cultural Studies Association* 5, no. 1 (Spring 2016), http://csalateral.org/issue/5-1/forum-alt-humanities-critical-disability-studies-now-minich/; Julie Avril Minich, "Thinking with Jina B. Kim and Sami Schalk," *Lateral: Journal of the Cultural Studies Association* 6, no. 1 (Spring 2017); Jina B. Kim, "Toward a Crip-of-Color Critique: Thinking with Minich's 'Enabling Whom?,'" *Lateral: Journal of the Cultural Studies Association* 6, no. 1 (Spring 2017); Sami Schalk, "Critical Disability Studies as Methodology," *Lateral: Journal of the Cultural Studies Association* 6, no. 1 (Spring 2017); Baynton, "Disability and the Justification of Inequality in American History," 17–33; Tobin Anthony Siebers, *Disability Theory* (Ann Arbor: University of Michigan Press, 2008); Kafer, *Feminist, Queer, Crip*; Rosemarie Garland-Thomson, "Integrating Disability, Transforming Feminist Theory," in *Feminist Disability Studies*, ed. Kim Q. Hall (Bloomington: Indiana University Press, 2011), 13–47; Susan Schweik, *The Ugly Laws: Disability in Public* (New York: New York University Press, 2010); and Nirmala Erevelles, *Disability and Difference in Global Contexts: Enabling a Transformative Body Politic* (New York: Palgrave Macmillan, 2011).

18. Kafer, *Feminist, Queer, Crip*; Kim E. Nielsen, *A Disability History of the United States* (Boston: Beacon Press, 2012); Schweik, *Ugly Laws*; and Carter, *Heart of Whiteness*.

19. Baynton, "Disability and the Justification of Inequality in American History," 17 (emphasis in original).

20. Kafer, *Feminist, Queer, Crip*; Erevelles, *Disability and Difference in Global Contexts*; Rickie Solinger, *Pregnancy and Power: A Short History of Reproductive Politics in America* (New York: New York University Press, 2007); and Dorothy Roberts, *Killing the Black Body: Race, Reproduction, and the Meaning of Liberty* (New York: Vintage, 1998).

21. For examples, see Nielsen, *Disability History of the United States*; Baynton, "Disability and the Justification of Inequality in American History"; and Solinger, *Pregnancy and Power*.

22. Jael Silliman et al., *Undivided Rights: Women of Color Organizing for Reproductive Justice* (Cambridge, MA: South End Press, 2004); Loretta Ross

and Rickie Solinger, *Reproductive Justice: An Introduction*, 1st edition (Oakland: University of California Press, 2017); Loretta Ross, "Reproductive Justice as Intersectional Feminist Activism," *Souls: A Critical Journal of Black Politics, Culture, and Society* 19, no. 3 (2017): 286–314; and Zakiya T. Luna, "From Rights to Justice: Women of Color Changing the Face of US Reproductive Rights Organizing," *Societies without Borders: Human Rights and the Social Sciences* 4 (2009): 343–65.

23. For examples, see Barbara Gurr, *Reproductive Justice: The Politics of Health Care for Native American Women*, 1st edition (New Brunswick, NJ: Rutgers University Press, 2014); Silliman et al., *Undivided Rights*; Andrea Smith, "Beyond Pro-Choice versus Pro-Life: Women of Color and Reproductive Justice," *NWSA Journal* 17, no. 1 (April 1, 2005): 119–40, https://doi.org/10.2307/4317105; Rickie Solinger, "The First Welfare Case: Money, Sex, Marriage, and White Supremacy in Selma, 1966, A Reproductive Justice Analysis," *Journal of Women's History* 22, no. 3 (Fall 2010): 13–38; and Lina-Maria Murillo, "Birth Control on the Border: Race, Gender, Religion, and Class in the Making of the Birth Control Movement, El Paso, Texas, 1936–1973," PhD dissertation, History, University of Texas–El Paso, 2016.

24. Loretta Ross, "Trust Black Women: Reproductive Justice and Eugenics," in *Radical Reproductive Justice: Foundations, Theory, Practice, Critique*, ed. Loretta Ross et al. (New York: Feminist Press, 2017), 62. Here I draw from the definition of white supremacy described in the introduction to *Radical Reproductive Justice*: "an ideology used to promote unequal laws, practices, and social outcomes. White supremacy is not a fact of genetics nor is it an accurate description of either a race of people or racial hierarchy. It is a totalizing system comprised of racism, sexism, homophobia, Christian nationalism, transphobia, ableism, and classism that differentiates who has access to institutionalized power" (17).

25. Loretta Ross, "Conceptualizing Reproductive Justice Theory," in *Radical Reproductive Justice: Foundations, Theory, Practice, Critique*, ed. Loretta Ross et al. (New York: Feminist Press, 2017), 187.

26. Ross, "Trust Black Women," 62.

27. Ross, "Conceptualizing Reproductive Justice Theory," 195.

28. Kim, "Toward a Crip-of-Color Critique."

29. Minich, "Enabling Whom?"

30. Schalk, "Critical Disability Studies as Methodology."

31. Erevelles, *Disability and Difference in Global Contexts*, 117.

32. Erevelles, *Disability and Difference in Global Contexts*, 6.

33. Erevelles, *Disability and Difference in Global Contexts*, 60.

34. Erevelles, *Disability and Difference in Global Contexts*, 117.

35. Ladd-Taylor, "'Sociological Advantages' of Sterilization," 281.

36. Roberts, *Killing the Black Body*, 81.

37. Solinger, *Pregnancy and Power*; Silliman et al., *Undivided Rights*; and Ross, "Conceptualizing Reproductive Justice Theory."

38. Natalia Molina, *Fit to Be Citizens?: Public Health and Race in Los Angeles, 1879–1939* (Berkeley: University of California Press, 2006); Mae M. Ngai, *Impossible Subjects: Illegal Aliens and the Making of Modern America* (Princeton, NJ: Princeton University Press, 2005); and Matthew Frye Jacobson, *Whiteness of a Different Color: European Immigrants and the Alchemy of Race* (Cambridge, MA: Harvard University Press, 1999).

39. David G. Gutiérrez, *Walls and Mirrors: Mexican Americans, Mexican Immigrants, and the Politics of Ethnicity* (Berkeley: University of California Press, 1995); Vicki L. Ruiz, *From out of the Shadows: Mexican Women in Twentieth-Century America*, 10th edition (New York: Oxford University Press, 2008); and George J. Sanchez, *Becoming Mexican American: Ethnicity, Culture, and Identity in Chicano Los Angeles, 1900–1945*, reprint (New York: Oxford University Press, 1995).

40. Sanchez, *Becoming Mexican American*, 13.

41. Sanchez, *Becoming Mexican American*; Ruiz, *From out of the Shadows*; William Deverell, *Whitewashed Adobe: The Rise of Los Angeles and the Remaking of Its Mexican Past*, reprint (Oakland: University of California Press, 2005); and Tomás Almaguer, *Racial Fault Lines: The Historical Origins of White Supremacy in California* (Berkeley: University of California Press, 1994).

42. Gonzalez, *Chicano Education in the Era of Segregation*; Edward J. Escobar, *Race, Police, and the Making of a Political Identity: Mexican Americans and the Los Angeles Police Department, 1900–1945*, 1st edition (Berkeley: University of California Press, 1999); and Chávez-García, *States of Delinquency*.

43. George Sanchez, "'Go after the Women': Americanization and the Mexican Immigrant Woman, 1915–1929," *Stanford Center for Chicano Research* 6 (1984).

44. Ruiz, *From out of the Shadows*, 28. This book builds on a vast body of literature that examines and documents the racialization of Mexicans in the United States including: Molina, *Fit to Be Citizens*; Molina, *How Race Is Made in America*; Sanchez, *Becoming Mexican American*; Gutiérrez, *Walls and Mirrors*; Escobar, *Race, Police, and the Making of a Political Identity*; Martha Menchaca, *Recovering History, Constructing Race: The Indian, Black, and White Roots of Mexican Americans*, 1st edition (Austin: University of Texas Press, 2002); Deverell, *Whitewashed Adobe*; John Mckiernan-González, *Fevered Measures: Public Health and Race at the Texas-Mexico Border, 1848–1942*, 1st edition (Durham, NC: Duke University Press Books, 2012); Cynthia E. Orozco, *No Mexicans, Women, or Dogs Allowed: The Rise of the Mexican American Civil Rights Movement*, 1st edition (Austin: University of Texas Press, 2009); and Ruiz, *From out of the Shadows*.

45. Ngai, *Impossible Subjects*.

46. Ngai, *Impossible Subjects*.

47. Douglas C. Baynton, *Defectives in the Land: Disability and Immigration in the Age of Eugenics* (Chicago: University of Chicago Press, 2016).

48. Amy L. Fairchild, *Science at the Borders: Immigrant Medical Inspection*

and the Shaping of the Modern Industrial Labor Force, 1st edition (Baltimore, MD: Johns Hopkins University Press, 2003); Howard Markel and Alexandra Minna Stern, "Which Face? Whose Nation? Immigration, Public Health, and the Construction of Disease at America's Ports and Borders, 1891–1928," *American Behavioral Scientist* 42, no. 9 (July 1999): 1314–31; and Mckiernan-González, *Fevered Measures.*

49. Olson's preface to Harry Hamilton Laughlin, *Eugenical Sterilization in the United States* (Chicago: Municipal Court of Chicago, 1922), v.

50. Olson in Laughlin, *Eugenical Sterilization in the United States*, v.

51. Ngai, *Impossible Subjects.*

52. Molina, *Fit to Be Citizens?.*

53. Mckiernan-González, *Fevered Measures*; Molina, *Fit to Be Citizens?*; Natalia Molina, "Medicalizing the Mexican: Immigration, Race, and Disability in the Early-Twentieth-Century United States," *Radical History Review*, no. 94 (December 21, 2006): 22–37; Markel and Stern, "Which Face? Whose Nation?"; and Fairchild, *Science at the Borders.*

54. Molina, *Fit to Be Citizens?*; Molina, "Medicalizing the Mexican"; Mckiernan-González, *Fevered Measures*; Laurie B. Green, John Mckiernan-González, and Martin Summers, eds., *Precarious Prescriptions: Contested Histories of Race and Health in North America* (Minneapolis: University of Minnesota Press, 2014); Markel and Stern, "Which Face? Whose Nation?"; and Fairchild, *Science at the Borders.*

55. Mckiernan-González, *Fevered Measures*; and Molina, *Fit to Be Citizens?.*

56. For more on public health, race, and immigration, see Shah, *Contagious Divides*; Alan M. Kraut, *Silent Travelers: Germs, Genes, and the Immigrant Menace* (Baltimore, MD: Johns Hopkins University Press, 1995); Fairchild, *Science at the Borders*; Emily K. Abel, "'Only the Best Class of Immigration,'" *American Journal of Public Health* 94, no. 6 (June 1, 2004): 932–39; and Markel and Stern, "Which Face? Whose Nation?"

57. Molina, *Fit to Be Citizens?*, 30.

58. "Fourth Biennial Report of the Department of Institutions of the State of California: Two Years Ending June 30, 1928" (Sacramento: California Department of Institutions, 1928), 18.

59. "Fifth Biennial Report of the Department of Institutions of the State of California: Two Years Ending June 30, 1930" (Sacramento: California Department of Institutions, 1930), 7.

60. "Fifth Biennial Report of the Department of Institutions of the State of California," 7.

61. This research was conducted under the approval of the California Committee for the Protection of Human Subjects under IRB number 12-04-0166.

62. Paul Popenoe, "Attitude of Patient's Relatives toward the Operation," *Journal of Social Hygiene* 14, no. 5 (1928): 271.

63. Emma Pérez, *Forgetting the Alamo, Or, Blood Memory: A Novel*, 1st edition (Austin: University of Texas Press, 2009); Emma Pérez, *The Decolonial Imaginary: Writing Chicanas into History* (Bloomington: Indiana University Press, 1999); Saidiya Hartman, *Wayward Lives, Beautiful Experiments: Intimate Histories of Social Upheaval*, 1st edition (New York: W. W. Norton & Company, 2019); Saidiya Hartman, "Venus in Two Acts," *Small Axe* 12, no. 2 (June 2008): 1–14; Sarah Haley, *No Mercy Here: Gender, Punishment, and the Making of Jim Crow Modernity* (Chapel Hill: University of North Carolina Press, 2016); and Marisa J. Fuentes, *Dispossessed Lives: Enslaved Women, Violence, and the Archive* (Philadelphia: University of Pennsylvania Press, 2016).

CHAPTER 1. THE PACIFIC PLAN

1. I pieced together the experiences of Mercedes, Margarita, Carlotta, Pauline, Rosa, and Betty by tracing them across three different archives: sterilization requests, admission ledgers kept by Pacific Colony, and index cards containing admission and treatment information for individual inmates of the institution. Facts about intelligence testing, commitment to Pacific Colony, their experience while committed, and their sterilization are drawn from documents in those archives. Sterilization Records, in California Department of Institutions, Department of Mental Hygiene, California State Archives; Patient Synopsis, 1927–1947, C01882, Department of Developmental Services, Lanterman Development Center, California State Archives; and Patient Card Files, 1930s–1960s, Department of Developmental Services, Lanterman Development Center, California State Archives.

2. This was an Indian boarding school established in Riverside in 1903.

3. "Fourth Biennial Report of the Department of Institutions of the State of California," 52.

4. "Fourth Biennial Report of the Department of Institutions of the State of California," 51.

5. I draw from Critical Disability Studies scholar Sami Schalk, who distinguished between *(dis)ability* as a "system of social norms which categorizes, ranks, and values bodyminds" and *disability* "as a historically and culturally variable category within this larger system." Schalk (in "Critical Disability Studies as Methodology") emphasizes the ways ability and disability operate in relation to one another in representations, medicine, history, law, and other social, political, and cultural realms. I elucidate how race, gender, and class operated alongside and through ideas about ability and disability within this historically specific system of (dis)ability to justify institutionalization, labor, and sterilization.

6. "Report of the 1915 Legislature: Committee on Mental Deficiency and the Proposed Institution for the Care of Feebleminded and Epileptic Persons," Whittier State School, Whittier, CA, 1917, ii and 6.

7. Lewis M. Terman, Virgil Dickson, and Lowry Howard, "Backward and Fee-ble-Minded Children in the Public Schools of 'X' County, California," in *Surveys in Mental Deviation in Prisons, Public Schools, and Orphanages in California* (Sacramento, CA: State Board of Charities and Corrections, 1918), 43.

8. Terman repeated the assertion that feeblemindedness was an inherent and hereditary condition that caused a number of social ills in various additional pub-lications, including Lewis M. Terman, "Introductory Statement," *Journal of Delin-quency* 1, no. 1 (March 1916): 54; Terman, *Measurement of Intelligence*; Lewis M. Terman, "Feeble-Minded Children in the Public Schools of California," *School and Society* 5, no. 111 (February 10, 1917): 161–65; and Lewis M. Terman, "Research on the Diagnosis of Pre-Delinquent Tendencies," *Journal of Delinquency* 9, no. 4 (July 1925): 124–30.

9. Nielsen, *Disability History of the United States*, 20–26; and Ben-Moshe, Carey, and Chapman, "Reconsidering Confinement."

10. Ben-Moshe, Carey, and Chapman, "Reconsidering Confinement," 4.

11. Carey, *On the Margins of Citizenship*, 51.

12. Susan Schweik, "Disability and the Normal Body of the (Native) Citizen," *Social Research* 78, no. 2 (Summer 2011): 417–42.

13. Andrea Smith, *Conquest: Sexual Violence and American Indian Genocide* (Cambridge, MA: South End Press, 2005), 35–37; and Gurr, *Reproductive Justice*.

14. Nielsen, *Disability History of the United States*, 120–21; Susan Burch, "'Dis-located Histories': The Canton Asylum for Insane Indians," *Women, Gender, and Families of Color* 2, no. 2 (Fall 2014): 141–62; Susan Burch, *Committed: Remem-bering Native Kindship in and Beyond Institutions* (Chapel Hill: University of North Carolina Press, 2021); Carla Joinson, *Vanished in Hiawatha: The Story of the Canton Asylum for Insane Indians* (Lincoln: University of Nebraska Press, 2016); Todd E. Leahy, *They Called It Madness: The Canton Asylum for Insane Indians 1899–1934* (Baltimore, MD: America Star Books, 2009); and Pemina Yel-low Bird, "Wild Indians: Native Perspectives on the Hiawatha Asylum for Insane Indians," National Empowerment Center, https://power2u.org/wild-indians -native-perspectives-on-the-hiawatha-asylum-for-insane-indians-by-pemima-yel low-bird/ (accessed June 15, 2020).

15. Yellow Bird, "Wild Indians," 4.

16. Yellow Bird, "Wild Indians," 5.

17. Yellow Bird, "Wild Indians," 5.

18. Dea H. Boster, *African American Slavery and Disability: Bodies, Prop-erty and Power in the Antebellum South, 1800–1860* (New York: Routledge, 2012); Nielsen, *Disability History of the United States*, 42; and Jenifer L. Barclay, "'The Greatest Degree of Perfection': Disability and the Construction of Race in Ameri-can Slave Law," *South Carolina Review* 2, no. 46 (2014): 27–43.

19. Carey, *On the Margins of Citizenship*, 46.

20. Roberts, *Killing the Black Body*; and Deborah Gray White, *Ar'n't I a*

Woman?: Female Slaves in the Plantation South, revised edition (New York: W. W. Norton & Company, 1999).

21. Jenifer L. Barclay, "Mothering the 'Useless': Black Motherhood, Disability, and Slavery," *Women, Gender, and Families of Color* 2, no. 2 (Fall 2014): 115–40.

22. Baynton, *Defectives in the Land.*

23. Baynton, *Defectives in the Land*; Schweik, *Ugly Laws*; and Fairchild, *Science at the Borders.*

24. Schweik, *Ugly Laws*, 165.

25. Sarah F. Rose, *No Right to Be Idle: The Invention of Disability, 1840s–1930s* (Chapel Hill: University of North Carolina Press, 2017).

26. Carey, *On the Margins of Citizenship*, 48.

27. Carey, *On the Margins of Citizenship*, 48.

28. The AMOAIIFP later became known as the American Association of Mental Retardation and is now the American Association on Intellectual and Developmental Disability.

29. Trent, *Inventing the Feeble Mind*, 67.

30. Trent, *Inventing the Feeble Mind*, 67–69.

31. Eric Foner, *The Second Founding: How the Civil War and Reconstruction Remade the Constitution* (New York: W. W. Norton & Company, 2019); and Martha S. Jones, *Birthright Citizens: A History of Race and Rights in Antebellum America* (Cambridge, UK: Cambridge University Press, 2018).

32. Trent, *Inventing the Feeble Mind*; and Carey, *On the Margins of Citizenship*, 53.

33. Trent, *Inventing the Feeble Mind*, 69–70.

34. For information on the use of statistics to validate the existence of feeblemindedness, see Rapley, *Social Construction of Intellectual Disability*, 16. Researchers and state authorities were using statistics to argue for immigration restriction around the same time, and statistics were vital in the construction of Black criminality. Khalil Gibran Muhammad, *The Condemnation of Blackness: Race, Crime, and the Making of Modern Urban America*, 2d edition (Cambridge, MA: Harvard University Press, 2019).

35. On eugenics, see the following: Daniel Kevles, *In the Name of Eugenics: Genetics and the Uses of Human Heredity* (Cambridge, MA: Harvard University Press, 1998); Dorr, *Segregation's Science*; Stern, *Eugenic Nation*; Nancy Ordover, *American Eugenics: Race, Queer Anatomy, and the Science of Nationalism*, 1st edition (Minneapolis: University of Minnesota Press, 2003); Diane B. Paul, *Controlling Human Heredity*, reprint (Amherst, NY: Humanity Books, 1995); Nancy Leys Stepan, *The Hour of Eugenics: Race, Gender, and Nation in Latin America* (Ithaca, NY: Cornell University Press, 1996); Kline, *Building a Better Race*; and Stephen Jay Gould, *The Mismeasure of Man*, revised and expanded edition (New York: W. W. Norton & Company, 1996).

36. This phrase comes from Nicole H. Rafter, "Claims-Making and Socio-

Cultural Context in the First U.S. Eugenics Campaign," *Social Problems* 39, no. 1 (February 1992): 17–34.

37. Carey, *On the Margins of Citizenship*, 65.

38. *Surveys in Mental Deviation in Prisons, Public Schools, and Orphanages in California* (California State Printing Office, 1918), 5.

39. Carey, *On the Margins of Citizenship*, 52.

40. Carey, *On the Margins of Citizenship*, 40.

41. In 1927 the United States Supreme Court upheld the validity of state statutes mandating compulsory sterilization with the case *Buck v. Bell*. This was a landmark victory for states that had eugenic sterilization laws on the books and gave the green light for states that would establish similar laws after 1927. For more on this Supreme Court case, see Lombardo, *Three Generations, No Imbeciles*.

42. For more on Sonoma, see Kline, *Building a Better Race*, 32–61.

43. *Proceedings of the Third California State Conference Charities and Corrections* (Preston School of Industry, 1904), 9.

44. "Report of the 1915 Legislature: Committee on Mental Deficiency and the Proposed Institution for the Care of Feebleminded and Epileptic Persons," 1–2.

45. See *Journal of Psycho-Asthenics* 5, no. 35 (June 1929–30): 47–48, for a list of previous conferences. The conference was previously held in the eastern and midwestern parts of the country and was even held in Canada but not in the West until the California conference.

46. Notably, Norman Fenton, then superintendent of the Whittier State School, a juvenile reform school in Southern California, was a key figure on organizing the joint committee and in early efforts to establish Pacific Colony. Fenton remained a key figure in Pacific Colony and elaborated the "Pacific Plan."

47. "Report of the 1915 Legislature: Committee on Mental Deficiency and the Proposed Institution for the Care of Feebleminded and Epileptic Persons," 45.

48. "Report of the 1915 Legislature: Committee on Mental Deficiency and the Proposed Institution for the Care of Feebleminded and Epileptic Persons," i.

49. Deverell, *Whitewashed Adobe*; Sanchez, *Becoming Mexican American*; Almaguer, *Racial Fault Lines*; Mike Davis, *City of Quartz: Excavating the Future in Los Angeles* (London: Verso, 1990); Chávez-García, *States of Delinquency*, 2012; Molina, *Fit to Be Citizens*; and Kelly Lytle Hernández, *City of Inmates: Conquest, Rebellion, and the Rise of Human Caging in Los Angeles, 1771–1965* (Chapel Hill: University of North Carolina Press, 2017).

50. Davis, *City of Quartz*.

51. Josh Sides, *L.A. City Limits: African American Los Angeles from the Great Depression to the Present* (Oakland: University of California Press, 2003), 14; and Sanchez, *Becoming Mexican American*, 70–71; and Deverell, *Whitewashed Adobe*.

52. Sides, *L.A. City Limits*, 15; and Sanchez, *Becoming Mexican American*.

53. Sides, *L.A. City Limits*, 17–21.

54. Hernández, *City of Inmates*; Escobar, *Race, Police, and the Making of a*

Political Identity; Molina, *Fit to Be Citizens?*; and Sanchez, *Becoming Mexican American*.

55. Hernández, *City of Inmates*; and Escobar, *Race, Police, and the Making of a Political Identity*.

56. Henry L. Minton, *Lewis M. Terman: Pioneer in Psychological Testing* (New York: New York University Press, 1988), 30. The advertised health benefits of living in Southern California were likely the selling points that drew Terman to the area. Ironically, Terman's own physical disabilities—the result of continuous bouts of tuberculosis—repeatedly disrupted his intellectual productivity. Moving to Southern California represented a therapeutic option to manage Terman's own impediments.

57. Widely known as G. Stanley Hall, this psychologist and educator was the first president of the American Psychological Association and is widely regarded as a pioneer in educational psychology and theories of adolescence.

58. Terman worked as a high school principal in San Bernardino and later accepted a position at the Los Angeles State Normal School, where he trained school teachers in child study and pedagogy. During this time, Terman and his family lived in Hollywood and the San Fernando Valley, where thanks to racially restrictive covenants, he was surrounded by other prosperous white settlers. Minton, *Lewis M. Terman*, 33.

59. Binet originally developed the test as a way to identify children in need of educational assistance. After performing a series of tasks, children were assigned an Intelligence Quotient (IQ), which was determined by the ratio of their mental age, a figure obtained by the test, and their chronological age. For Binet the IQ was merely a rough guide, not a fixed measure of intelligence. He did not associate the IQ with inherent or hereditary intelligence, nor did he advocate using intelligence as an indicator of individual worth or capability. It was American psychologists, like Terman in particular, who imbued the IQ score with hereditary significance and social value. See Gould, *Mismeasure of Man*, 180–90.

60. Minton, *Lewis M. Terman*, 6.

61. Terman, *Measurement of Intelligence*, 19–20.

62. Terman, *Measurement of Intelligence*, 79.

63. Terman, *Measurement of Intelligence*, 80.

64. Henry H. Goddard, *Feeble-Mindedness: Its Causes and Consequences* (New York: Macmillan Company, 1914), 4.

65. Terman, *Measurement of Intelligence*, 78–104 and 121–40.

66. Wendy Kline provides an excellent analysis of the concern over the "moron" level of intelligence in chapter 1 of *Building a Better Race*. See also Goddard, *Feeble-Mindedness*; and Terman, *Measurement of Intelligence*.

67. Siobhan B. Somerville, *Queering the Color Line: Race and the Invention of Homosexuality in American Culture*, 1st edition (Durham, NC: Duke University Press Books, 2000).

68. Terman, *Measurement of Intelligence*, 91.

69. Terman, *Measurement of Intelligence*, 90–92.

70. Terman, *Measurement of Intelligence*, 92.

71. Terman, *Measurement of Intelligence*, 92.

72. Terman, *Measurement of Intelligence*, 81.

73. Terman, *Measurement of Intelligence*, 96. By "native-born" he means Anglo-Americans. Terman was known to test the children of his colleagues and even tested his own children. Minton, *Lewis M. Terman*, 58.

74. Quoted in Minton, *Lewis M. Terman*, 99.

75. *Surveys in Mental Deviation in Prisons, Public Schools, and Orphanages in California*, 13–19.

76. Adjusted for inflation, that figure translates to more than $1 million in 2020. *Surveys in Mental Deviation in Prisons, Public Schools, and Orphanages in California*, 42.

77. *Surveys in Mental Deviation in Prisons, Public Schools, and Orphanages in California*, 42.

78. *Surveys in Mental Deviation in Prisons, Public Schools, and Orphanages in California*, 45.

79. Adding a visual to the data, the surveys illustrate the rates of feeblemindedness among Mexican, Spanish, and Portuguese at the top, despite the fact that they aren't the largest groups among the men. Europeans (excluding Spanish and Portuguese) were the biggest group, but they were third under Mexican, Spanish, and Portuguese, at the top, "Negroes" after, then Europeans, and then Americans.

80. "Report of the 1915 Legislature: Committee on Mental Deficiency and the Proposed Institution for the Care of Feebleminded and Epileptic Persons," 46.

81. "Report of the 1915 Legislature: Committee on Mental Deficiency and the Proposed Institution for the Care of Feebleminded and Epileptic Persons," 47.

82. "Report of the 1915 Legislature: Committee on Mental Deficiency and the Proposed Institution for the Care of Feebleminded and Epileptic Persons," 51.

83. In his opinion on the *Buck v. Bell* ruling—which upheld state's rights to enforce compulsory sterilization—Justice Oliver Wendell Holmes wrote: "It is better for all the world, if instead of waiting to execute degenerate offspring for crime, or to let them starve for their imbecility, society can prevent those who are manifestly unfit from continuing their kind. The principle that sustains compulsory vaccination is broad enough to cover cutting the fallopian tubes." Holmes concluded with the now infamous statement: "Three generations of imbeciles are enough." For a comprehensive history of *Buck v. Bell*, see Lombardo, *Three Generations, No Imbeciles*. "Report of the 1915 Legislature: Committee on Mental Deficiency and the Proposed Institution for the Care of Feebleminded and Epileptic Persons," 51.

84. Gayle Gullett, *Becoming Citizens: The Emergence and Development of the*

California Women's Movement, 1880–1911 (Urbana: University of Illinois Press, 2000).

85. "League Center Approves of Three Bills out of Eleven," *San Francisco Chronicle*, June 23, 1916.

86. "Pacific Colony Battle Is Won," *Los Angeles Times*, May 10, 1923.

87. *Eighth Biennial Report of the State Board of Charities and Corrections of the State of California from July 1, 1916 to June 30, 1918* (Sacramento: California State Printing Office, 1918), 50–55.

88. "Seek to Keep Moron Colony," *Los Angeles Times*, March 23, 1923, sec. I; and "Pacific to Establish Moron Colony," *Los Angeles Times*, June 5, 1918.

89. "For Feeble-Minded: Expert Adviser to Pacific Colony Guest at Dinner Given by Friday Morning Club," *Los Angeles Times*, July 11, 1918.

90. Sharon Lamp and W. Carol Cleigh, "A Heritage of Ableist Rhetoric in American Feminism from the Eugenics Period," in *Feminist Disability Studies*, ed. Kim Q. Hall (Bloomington: Indiana University Press, 2011), 177.

91. Baynton, "Disability and the Justification of Inequality in American History"; and Lamp and Cleigh, "Heritage of Ableist Rhetoric in American Feminism from the Eugenics Period."

92. "Report Escape of Five Boys from Cal. Reform School," *Los Angeles Herald*, July 2, 1921; and "Pacific Colony Is Not in Shape for Patients," *San Bernardino Sun*, May 3, 1921.

93. *Tenth Biennial Report of the State Board of Charities and Corrections of the State of California From July 1, 1920, to June 30, 1922* (Sacramento: California State Printing Office, 1923), 32.

94. "Prepared to Build Largest School for Feebleminded," *Madera Weekly Tribune*, December 5, 1918; and "Pacific Colony to Start Soon," *Los Angeles Times*, July 6, 1919, sec. V.

95. "Report Escape of Five Boys from Cal. Reform School." The young men's act of rebellion represents the first of many documented escapes from Pacific Colony. Escaping from the institution was one of the few ways that individuals confined to state institutions could reclaim bodily autonomy. In chapter 4, I discuss escapes from Pacific Colony and what they tell us about experiences of institutionalization, agency, and defiance under conditions of confinement.

96. Hugh Kohler, "Pacific State Hospital, 1921–1965," *The Pomona Valley Historian* 8, no. 1 (January 1972): 4.

97. The Walnut land and the buildings that the young men built were leased to the Protestant Welfare Association of Los Angeles County. They used it as a "home for wayward boys" called the Pacific Lodge Boys Home. Kohler, "Pacific State Hospital, 1921–1965," 6.

98. Norman Fenton, "Pacific Colony Plan," *Journal of Juvenile Research* 16 (October 1932): 301.

99. Kohler, "Pacific State Hospital, 1921–1965," 10.

100. Kohler, "Pacific State Hospital, 1921–1965," 10. This figure would be more than $11 million today.

101. Abel, "'Only the Best Class of Immigration,'" *American Journal of Public Health* 94, no. 6 (June 1, 2004): 932–39; and Francisco E. Balderrama and Raymond Rodríguez, *Decade of Betrayal: Mexican Repatriation in the 1930s*, revised edition (Albuquerque: University of New Mexico Press, 2006)..

102. "Rolph Aides Dedication," *Los Angeles Times*, March 31, 1931, 8.

103. Faith C. Barber, "A Study of the Program of a State Institution for the Feebleminded and Epileptic," master's thesis, Claremont Colleges, 1935, p. 8.

104. Barber, "Study of the Program of a State Institution for the Feebleminded and Epileptic," 1935; and Charles Alvah Dickinson, *An Evening Recreational Program in a State Institution for the Feebleminded*, master's thesis, Claremont Colleges, 1934.

105. Barber, "Study of the Program of a State Institution for the Feebleminded and Epileptic," 10.

106. Barber, "Study of the Program of a State Institution for the Feebleminded and Epileptic," 9–11.

107. Dickinson, *Evening Recreational Program in a State Institution for the Feebleminded*, 5.

108. Kohler, "Pacific State Hospital, 1921–1965," 1–29.

109. Kohler, "Pacific State Hospital, 1921–1965," 12. "Feebleminded and Degenerate Juveniles," *Los Angeles Times*, 1937. This would be approximately $18 million today.

110. Al Ostrow, "People in the Dark: A Series of Ten Articles on California's Hospital System," *San Francisco News*, 1946.

111. Kohler, "Pacific State Hospital, 1921–1965," 14–20. This construction took place over three years, and in 1953 Pacific Colony changed its name to Pacific State Hospital due to a law passed by the legislature, which "reflected the changing attitude" that Pacific Colony "was to be designated as a hospital rather than a home or institution."

112. "To Establish Moron Colony," *Los Angeles Times*, June 5, 1918, sec. I.

113. Janice Brockley, "Rearing the Child Who Never Grew: Ideologies of Parenting and Intellectual Disability in American History," in *Mental Retardation in America*, ed. Steven Noll and James W. Trent (New York: New York University Press, 2004), 130–64.

114. Data on age and economic status was collected from the third through fifth Biennial Reports of the Department of Institutions (Sacramento: California Department of Institutions), and the Statistical Reports of the Department of Institutions of the State of California for the years 1936–1946 (Sacramento: California Department of Institutions).

115. Winifred Ruth Wardell, "Care of the Feeble-Minded in California Illus-

trated by Care Given Three Generations in a Single Family," master's thesis, University of California, 1944, p. 4.

116. Jewel Minna Rouble, "Social and Industrial Adjustment of the Feebleminded on Parole," master's thesis, University of California, 1942, p. 27.

117. Barber, "Study of the Program of a State Institution for the Feebleminded and Epileptic," 11; and Dickinson, *An Evening Recreational Program in a State Institution for the Feebleminded*, 7.

118. Robert B. Edgerton, *The Cloak of Competence*, 1st edition (Berkeley: University of California Press, 1993), 54.

119. Florence Frisch, "Factors in the Decision of Parents to Apply for Commitment of Mentally Defective Children to Pacific Colony," master's, social work, University of Southern California, 1952.

120. Chávez-García, *States of Delinquency*, 143.

121. Wardell, "Care of the Feeble-Minded in California," 34; and Kohler, "Pacific State Hospital, 1921–1965," 16. Kohler writes that the waitlist throughout the 1940s held around six hundred names.

122. Siebers, *Disability Theory*, 14.

123. Molly Ladd-Taylor, *Mother-Work: Women, Child Welfare, and the State, 1890–1930* (Champaign: University of Illinois Press, 1995); Rembis, *Defining Deviance*; Murphy, *Voices of Pineland*; and Zipf, *Bad Girls at Samarcand*.

124. Barber, "Study of the Program of a State Institution for the Feebleminded and Epileptic," 28. Individuals labeled "Black" and "Indian" were also confined at rates that were disproportionate to their population in the state. "Black" individuals represented 2.6 percent of the Pacific Colony population and 1.4 percent of the state population, and "Indian" individuals represented 1.1 percent of the Pacific Colony population but 0.3 percent of the state population. The racial category "Yellow" was also used to refer to people of "Japanese, Chinese, Filipino, Hindu, Korean, Hawaiian, Malay, Siamese and Samoan" descent. Individuals labeled "Yellow" represented 0.8 percent of the Pacific Colony population and 3 percent of the state population.

125. "Report to Governors Council Psychology Department Pacific Colony," May 1947, Boxed Records, Box 1, Department of Developmental Services, Lanterman Development Center, California State Archives.

126. Patient Synopsis, 1927–1947, C01882, Department of Developmental Services, Lanterman Development Center California State Archives.

127. Analysis of "nativity" data shows that only fifty-four Pacific Colony inmates were born in Mexico. See California Department of Institutions, Biennial and Annual Reports, 1926–1944.

128. "New Era Seen in Mental Ills," *Los Angeles Times*, July 13, 1932.

129. Fenton, "Pacific Colony Plan," 298.

130. Fenton, "Pacific Colony Plan," 298.

131. Lawrence B. Goodheart, "Rethinking Mental Retardation: Education and

Eugenics in Connecticut, 1818–1917," *Journal of the History of Medicine and Allied Science* 59, no. 1 (2004): 103; and Nielsen, *Disability History of the United States*, 118. Goodheart and Nielsen draw important connections between Jim Crow, the colonization of the Philippines, Puerto Rico, and Cuba, and the development of the "colony plan" in the late nineteenth century. For an excellent analysis of eugenics and race in the South, see Dorr, *Segregation's Science*.

132. Mary T. Waggaman, "Labor Colonies for the Feeble-Minded," *Monthly Labor Review* 11, no. 3 (September 1920): 12.

133. "Report of the 1915 Legislature: Committee on Mental Deficiency and the Proposed Institution for the Care of Feebleminded and Epileptic Persons," 11.

134. "Report of the 1915 Legislature: Committee on Mental Deficiency and the Proposed Institution for the Care of Feebleminded and Epileptic Persons," 13.

135. Fenton, "Pacific Colony Plan," 298–301.

136. Barber, "Study of the Program of a State Institution for the Feebleminded and Epileptic," 48.

137. Barber, "Study of the Program of a State Institution for the Feebleminded and Epileptic," 11.

138. Dickinson, *Evening Recreational Program in a State Institution for the Feebleminded*, 11. In his thesis Dickinson states that the daily schedule was similar to that of institutions in the East Coast and provides an example. I base my timeline of a typical day on his description.

139. Barber, "Study of the Program of a State Institution for the Feebleminded and Epileptic," 59.

140. Barber, "Study of the Program of a State Institution for the Feebleminded and Epileptic," 14–16.

141. Barber, "Study of the Program of a State Institution for the Feebleminded and Epileptic," 15–16.

142. Barber, "Study of the Program of a State Institution for the Feebleminded and Epileptic," 14–15.

143. Barber, "Study of the Program of a State Institution for the Feebleminded and Epileptic," 48.

144. Edgerton, *Cloak of Competence*, 72; and Barber, "Study of the Program of a State Institution for the Feebleminded and Epileptic," 17–18, 55–58.

145. Barber, "Study of the Program of a State Institution for the Feebleminded and Epileptic," 18–20.

146. Edgerton, *Cloak of Competence*, 54–55.

147. Edgerton, *Cloak of Competence*, 153.

148. For more on the ways states create disability and disabling conditions, see Erevelles, *Disability and Difference in Global Contexts*; Kim, "Toward a Crip-of-Color Critique"; Julie Avril Minich, *Accessible Citizenships: Disability, Nation, and the Cultural Politics of Greater Mexico* (Philadelphia: Temple University

Press, 2013); and Jasbir K. Puar, *The Right to Maim: Debility, Capacity, Disability* (Durham, NC: Duke University Press, 2017).

149. Rouble, "Social and Industrial Adjustment of the Feebleminded on Parole," 3, 55; Barber, "Study of the Program of a State Institution for the Feebleminded and Epileptic," 57; and "Second Biennial Report of the Department of Institutions If the State of California: Two Years Ending June 30, 1924" (Sacramento: California Department of Institutions, 1924), 90.

150. Paul Popenoe and E. S. Gosney, *Twenty-Eight Years of Sterilization in California* (Pasadena, CA: Human Betterment Foundation, 1938), 35.

CHAPTER 2. THE MEXICAN SEX MENACE

1. I pieced together this narrative of Valentina's life from her patient card file, her sterilization request, and the sterilization requests for her siblings (from Sonoma), aunt, and mother (from Pacific Colony). While I speculate about how she felt about her date, all other details are drawn directly from her and her family's records, including that Valentina was "interested in her appearance," her anger at being sent to live at St. Vincent's, the fact that she tried to keep her date a secret and lied to the doctor who employed her, that she was unsatisfied with working long hours at the doctor's house, and that she simply left the doctor's house one day and never returned. Valentina was eventually discharged while on escape, indicating that she remained out of Pacific Colony. Patient Card Files, 1930s–1960s, Department of Developmental Services, Lanterman Development Center, California State Archives; and "Sterilization Records."

2. Barber, "Study of the Program of a State Institution for the Feebleminded and Epileptic," 17.

3. Ruiz, *From out of the Shadows*; Vicki L. Ruiz, ed., *Las Obreras: Chicana Politics of Work and Family* (Los Angeles: UCLA Chicano Studies Research Center Publications, 2000); Catherine S. Ramírez, *The Woman in the Zoot Suit: Gender, Nationalism, and the Cultural Politics of Memory*, 1st edition (Durham, NC: Duke University Press Books, 2009); Elizabeth R. Escobedo, *From Coveralls to Zoot Suits: The Lives of Mexican American Women on the World War II Home Front*, 1st edition (Chapel Hill: University of North Carolina Press, 2013); Gutiérrez, *Fertile Matters*; Patricia Zavella, *Women's Work and Chicano Families: Cannery Workers of the Santa Clara Valley* (Ithaca, NY: Cornell University Press, 1987); Adelaida R. Del Castillo, "Sterilization: An Overview," in *Mexican Women in the United States: Struggles Past and Present*, ed. Magdalena Mora and Adelaida R. Del Castillo (Los Angeles: UCLA Chicano Studies Research Center Publications, 1980), 65–70; Magdalena Mora and Adelaida R. Del Castillo, *Mexican Women in the United States: Struggles Past and Present*, Occasional Paper No. 2 (Los Angeles: Chicano Studies Research Center Publications, University of California, 1980),

4. Haley, *No Mercy Here*, 4.

5. As Solinger writes in *Pregnancy and Power* (2), "sex-and-pregnancy" or reproductive capacity has carried profoundly different meanings and consequences depending on a person's subject position. For more on how sexual agency and reproductive capacity of Women of Color in the United States has been denigrated and attacked by the state, see Silliman et al., *Undivided Rights*; Roberts, *Killing the Black Body*; Gurr, *Reproductive Justice*; and Gutiérrez, *Fertile Matters*. For information on how the sexual agency and reproduction of people with a disability label has been similarly denigrated and subject to control by the state or other authorities (family, hospitals, etc.), see Lamp and Cleigh, "Heritage of Ableist Rhetoric in American Feminism from the Eugenics Period"; Carey, *On the Margins of Citizenship*; Kafer, *Feminist, Queer, Crip*; and Rembis, *Defining Deviance*.

6. I draw this phrasing of being "marked for management" from Gurr, *Reproductive Justice*, 30.

7. Antonia Castañeda, "The Political Economy of Nineteenth-Century Stereotypes of Californianas," in *Three Decades of Engendering History: Selected Works of Antonia I. Castañeda* (Denton: University of North Texas Press, n.d.), 37–63; and Miroslava Chávez-García, *Negotiating Conquest: Gender and Power in California, 1770s to 1880s*, 3rd edition (Tucson: University of Arizona Press, 2006).

8. Castañeda, "Political Economy of Nineteenth-Century Stereotypes of Californianas."

9. Gutiérrez, *Fertile Matters*, 5.

10. Martha Gardner, *The Qualities of a Citizen: Women, Immigration, and Citizenship, 1870–1965* (Princeton, NJ: Princeton University Press, 2009), 157.

11. Gardner, *Qualities of a Citizen*.

12. Silliman et al., *Undivided Rights*; and Gutiérrez, *Fertile Matters*.

13. Ruiz, *From out of the Shadows*, 11; and Gutiérrez, *Fertile Matters*.

14. Gutiérrez, *Fertile Matters*.

15. Gutiérrez, *Fertile Matters*, 56–58.

16. Molina, *Fit to Be Citizens?*, 144. These discussions ultimately paved the way for cultural constructions of Mexican women as hyperfertile "welfare queens" who were prone to living in a "culture of poverty" (see Molina, *Fit to Be Citizens?*, 146; and Gutierrez, *Fertile Matters*).

17. "Aliens Load Relief Roll," *Los Angeles Times*, March 4, 1934.

18. For a discussion on the "Mexican problem" of assimilation, see Sanchez, *Becoming Mexican American*.

19. Sanchez, "'Go after the Women,'" 12.

20. Sanchez (in "'Go after the Women,'" 13) writes that this was an open market for Mexican immigrant women because African American and European immigrant women had not migrated to the American Southwest in large enough numbers to fill the demand.

21. Sanchez, "'Go after the Women,'" 16.

22. Sanchez, "'Go after the Women,'" 11.

23. As gender historians of the period describe, efforts to pathologize and criminalize the sexual acts of certain women reflected ideological shifts in how upper- and middle-class white Americans understood and intervened upon the sexual behavior of marginalized populations. During the Progressive Era, reformers shifted their thinking on sexual immorality. Young women who engaged in sex outside of marriage were no longer seen as victims of male predators, as the traditional Victorian model dictated. Instead, some of these young women, they argued, were disturbed, deviant, and wayward and thus required state attention and intervention. See Odem, *Delinquent Daughters*.

24. Mary Odem, in *Delinquent Daughters*, writes that instead of blaming evil men for taking advantage of women—a Victorian notion that women who engaged in illicit sex were victims—they began looking at heredity, family, and social environment to explain immorality. Odem's research focuses mostly on white purity activists who launched a national effort to establish age-of-consent laws in the 1880s and the development of antiprostitution campaigns and vice committees during the first two decades of the twentieth century. She asserts that during these shifts some women were cast as threats, while others were seen as victims of "white slavers." It should be noted that discourses of victimization and deviance were racialized because women of color were often seen as hypersexual and thus rarely seen as victims of male lust. Legally, Black and enslaved women were excluded from any claims of rape and sexual violence.

25. Odem, *Delinquent Daughters*; and Hazel V. Carby, "Policing the Black Woman's Body in an Urban Context," *Critical Inquiry* 18, no. 4 (1992): 738–55.

26. Odem, *Delinquent Daughters*.

27. Laura S. Abrams and Laura Curran, "Wayward Girls and Virtuous Women: Social Workers and Female Juvenile Delinquency in the Progressive Era," *Affilia* 15, no. 1 (February 1, 2000): 49, https://doi.org/10.1177/08861099000150104; Odem, *Delinquent Daughters*; and Steven Schlossman and Stephanie Wallach, "The Crime of Precocious Sexuality: Female Juvenile Delinquency in the Progressive Era," *Harvard Educational Review* 48, no. 1 (February 1978): 65–94.

28. Odem, *Delinquent Daughters*; Zipf, *Bad Girls at Samarcand*; Rembis, *Defining Deviance*; and Schlossman and Wallach, "Crime of Precocious Sexuality."

29. As historian Vicki Ruiz's oral histories illustrate, some Mexican-origin parents used the fear of institutionalization to warn their daughters to avoid unwed pregnancy. One woman that Ruiz interviewed recalled how her mother threatened to send her to a Florence Crittenton Home if she ever became pregnant Ruiz, *From out of the Shadows*, 71.

30. Ruiz, *From out of the Shadows*.

31. Ramírez, *Woman in the Zoot Suit*, 36.

32. Escobedo, *From Coveralls to Zoot Suits*; and Ramírez, *Woman in the Zoot Suit*.

33. Ramírez, *Woman in the Zoot Suit*, 31. Although the young men who were

convicted in the case benefited from legal help of the Sleepy Lagoon Defense Committee, the young women sent to Ventura could not be assisted because their parents had "consented" to their placement at the reform school. However, in her interview with Sleepy Lagoon Defense Committee executive secretary Alice Greenfield McGrath, Ramírez quotes her as saying that "once consent is given—and it isn't informed consent, it's a really contrived, manipulated event. but once the parent has given consent, it is very hard to do anything about it" (McGrath as quoted in Ramírez, *Woman in the Zoot Suit*, 36). Girls did more time than the boys; see Schlossman and Wallach, "Crime of Precocious Sexuality."

34. Ralph Banay, "A Psychiatrist Looks at the Zoot Suit," *Probation* 22 (1944): 85.

35. Banay, "Psychiatrist Looks at the Zoot Suit," 85.

36. Rembis, *Defining Deviance*, 42.

37. Zipf, *Bad Girls at Samarcand*; Ladd-Taylor, *Mother-Work*; Rembis, *Defining Deviance*; and Mary Zaborskis, "Queering Black Girlhood at the Virginia Industrial School," *Signs: Journal of Women in Culture and Society* 45, no. 2 (2020): 373–94.

38. Rembis, *Defining Deviance*, 42–43.

39. George Ordahl, "Mental Defectives and the Juvenile Court," *Journal of Delinquency* 2, no. 1 (January 1917): 2–4.

40. Ordahl, "Mental Defectives and the Juvenile Court," 7.

41. Louise E. Ordahl and George Ordahl, "Delinquent and Dependent Girls," *Journal of Delinquency* 3, no. 2 (March 1918): 63.

42. Ordahl and Ordahl, "Delinquent and Dependent Girls," 66.

43. Ordahl, "Mental Defectives and the Juvenile Court," 9.

44. Historian Wendy Kline's research on Northern California's Sonoma State Home for the Feebleminded illustrates very clearly the ways in which "anxiety about working-class female sexuality was channeled into anxiety about the 'menace of the feebleminded.'" Kline's important study shows how institutional authorities in California used the broadness of categories within the diagnosis of feeblemindedness, such as "moron" and "borderline," to figure social acts such as unwed motherhood and "promiscuity" as symptoms requiring diagnosis and intervention. In effect, Kline documented, Sonoma "served as a laboratory where strategies for analyzing and controlling female sexual and reproductive behavior" were tested. Kline, *Building a Better Race*, 24 and 34.

45. Rembis, *Defining Deviance*; Trent, *Inventing the Feeble Mind*; Carey, *On the Margins of Citizenship*; and Zipf, *Bad Girls at Samarcand*.

46. *Tenth Biennial Report of the State Board of Charities and Corrections of the State of California from July 1, 1920, to June 30, 1922*, 30.

47. Popenoe and Gosney, *Twenty-Eight Years of Sterilization in California*, 35. The section on the sterilization of individuals deemed feebleminded in general

was the longest section in the study, but the authors pay considerably more attention to the sterilization of feebleminded women.

48. Popenoe and Gosney, *Twenty-Eight Years of Sterilization in California*, 23.

49. Popenoe and Gosney, *Twenty-Eight Years of Sterilization in California*, 23.

50. Popenoe and Gosney, *Twenty-Eight Years of Sterilization in California*, 24.

51. Popenoe and Gosney, *Twenty-Eight Years of Sterilization in California*, 31.

52. Popenoe and Gosney, *Twenty-Eight Years of Sterilization in California*, 30.

53. Popenoe and Gosney, *Twenty-Eight Years of Sterilization in California*, 31.

54. Abrams and Curran, "Wayward Girls and Virtuous Women."

55. Abrams and Curran, "Wayward Girls and Virtuous Women"; and Angie C. Kennedy, "Eugenics, 'Degenerate Girls,' and Social Workers during the Progressive Era," *Affilia* 23, no. 1 (February 1, 2008): 22–37.

56. Excerpt from Minutes of Meeting, August 9, 1927, R350.005 10/19, Social Welfare, Admin-Subject Files, Hospitals and Institutions, California State Archives.

57. Excerpts from Minutes of Meeting, December 10, 1930, R350.005 10/19, Social Welfare, Admin-Subject Files, Hospitals and Institutions, California State Archives; and Letter, January 26, 1931, R350.005 10/19, Social Welfare, Admin-Subject Files, Hospitals and Institutions, California State Archives.

58. Correspondence, November 1936, R350.005 10/20, Social Welfare, Admin-Subject Files, Hospitals and Institutions, California State Archives.

59. "Sterilization Records," n.d.

60. Correspondence, November 1936.

61. "Sterilization Records," Reels 119 and 120.

62. Most residents included in this figure were explicitly labeled "sexual delinquent" either in the clinical history or diagnosis section of their sterilization request. In some cases they were labeled "sex delinquents" in supplemental letters regarding their need for sterilization. Also included in this figure were residents whose records made references to sexual delinquency. That is, if they were described as "promiscuous," "sexually aggressive," "immoral," engaging in "prostitution," or having "illegitimate children," they were included in the count of residents described as "sexually delinquent."

63. Arthur Lawrence Palace, "A Comparative Description of Anglo-White and Mexican-White Boys Committed to Pacific Colony," master's thesis, School of Social Work, University of Southern California, 1950, p. 23.

64. Of these, 7 percent were born in Arizona, 5 percent were born in New Mexico, and 6 percent were born in Texas. The rest were born in other states of the country.

65. "Sterilization Records," n.d., Reel 123.

66. A note next to Gomez's diagnosis reads: "Does not function up to this level." This reveals the weakness of these diagnoses. The sexual agency of young Mexican-origin women was also used as evidence of mental deficiency in the steriliza-

tion records at Sonoma. There, out of the 371 Spanish-surnamed women deemed in need of sterilization between 1935 and 1944, 47 percent were explicitly described as sexual delinquents. While the sterilization records at Pacific Colony cited the sexual transgressions of Mexican-origin women as evidence of their need for sterilization more frequently, the Sonoma requests also reveal that young Mexican-origin women were sterilized there for admitting to "illicit relations" and being "aggressive sexually" ("Sterilization Records").

67. Rickie Solinger, *Wake up Little Susie: Since Pregnancy and Race before Roe v. Wade* (London: Routledge, 1992).

68. Ruiz, *From out of the Shadows*, 62–63.

69. "Sterilization Records," Reel 121, 1939.

70. "Sterilization Records," Reel 122, 1940.

71. Rembis, *Defining Deviance*, 34.

72. Lombardo, *Three Generations, No Imbeciles*.

73. "Sterilization Records," Reel 119.

74. "Sterilization Records," Reel 122, 1941.

75. "Sterilization Records," Reel 119.

76. "Sterilization Records," Reel 121.

77. "Sterilization Records," Reel 122.

78. Abrams and Curran, "Wayward Girls and Virtuous Women"; and Kennedy, "Eugenics, 'Degenerate Girls,' and Social Workers during the Progressive Era."

79. "Sterilization Records," Reel 123.

80. Garland-Thomson, "Integrating Disability, Transforming Feminist Theory," 19. For more on how disabled women's (reproductive) bodies are figured in legal and institutional settings, see Kafer, *Feminist, Queer, Crip*.

81. Garland-Thomson, "Integrating Disability, Transforming Feminist Theory," 19.

82. Butler as quoted in "Third Biennial Report of the Department of Institutions of the State of California: Two Years Ending June 30, 1926" (Sacramento: California Department of Institutions, 1926), 96.

83. Patient Card Files, 1930s–1960s.

84. Lee Shropshire, William M. Morris, and Edward L. Foote, "Suppression of Menstruation: A Hygienic Measure in the Care of Mentally Retarded Patients," *Journal of the American Medical Association* 200, no. 5 (May 1, 1967): 414–15.

85. All information on Rosie comes from Elizabeth Ballantyne Brainard, "Individual Summaries and Intake Interviews in Social Group Work Practice: A Study of the Participation of Five Members of a Club Group in a State Hospital for the Mentally Deficient," master's, social work, University of Southern California, 1955, pp. 34–39.

86. "A Survey of the Mental Institutions of the State of California," December 27, 1949, 155, F3640:2709, Earl Warren Papers, Administrative Files, Department of Mental Hygiene, California State Archives; Barber, "Study of the Program of a

State Institution for the Feebleminded and Epileptic"; "Statistical Report of the Department of Institutions of the State of California: Year Ending June 30, 1936" (Sacramento: California Department of Institutions, 1936), 12; and "Statistical Report of the Department of Institutions of the State of California: Year Ending June 30, 1940" (Sacramento: California Department of Institutions, 1940).

87. Robert B. Edgerton, "A Patient Elite: Ethnography in a Hospital for the Mentally Retarded," *Journal of Mental Deficiency* 68, no. 3 (November 1963): 372–84, 380.

88. Edgerton, "Patient Elite"; and Brainard, "Individual Summaries and Intake Interviews in Social Group Work Practice."

89. Brainard, "Individual Summaries and Intake Interviews in Social Group Work Practice," 21.

90. Brainard, "Individual Summaries and Intake Interviews in Social Group Work Practice," 17.

91. Zaborskis, "Queering Black Girlhood at the Virginia Industrial School."

92. Zipf, *Bad Girls at Samarcand*, 173–74; and Zaborskis, "Queering Black Girlhood at the Virginia Industrial School."

93. Zipf, *Bad Girls at Samarcand*; Robert Bogdan and Steven J. Taylor, *Inside Out: Two First-Person Accounts of What It Means to Be Labeled "Mentally Retarded"* (Toronto: University of Toronto Press, 1982); D'Antonio, *State Boys Rebellion*; Rembis, *Defining Deviance*; and Zaborskis, "Queering Black Girlhood at the Virginia Industrial School."

94. Edgerton, "Patient Elite," 381.

95. D'Antonio, *State Boys Rebellion*; Edgerton, *Cloak of Competence*; and Bogdan and Taylor, *Inside Out*.

96. Bogdan and Taylor, *Inside Out*, 45.

97. Bogdan and Taylor, *Inside Out*, 142.

98. Edgerton, "Patient Elite," 381.

99. Brainard, "Individual Summaries and Intake Interviews in Social Group Work Practice," 34.

100. Robert B. Edgerton, George Tarjan, and Harvey F. Dingman, "Free Enterprise in a Captive Society," *Journal of Mental Deficiency* 66, no. 1 (July 1961): 35–41.

101. Barber, "Study of the Program of a State Institution for the Feebleminded and Epileptic," 56–57.

102. Edgerton, *Cloak of Competence*, 72.

103. "Survey of the Mental Institutions of the State of California," 152.

104. Brainard, "Individual Summaries and Intake Interviews in Social Group Work Practice," 11.

105. Edgerton, *Cloak of Competence*, 72.

106. Edgerton, *Cloak of Competence*, 83.

107. Sabagh and Edgerton, "Sterilized Mental Defectives Look at Eugenic Sterilization," 219–20.

108. Brainard, "Individual Summaries and Intake Interviews in Social Group Work Practice," 36–37.

109. Bogdan and Taylor, *Inside Out*, 56.

CHAPTER 3. THE LABORATORY OF DEFICIENCY

1. Information on Raul comes from sterilization request forms, consent forms, and interdepartmental letters contained in "Sterilization Records," Reel 124. Mildred Malm was listed as an examiner at the Los Angeles Juvenile Hall during the time that Raul was brought before the courts, and although his sterilization records do not name her, it is possible that she or one of her colleagues performed Raul's intelligence test. The Lanterman Development Center (formerly Pacific Colony) accession at the California State Archives contains several intelligence test kits used on youth committed to Pacific Colony. A number of these kits included signs that examiners were instructed to hang on doors while testing.

2. The murder of José Diaz in August of 1942 was the impetus for a mass roundup of Mexican-origin youth led by the Los Angeles Police Department. In October the state waged the largest mass trial in California history, *People v. Zamora*, wherein prosecutors highlighted the pachuco style and supposed gang affiliations of Mexican-origin youth as evidence of their guilt. This chapter builds on Chicano Studies scholarship that investigates the racial profiling and criminalization of Mexican-origin men during the 1940s and highlights *People v. Zamora* and the Zoot Suit Riots as important flashpoints in Mexican American history. Among the works consulted for this chapter are Eduardo Obregon Pagan, *Murder at the Sleepy Lagoon: Zoot Suits, Race, and Riot in Wartime L.A.*, 1st edition (Chapel Hill: University of North Carolina Press, 2003); Luis Alvarez, *The Power of the Zoot: Youth Culture and Resistance during World War II* (Berkeley: University of California Press, 2009); Escobar, *Race, Police, and the Making of a Political Identity*; and Mauricio Mazón, *The Zoot-Suit Riots: The Psychology of Symbolic Annihilation* (Austin: University of Texas Press, 2010).

3. John E. Rankin, "Zoot Suiter Termites," Congressional Record, 78th Congress, 1st Session, June 15, 1943.

4. Banay, "Psychiatrist Looks at the Zoot Suit," 85.

5. Alvarez, *Power of the Zoot*; Escobedo, *From Coveralls to Zoot Suits*; and Ramírez, *Woman in the Zoot Suit*.

6. Chávez-García, *States of Delinquency*; and Anthony M. Platt, *The Child Savers: The Invention of Delinquency* (New Brunswick, NJ: Rutgers University Press, 2009). For more on differentiation and the construction of penal institutions in the United States, see Ben-Moshe, Carey, and Chapman, "Reconsidering Confinement"; Nielsen, *Disability History of the United States*; and David Rothman, *The Discovery of the Asylum: Social Order and Disorder in the New Republic* (London: Routledge, 2002).

7. Platt (*Child Savers*, 3) defines the "child savers" as a term "used to characterize a group of 'disinterested' reformers who regarded their cause as a matter of conscience and morality, serving no particular class or political interests. The child savers viewed themselves as altruists and humanitarians dedicated to rescuing those who were less fortunately placed in the social order."

8. Chávez-García, *States of Delinquency*; and Platt, *Child Savers*. The first juvenile tribunal was established in Chicago in 1899. By 1917 legislation establishing juvenile courts had been passed in all states with the exception of three. By 1932 there were more than six hundred juvenile courts in the United States. This was widely regarded as an advance in child welfare (Platt, *Child Savers*, 10).

9. The Whittier State School was a reform school established in 1891 to confine young women and men who were accused of delinquency. In 1913 it became a boys-only school, and the young women were transferred to a new institution, Ventura School for Girls. Chávez-García, *States of Delinquency*.

10. Chávez-García, *States of Delinquency*. Established by Davenport in 1910, the Eugenics Records Office was the foremost eugenics research center in the nation.

11. Chávez-García, *States of Delinquency*, 62.

12. Chávez-García, *States of Delinquency*, 6 and 62–70.

13. While the CBJR was located at the Whittier State School, Fred C. Nelles and J. Harold Williams established branches and appointed resident psychologists at the other state institutions. In addition to creating a broader scope of research options, this organizational structure allowed for direct access to subjects "on which to experiment, conduct research, and deepen understandings of intelligence, delinquency, race, and eugenics" (Chávez-García, *States of Delinquency*, 86).

14. Muhammad, *Condemnation of Blackness*.

15. Platt, *Child Savers*; and Nicole Rafter, *Creating Born Criminals* (Urbana: University of Illinois Press, 1998).

16. Platt, *Child Savers*, 18.

17. Platt, *Child Savers*, 19.

18. Terman, "Introductory Statement," 10.

19. Terman, "Introductory Statement," 10.

20. "The Present Status of Juvenile Delinquency in California," *Journal of Delinquency* 5, no. 5 (September 1920): 188.

21. Platt (*Child Savers*, 36) writes that the shift away from pure biological determinism occurred in tandem with "the rise of a professional class of correctional administrators and social servants who promoted a medical model of deviant behavior and suggested techniques of remedying 'natural' imperfections."

22. "Present Status of Juvenile Delinquency in California," 188.

23. J. Harold Williams, "Delinquent Boys of Superior Intelligence," *Journal of Delinquency* 1, no. 1 (March 1916): 35–36.

24. Williams, "Delinquent Boys of Superior Intelligence," 36.

25. L. W. Crafts and E. A. Doll, "The Proportion of Mental Defectives among Juvenile Delinquents (I)," *Journal of Delinquency* 2, no. 3 (May 1917): 126, 123. Edgar Doll was a researcher and psychologist at the Vineland Training School for Feeble-Minded Girls and Boys in New Jersey, one of the first large-scale institutions for the feebleminded.

26. Crafts and Doll, "Proportion of Mental Defectives among Juvenile Delinquents (I)," 123.

27. "Present Status of Juvenile Delinquency in California," 188.

28. Feeblemindedness and mental deficiency broke down into grades that were tied to scores on intelligence tests (IQ scores) and mental/physical capacity. The grades included "idiot", "imbecile," "moron," and "borderline."

29. Crafts and Doll, "Proportion of Mental Defectives among Juvenile Delinquents (I)," 141.

30. Crafts and Doll, "Proportion of Mental Defectives among Juvenile Delinquents (I)," 141.

31. "Present Status of Juvenile Delinquency in California," 186.

32. Ramiro Martinez Jr. and Abel Valenzuela Jr., eds., *Immigration and Crime: Race, Ethnicity, and Violence*, 1st edition (New York: New York University Press, 2006); Escobar, *Race, Police, and the Making of a Political Identity*; Platt, *Child Savers*; William S. Bush, *Who Gets a Childhood?: Race and Juvenile Justice in Twentieth-Century Texas* (Athens: University of Georgia Press, 2010); and Muhammad, *Condemnation of Blackness*.

33. Muhammad writes that statistical comparisons between the "foreign-born" and the "Negro" were "foundational to the emergence of distinctive modern discourses on race and crime." Although some European immigrants were criminalized and incarcerated in the mid- and late nineteenth century, Muhammad writes, Progressive Era reformers established a "pathway for their redemption and rehabilitation" while crime continued to be discussed as a component of Black pathology. Muhammad, *Condemnation of Blackness*, 6.

34. Crafts and Doll, "Proportion of Mental Defectives Among Juvenile Delinquents (I)," 138.

35. Crafts and Doll, "Proportion of Mental Defectives Among Juvenile Delinquents (I)," 138.

36. Crafts and Doll, "Proportion of Mental Defectives Among Juvenile Delinquents (I)," 138.

37. Citing a study performed by Byron A. Philips, Crafts and Doll wrote: "The colored children are retarded to a much greater extent both pedagogically and psychologically than the white children." See L. W. Crafts and E. A. Doll, "The Proportion of Mental Defectives Among Juvenile Delinquents (II)," *Journal of Delinquency* 2, no. 4 (July 1917): 203.

38. Crafts and Doll, "Proportion of Mental Defectives Among Juvenile Delinquents (II)," 203.

39. Crafts and Doll, "Proportion of Mental Defectives Among Juvenile Delinquents (II)," 204.

40. Crafts and Doll, "Proportion of Mental Defectives Among Juvenile Delinquents (II)," 204.

41. Crafts and Doll, "Proportion of Mental Defectives Among Juvenile Delinquents (II)," 204.

42. Escobar, *Race, Police, and the Making of a Political Identity*; Chávez-García, *States of Delinquency*; and Bush, *Who Gets a Childhood?*.

43. Willis W. Clark, "A Statistical Study of 102 Truants," *Journal of Delinquency* 3, no. 5 (September 1918): 214. In his study Clark splits his subjects into groups according to race, revealing the particular racialization of Mexicans in California. He writes that he split "the truants according to race as White, Colored, or Mexican-Indians (i.e., Mexicans having Indian blood)" (214).

44. Clark, "Statistical Study of 102 Truants," 232.

45. Clark, "Statistical Study of 102 Truants," 232.

46. Clark, "Statistical Study of 102 Truants," 232.

47. He wrote that 68.6 percent of the homes had "abnormal parental conditions, one or both parents being dead, or divorced, separated or deserted" (see Clark, "Statistical Study of 102 Truants," 232).

48. Clark, "Statistical Study of 102 Truants," 233.

49. Terman, *Measurement of Intelligence*, 11.

50. "Report of the 1915 Legislature," 57 and 61.

51. "Report of the 1915 Legislature," 61.

52. "Report of the 1915 Legislature," 62.

53. In their work Tufuku Zuberi and Eduardo Bonilla-Silva define "white logic" as the "context in which White supremacy has defined the techniques and processes of reasoning about social facts" and "white methods" as the "practical tools used to manufacture empirical data and analysis to support the racial stratification in society." See Zuberi and Bonilla-Silva, *White Logic, White Methods: Racism and Methodology* (New York: Rowman & Littlefield Publishers, 2008), 17–18.

54. Willis W. Clark and J. Harold Williams, *A Guide to the Grading of Neighborhoods: Directions for Using the Whittier Scale for Grading Neighborhood Conditions, with the Standard Score Sheet of Comparative Data*, Whittier State School Department of Research Bulletin 8 (Whittier, CA: Whittier State School Department of Printing Instruction, 1919); and J. Harold Williams, *A Guide to the Grading of Homes: Directions for Using the Whittier Scale for Grading Home Conditions, with the Standard Score Sheet of Comparative Data*, Whittier State School Department of Research Bulletin 7 (Whittier, CA: Whittier State School Department of Printing Instruction, 1918).

55. Clark and Williams, *Guide to the Grading of Neighborhoods*, 1.

56. Shah, *Contagious Divides*; and Molina, *Fit to Be Citizens?*.

57. Terman, "Feeble-Minded Children in the Public Schools of California," 162.

58. For an excellent legal analysis of the ways privacy rights continue to be denied to low-income people, see Khiara M. Bridges, *The Poverty of Privacy Rights* (Stanford, CA: Stanford Law Books, 2017).

59. Harry Maynard Perry, "A Study of Origin, Background, Intelligence, Race, and Other Factors Contributing to the Behavior of Boys Committed to Los Angeles Welfare Centers 1930–1934," master's, science in education, University of Southern California, 1938, p. 21.

60. Perry, "Study of Origin, Background, Intelligence, Race, and Other Factors," 55.

61. Perry, "Study of Origin, Background, Intelligence, Race, and Other Factors," 66.

62. Perry, "Study of Origin, Background, Intelligence, Race, and Other Factors," 70.

63. Florence Perrigo Van Sickle, "The Function of the Mental Hygiene Clinic at Juvenile Hall in Los Angeles, California," master's, social work, University of Southern California, 1944, p. 29. This practice originated in Chicago under the guidance of Dr. William Healy. During the early period, psychologists relied largely on Terman's revised Stanford-Binet test but later added many more. By the 1940s the Stanford-Binet had been translated into Spanish, and they had developed tests for people with "language handicaps," both of which were considered useful for evaluating Mexican children.

64. Sickle, "Function of the Mental Hygiene Clinic at Juvenile Hall," 67.

65. Platt, *Child Savers*, 145.

66. Platt, *Child Savers*, 145.

67. Sickle, "Function of the Mental Hygiene Clinic at Juvenile Hall," 30–32.

68. Patient Card Files, 1930s–1960s.

69. Alvin P. Sion, "Mentally Deficient Mexican-American Delinquent Boys Who Made Good after Institutional Care: An Analysis of Six Cases," master's, social work, University of Southern California, 1951, pp. 16–20.

70. Sion, "Mentally Deficient Mexican-American Delinquent Boys," 31.

71. Sion, "Mentally Deficient Mexican-American Delinquent Boys," 32.

72. Fred O. Butler, "California's Legal Approach and Progress in the Rehabilitation of the Defective and Psychopathic Delinquent," *Journal of Mental Deficiency* 53, no. 1 (July 1948): 76–79.

73. Patient Card Files, 1930s–1960s.

74. Chávez-García, *States of Delinquency*, 4.

75. J. Harold Williams, "Delinquency and Mental Deficiency," *Journal of Delinquency* 1, no. 2 (May 1916): 101.

76. "Present Status of Juvenile Delinquency in California," 188.

77. "Third Biennial Report of the Department of Institutions of the State of California: Two Years Ending June 30, 1926," 96.

78. Escobar, *Race, Police, and the Making of a Political Identity*, 7.

79. Crafts and Doll, "Proportion of Mental Defectives among Juvenile Delinquents (II)," 203.

80. Escobar, *Race, Police, and the Making of a Political Identity*; Pagan, *Murder at the Sleepy Lagoon*; and Ruiz, *From out of the Shadows*.

81. Garis as quoted in Escobar, *Race, Police, and the Making of a Political Identity*, 9.

82. Fred C. Nelles, "Juvenile Delinquency Measures Adopted by the California Legislature of 1921," *Journal of Delinquency* 6, no. 3 (May 1921): 402–409, 408.

83. "Sterilization Records," Reel 122.

84. "Sterilization Records," Reel 121.

85. "Sterilization Records," Reel 121.

86. "Sterilization Records," Reel 120.

87. "Sterilization Records," Reel 121.

88. "Sterilization Records," Reel 121.

89. "Sterilization Records," Reel 124.

90. Preston was a state reform school for juvenile delinquents that were not labeled "defective."

91. "Sterilization Records," Reel 124.

92. "Sterilization Records," Reels 120, 122, and 124.

93. Patient Card Files, 1930s–1960s.

94. Patient Card Files, 1930s–1960s.

95. "Dr. Fenton to Join Faculty: Head of State Research in Juvenile Work," *Pomona Progress*, August 26, 1932.

96. Carey, *On the Margins of Citizenship*, 53; Rafter, *Creating Born Criminals*; and Liat Ben-Moshe, "Disabling Incarceration: Connecting Disability to Divergent Confinements in the USA," *Critical Sociology* 39, no. 3 (2011): 385–403, 391.

97. Patient Card Files, 1930s–1960s.

98. Palace, "Comparative Description of Anglo-White and Mexican-White Boys," 69. The California Youth Authority was the name of the state agency in charge of juvenile justice in California. In 2005 it was renamed the Division of Juvenile Justice.

99. Palace, "Comparative Description of Anglo-White and Mexican-White Boys," 69–70.

100. Palace, "Comparative Description of Anglo-White and Mexican-White Boys," 70. Later on in his study Palace makes an interesting statement regarding the role of educators in the commitment process. He writes that because a higher proportion of the Mexican-origin male youths he observed were "behavior and truancy problems, despite better progress scholastically," the educator's opinion in commitment to a state institution was a decisive factor (84 and 91). This comment

suggests that further research should be done regarding the role of schools and teachers in identifying "defective delinquents" for admission to state institutions for the feebleminded.

101. Palace, "Comparative Description of Anglo-White and Mexican-White Boys," 17.

102. Palace, "Comparative Description of Anglo-White and Mexican-White Boys," 17.

103. Palace, "Comparative Description of Anglo-White and Mexican-White Boys," 19.

104. Palace, "Comparative Description of Anglo-White and Mexican-White Boys," 19. The social work theses of the late 1940s and 1950s reveal the ways in which emotions get framed as deviant and abnormal marking a shift in psychological focus. They foreshadow a shift in the field of psychology to an emphasis on the "emotional disturbance" of young women and men of color and theories around cultural and emotional "deficit" that is examined in Mical Raz, *What's Wrong with the Poor?: Psychiatry, Race, and the War on Poverty* (Chapel Hill: University of North Carolina Press, 2013). There is also a clear mixing of ideas about the culture of poverty that shows that there wasn't really a clear transition from hereditarian ideas of deviant and cultural ideas.

105. Palace, "Comparative Description of Anglo-White and Mexican-White Boys," 23.

106. Palace, "Comparative Description of Anglo-White and Mexican-White Boys," 36–37.

107. Palace, "Comparative Description of Anglo-White and Mexican-White Boys," 23.

108. Palace, "Comparative Description of Anglo-White and Mexican-White Boys," 63.

109. Palace, "Comparative Description of Anglo-White and Mexican-White Boys," 67.

110. Palace, "Comparative Description of Anglo-White and Mexican-White Boys," 19.

111. G. Sabagh, G. Tarjan, and S. W. Wright, "Social Class and Ethnic Status of Patients Admitted to a State Hospital for the Retarded," *Pacific Sociology Review* 2 (1959): 76–80.

112. Raz, *What's Wrong with the Poor?*.

113. Ben-Moshe, Carey, and Chapman, "Reconsidering Confinement," 2014; and Ben-Moshe, "Disabling Incarceration."

114. Rachel Roth, "'She Doesn't Deserve to Be Treated Like This': Prisons as Sites of Reproductive Injustice," in *Radical Reproductive Justice: Foundation, Theory, Practice, Critique*, ed. Loretta Ross et al. (New York: Feminist Press, 2017), 285–301; and Ross and Solinger, *Reproductive Justice*, 215–17.

CHAPTER 4. RIOTS, REFUSALS, AND OTHER
DEFIANT ACTS

1. All information on Teresa comes from Margaret Frank, "Factors Contributing to Indefinite Leave Failures of Five Adolescent Female Patients from Pacific Colony," master's, social work, University of Southern California, 1953, pp. 47–51.

2. Frank, "Factors Contributing to Indefinite Leave Failures," 48.

3. In this chapter I build on literature that examines histories and historical narratives of deviance, resistance, and agency, particularly the following: Lila Abu-Lughod, "The Romance of Resistance: Tracing Transformations of Power through Bedouin Women," *American Ethnologist* 17, no. 1 (1990): 41–55; Robin D. G. Kelley, *Race Rebels: Culture, Politics, and the Black Working Class* (New York: Free Press, 1996); Miroslava Chávez-García, "Youth, Evidence, and Agency: Mexican and Mexican American Youth at the Whittier State School, 1890–1920," *Aztlán: A Journal of Chicano Studies* 31, no. 2 (2006): 55–83; Alvarez, *Power of the Zoot*; Cathy J. Cohen, "Deviance as Resistance: A New Research Agenda for the Study of Black Politics," *Du Bois Review* 1, no. 1 (2004): 27–45; James C. Scott, *Weapons of the Weak: Everyday Forms of Peasant Resistance*, reprint edition (New Haven, CT: Yale University Press, 1987); Haley, *No Mercy Here*; and Zipf, *Bad Girls at Samarcand.*

4. Carey, *On the Margins of Citizenship.*

5. Erevelles and Minear, "Unspeakable Offenses," 129 (emphasis in original).

6. Johanna Hedva, "Sick Woman Theory," *Mask Magazine*, www.maskmagaz ine.com/not-again/struggle/sick-woman-theory, accessed April 12, 2016. Hedva's "Sick Woman Theory" is an effort to redefine historically feminized pathologies into modes of political protest. She insists that "most modes of political protest are internalized, lived, embodied, suffered, and no doubt invisible." She writes that the Sick Woman is "all of the 'dysfunctional,' 'dangerous' and 'in danger,' 'badly behaved,' 'crazy,' 'incurable,' 'traumatized,' 'disordered,' 'diseased,' 'chronic,' 'uninsurable,' 'wretched,' 'undesirable' and altogether 'dysfunctional' bodies belonging to women, people of color, poor, ill, neuro-atypical, differently abled, queer, trans, and genderfluid people, who have been historically pathologized, hospitalized, institutionalized, brutalized, rendered 'unmanageable,' and therefore made culturally illegitimate and politically invisible."

7. Kelley, *Race Rebels*; Chávez-García, "Youth, Evidence, and Agency," 55–83; and Cohen, "Deviance as Resistance," 27–45.

8. Excerpts from Minutes of Meeting of State Department of Social Welfare, June 26, 1929, R350.005, Social Welfare, Admin-Subject Files, Hospitals and Institutions.

9. Margaret P. Pratt, letter dated October 3, 1929, R350.005, Social Welfare, Admin-Subject Files, Hospitals and Institutions.

10. Barber, "Study of the Program of a State Institution for the Feebleminded and Epileptic," 24.

11. Edgerton, "Patient Elite," 374 and 378.

12. Frank, "Factors Contributing to Indefinite Leave Failures," 36.

13. Edgerton, "Patient Elite," 374.

14. Edgerton, "Patient Elite," 381.

15. Edgerton, "Patient Elite," 381–82.

16. William F. Meredith, "Factors Contributing to Indefinite Leave Failures of Nine Adolescent Male Patients from Pacific Colony," master's, social work, University of Southern California, 1953, pp. 62–63.

17. Frank, "Factors Contributing to Indefinite Leave Failures," 36.

18. Frank, "Factors Contributing to Indefinite Leave Failures," 36.

19. Frank, "Factors Contributing to Indefinite Leave Failures," 40.

20. "Sterilization Records," Reel 124.

21. Edgerton, "Patient Elite," 381.

22. Meredith, "Factors Contributing to Indefinite Leave Failures of Nine Adolescent Male Patients from Pacific Colony," 70–72.

23. Edgerton, "Patient Elite," 381.

24. Edgerton, "Patient Elite," 382.

25. Edgerton, *Cloak of Competence*, 54.

26. Quoted in Bogdan and Taylor, *Inside Out*, 142.

27. D'Antonio, *State Boys Rebellion*.

28. Frank, "Factors Contributing to Indefinite Leave Failures," 36.

29. Memorandum, June 21, 1949, F3640:2772, Earl Warren Papers, Administrative Files, Department of Mental Hygiene, California State Archives.

30. Meredith, "Factors Contributing to Indefinite Leave Failures of Nine Adolescent Male Patients from Pacific Colony," 70.

31. Norman Fenton quoted in Barber, "Study of the Program of a State Institution for the Feebleminded and Epileptic," 48.

32. Edgerton, *Cloak of Competence*, 21.

33. Stacy Diaz-Cordova, phone interview by Natalie Lira regarding Stacy Diaz-Cordova's Aunt Mary Franco, January 12, 2017; "Take Two® | Audio: In the Eugenics Era, Mexican American Women Were Prime Targets of Sterilization in California | 89.3 KPCC," aired May 4, 2019, www.scpr.org/programs/take-two/20 18/04/05/62481/in-the-eugenics-era-mexican-american-women-were-pr/.

34. Chávez-García, "Youth, Evidence, and Agency," 64.

35. Excerpt from Minutes of Meeting, September 11, 1929, R350.005, Social Welfare, Admin-Subject Files, Hospitals and Institutions.

36. Administrative Files, 1949, 1943, F3640:2709, F3640:2772, Earl Warren Papers; and Admin-Subject Files, Hospitals and Institutions, n.d., R350.005 10/20, 10/19, Social Welfare, California State Archives.

37. Edward Bunker, *Education of A Felon: A Memoir* (New York: St. Martin's Griffin, 2000), 20–21.

38. A letter to then governor Earl Warren alleges the same practice of having youths fight each other for the entertainment of staff at the Sonoma State Home. This claim echoes the experiences of people in other state institutions. See D'Antonio, *State Boys Rebellion*; Bogdan and Taylor, *Inside Out*; and Edgerton, *Cloak of Competence*.

39. Memorandum for Information of U.S. Public Health Service in Surveying Department of Mental Health, December 27, 1949, 5, F3640:2709, Earl Warren Papers, Administrative Files, Department of Mental Hygiene, California State Archives.

40. "Martha" is the pseudonym that anthropologist Robert Edgerton gave to a woman he interviewed after she had been discharged from Pacific Colony. Her mother was from North Carolina, and when she got pregnant with Martha at age fifteen, she ran away to California. Because she was poor, she was forced to place Martha in an orphanage. Martha was adopted but then abandoned by her adoptive parents and placed in various foster homes until she was fourteen. Edgerton writes that Martha was "highly irritable" and had a problem with bed wetting and "open masturbation," but that several episodes of menorrhagia were the "immediate reason for her commitment to pacific." "Menorrhagia" is a term that refers to very long and heavy menstrual cycles.

41. Martha as quoted in Edgerton, *Cloak of Competence*, 44–45.

42. D'Antonio, *State Boys Rebellion*; Bogdan and Taylor, *Inside Out*; Zipf, *Bad Girls at Samarcand*; and Murphy, *Voices of Pineland*.

43. Martha as quoted in Edgerton, *Cloak of Competence*, 54–55.

44. Fred as quoted in Edgerton, *Cloak of Competence*, 39.

45. "Short History of Mental Institution of the State of California under the Administration of Governor Earl Warren," September 1948, F3640:2695, Earl Warren Papers, Administrative Files, Department of Mental Hygiene, California State Archives.

46. Al Ostrow, "People in the Dark: A Series of Articles on California's Hospital System for the Mentally Sick," *San Francisco News*, December 1946.

47. "Report Escape of Five Boys from Cal. Reform School."

48. "Sterilization Records," Reel 116.

49. "Juvenile Prisoners Escape; Three Boys Overpower Guards," *Los Angeles Times*, December 2, 1943.

50. "Statistical Report of the Department of Institutions of the State of California: Year Ending June 30, 1941" (Sacramento: California Department of Institutions, 1941); "Statistical Report of the Department of Institutions of the State of California: Year Ending June 30, 1942" (Sacramento: California Department of Institutions, 1942); and "Statistical Report of the Department of Institutions

of the State of California: Year Ending June 30, 1943" (Sacramento: California Department of Institutions, 1943).

51. "Colony Children Sought," *Los Angeles Times*, October 27, 1930.

52. "Three Young Colony Fugitives Hunted," *The Pomona Progress Bulletin*, November 10, 1941.

53. "Hunt Four Missing Colony Inmates," *The Pomona Progress Bulletin*, October 6, 1942.

54. Meredith, "Factors Contributing to Indefinite Leave Failures of Nine Adolescent Male Patients from Pacific Colony," 19.

55. "Boys Flee Spadra Colony," *Los Angeles Times*, October 15, 1930.

56. "Pacific Colony Youths Escape: Two Guards Overpowered as 21 Make Getaway From State Institution," *Los Angeles Times*, December 10, 1942.

57. "Pacific Colony Youths Escape."

58. "Pacific Colony Youths Escape."

59. "Nine of Delinquents Escaping from Pacific Colony Caught," *Los Angeles Times*, December 11, 1942.

60. "Nine of Delinquents Escaping from Pacific Colony Caught."

61. "Eight Escaped Youths Sought," *Los Angeles Times*, May 10, 1946.

62. Meredith, "Factors Contributing to Indefinite Leave Failures of Nine Adolescent Male Patients from Pacific Colony," 71.

63. Sion, "Mentally Deficient Mexican-American Delinquent Boys," 33.

64. Brainard, "Individual Summaries and Intake Interviews in Social Group Work Practice."

65. "Sterilization Records," Reel 120.

66. "Youth Hangs Self in Jail," *Los Angeles Times*, April 19, 1941.

67. Chávez-García, *States of Delinquency*, 182–212.

68. On Joe Avila, see Patient Card Files, 1930s–1960s. On Ralph, see Meredith, "Factors Contributing to Indefinite Leave Failures of Nine Adolescent Male Patients from Pacific Colony," 19.

69. Sion, "Mentally Deficient Mexican-American Delinquent Boys"; and Meredith, "Factors Contributing to Indefinite Leave Failures of Nine Adolescent Male Patients from Pacific Colony."

70. Sion, "Mentally Deficient Mexican-American Delinquent Boys"; and Meredith, "Factors Contributing to Indefinite Leave Failures of Nine Adolescent Male Patients from Pacific Colony."

71. Meredith, "Factors Contributing to Indefinite Leave Failures of Nine Adolescent Male Patients from Pacific Colony," 19.

72. Sion, "Mentally Deficient Mexican-American Delinquent Boys," 38.

73. Sion, "Mentally Deficient Mexican-American Delinquent Boys," 38.

74. "Sterilization Records," Reels 120, 121, 122, and 124.

75. Patient Card Files, 1930s–1960s.

76. "Statistical Report of the Department of Institutions of the State of Califor-

nia: Year Ending June 30, 1942," 106; and "Statistical Report of the Department of Institutions of the State of California: Year Ending June 30, 1943," 97.

77. Sion, "Mentally Deficient Mexican-American Delinquent Boys," 38.

78. Hatch as quoted in D'Antonio, *State Boys Rebellion*.

79. Allison C. Carey and Lucy Gu, "Walking the Line between the Past and the Future: Parents' Resistance and Commitment to Institutionalization," in *Disability Incarcerated: Imprisonment and Disability in the United States and Canada*, ed. Liat Ben-Moshe, Chris Chapman, and Allison C. Carey (London: Palgrave Macmillan, 2014), 101–20.

80. Kline, *Building a Better Race*, 95–124.

81. Kline, *Building a Better Race*.

82. Ruiz, *From out of the Shadows*, 71.

83. Trent, *Inventing the Feeble Mind*; Carey and Gu, "Walking the Line between the Past and the Future"; and Carey, *On the Margins of Citizenship*.

84. "Governor's Office- Institutions- Hospitals- Sonoma State," 44 1943, F3640: 2413, Earl Warren Papers, Administrative Files, California State Archives.

85. Sion, "Mentally Deficient Mexican-American Delinquent Boys," 33.

86. Sion, "Mentally Deficient Mexican-American Delinquent Boys," 33.

87. Sion, "Mentally Deficient Mexican-American Delinquent Boys," 24.

88. Sion, "Mentally Deficient Mexican-American Delinquent Boys," 29.

89. In an analysis of sterilization requests processed by both Sonoma and Pacific Colony between 1935 and 1944, the peak of sterilization in California (n = 3,014), only five Spanish-surnamed patients were described as desiring sterilization. This, of course, does not represent full consent in the way we understand it now. In a context where sterilization was tied to release from the institution, it is hard to parse out when a desire for sterilization was about not wanting to have children and when it was about wanting to be released from the institution.

90. Wellerstein, "States of Eugenics"; and Stern, *Eugenic Nation*.

91. Popenoe, "Attitude of Patient's Relatives toward the Operation," 271.

92. Popenoe, "Attitude of Patient's Relatives toward the Operation"; and Kline, *Building a Better Race*, 58.

93. Popenoe, "Attitude of Patient's Relatives toward the Operation," 271; and Rouble, "Social and Industrial Adjustment of the Feebleminded on Parole," 3.

94. Edgerton, *Cloak of Competence*, 140.

95. "Sterilization Records."

96. "Sterilization Records," Reel 124.

97. Popenoe, "Attitude of Patient's Relatives toward the Operation."

98. "Sterilization Records."

99. Smith, *Conquest*; and Bush, *Who Gets a Childhood?*

100. Dorothy Roberts, *Shattered Bonds: The Color of Child Welfare* (New York: Hachette Book Group, 2002).

101. "Sterilization Records."

102. "Sterilization Records," Reel 121.

103. "Sterilization Records."

104. "Sterilization Records," Reels 120, 122, and 124.

105. This, in large part, reflected the historical role of the consulate as a source of support for the Mexican-origin community in California. Established to protect a largely working-class group of compatriots, the consulate's charge to "protect the interests and rights of Mexican Nationals" resulted in the provision of a whole host of services, including organizing informational sessions and conferences on U.S. laws, assisting workers in labor disputes and work-related accidents, intervening in civil and criminal cases, and investigating deaths and disappearances. See Francisco E. Balderrama, *In Defense of La Raza, the Los Angeles Mexican Consulate, and the Mexican Community, 1929 to 1936* (Tucson: University of Arizona Press, 1982).

106. Balderrama, *In Defense of La Raza*, 7.

107. Balderrama, *In Defense of La Raza*, 8.

108. "Sterilization Records," Reel 122. Although the consulate official may have said this, they did not have the legal authority intervene in regard to institutional decisions.

109. Administrative Files 1950, n.d., F3640: 2764, Earl Warren Papers, California State Archives.

110. "Informe de Proteccion," May 1935, Secretaria de Relaciones Exteriores, Archivo Histórico Genaro Estrada.

111. Consulate attorneys were U.S. citizens and members of the state bar association. They typically "prepared legal briefs, defended Mexican nationals who lacked funds, submitted petitions for pardons or paroles for Mexicans serving jail sentences, reviewed requests of victims of criminal offenses, and presented claims from industrial accidents to appropriate authorities" (Balderrama, *In Defense of La Raza*, 10).

112. At the time, David C. Marcus was working for the Mexican consulate as the consular attorney in Los Angeles. He went on to file and litigate *Mendez v. Westminster* (1946). For more on Marcus, see Genevieve Carpio, "Unexpected Allies: David C. Marcus and His Impact on the Advancement of Civil Rights in the Mexican-American Legal Landscape of Southern California," ed. George Sanchez, *Beyond Alliances: The Jewish Role in Reshaping the Racial Landscape of Southern California* (West Lafayette, IN: Purdue University Press, 2012), 1–31.

113. *Garcia v. State Dept. of Institutions*, No. Civ. No. 12533 (Second Appellate District December 18, 1939).

114. Sara Garcia and David Marcus were specifically arguing against Section 6224 of the Welfare and Institutional Code of the State of California as enacted in 1937, which was the version of California's sterilization law being used at the time. It provided for the sterilization of any person legally committed to any one of California's institutions for the feebleminded or mentally ill. They presented five rea-

sons why the statute was void: (1) It is "a contravention of the XIV Amendment . . . in that it violates the fundamental and inalienable right of said minor, Andrea Garcia, to life, liberty and the pursuit of happiness and therefore exceeds the police power of the State of California to perform said sterilization operation"; (2) It is a "violation of the equal protection clause . . . in that only inmates of the institution mentioned in said statute shall be sterilized, and only those whom the officers and employees of said institution may in their discretion cause to be sterilized"; (3) It is a "violation of the due process of law . . . in that no appeal or hearing is provided from the discretion vested in the employees and officers of said institution which officers and employees are a non-judicial body"; (4) It is void and in violation of the state constitution in that "said statute does not provide for a hearing, notice or appeal from the discretion vetted in the non-judicial body or persons contemplating said sterilization"; and (5) It is in violation of state constitution "because it is discriminatory, denies equal protection of the law and due process of the law" (*Garcia v. State Dept. of Institutions*, 5–6).

115. *Garcia v. State Dept. of Institutions*, 7.

116. For more on reproductive politics and slavery, see Deirdre Cooper Owens, *Medical Bondage: Race, Gender, and the Origins of American* Gynecology (Athens: University of Georgia Press, 2018); Roberts, *Killing the Black Body*; Angela Davis, "Racism, Birth Control, and Reproductive Rights," in *Women, Race & Class* (New York: Vintage Books, 1983), 202–21; Peggy Cooper Davis, *Neglected Stories* (New York: Hill and Wang, 1998); Barclay, "'Greatest Degree of Perfection'"; and Barclay, "Mothering the 'Useless.'"

117. "Sterilization Records"; and Patient Card Files, 1930s–1960s.

118. Patient Synopsis, 1927–1947, C01882, Department of Developmental Services, Lanterman Development Center, California State Archives.

119. Kelley, *Race Rebels*; and Hedva, "Sick Woman Theory."

CONCLUSION

1. Quoted in Sabagh and Edgerton, "Sterilized Mental Defectives Look at Eugenic Sterilization," 220.

2. As detailed in the introduction, the three pillars of Reproductive Justice include: the right to not have children using the method of one's choice, the right to have children, and the right to raise your children in safe environments.

3. Kafer, *Feminist, Queer, Crip*, 4.

4. Ruha Benjamin, "Catching Our Breath: Critical Race STS and the Carceral Imagination," *Engaging Science, Technology, and Society* 2 (2016): 145–56, 149.

5. Sabagh and Edgerton, "Sterilized Mental Defectives Look at Eugenic Sterilization," 116.

6. Raz, *What's Wrong with the Poor?*; and Jonathan Metzl, *The Protest Psychosis: How Schizophrenia Became a Black Disease* (Boston: Beacon Press, 2011).

7. Raz, *What's Wrong with the Poor?*.

8. Anne E. Parsons, *From Asylum to Prison: Deinstitutionalization and the Rise of Mass Incarceration after 1945* (Chapel Hill: University of North Carolina Press, 2018); and Ben-Moshe, *Decarcerating Disability*.

9. Del Castillo, "Sterilization," 67.

10. Elena R. Gutiérrez, *Fertile Matters*; and Virginia Espino, "'Woman Sterilized As Gives Birth': Forced Sterilization and Chicana Resistance in the 1970s," in *Las Obreras: Chicana Politics of Work and Family*, ed. Vicki L. Ruiz (Los Angeles, CA: Chicano Studies Research Center Publications, University of California, 2000), 65–81.

11. Gutiérrez, *Fertile Matters*; Del Castillo, "Sterilization"; Espino, "'Woman Sterilized As Gives Birth,'" 65–81; Gurr, *Reproductive Justice*; and Silliman et al., *Undivided Rights*.

12. Del Castillo, "Sterilization."

13. Johanna Schoen, "Between Choice and Coercion: Women and the Politics of Sterilization in North Carolina, 1929–1975," *Journal of Women's History* 13, no. 1 (Spring 2001): 132–56.

14. Gutiérrez, *Fertile Matters*; Ana María García, *La Operación* (Latin American Film Project, 1982); *No Más Bebés*, directed by Rene Tajima-Peña (Moon Canyon Films, 2015); and Lorna Tucker, *Amá* (Raindog Films, 2018).

15. Bogdan and Taylor, *Inside Out*, 88.

16. Annamma, *Pedagogy of Pathologization*; and Erevelles and Minear, "Unspeakable Offenses," 127–45.

17. Diana Lambert, "Lawsuit Challenges Use of Restraint, Seclusion in California Special Education School," *EdSource*, May 20, 2019, https://edsource.org/20 19/lawsuit-challenges-use-of-restraint-seclusion-in-california-special-education -school/612690; and Jodi S. Cohen, "How Often Do Schools Use Seclusion and Restraint? The Federal Government Isn't Properly Tracking the Data, According to a New Report," *ProPublica*, April 23, 2020, www.propublica.org/article/how-of ten-do-schools-use-seclusion-and-restraint-the-federal-government-isnt-proper ly-tracking-the-data-according-to-a-new-report.

18. Nicole Chavez and Melissa Alonso, "Police Took a 6-Year-Old Girl to a Mental Health Facility in Florida Because She Was 'out of Control' at School," CNN, February 16, 2020, www.cnn.com/2020/02/15/us/florida-girl-mental-heal th-baker-act/index.html.

19. Jodi S. Cohen, "A Teenager Didn't Do Her Online Schoolwork. So a Judge Sent Her to Juvenile Detention," *ProPublica*, July 14, 2020, www.propublica.org /article/a-teenager-didnt-do-her-online-schoolwork-so-a-judge-sent-her-to-juve nile-detention.

20. For an overview of how this policy evolved over time, see "Family Separation under the Trump Administration—a Timeline," Southern Poverty Law Center,

June 17, 2020, www.splcenter.org/news/2020/06/17/family-separation-under-tru mp-administration-timeline.

21. Justin Wise, "HHS Secretary: We're Doing 'Great Acts of American Generosity' for Migrant Children," *The Hill*, July 7, 2018, https://thehill.com/latino /396442-hhs-secretary-what-were-doing-for-migrant-children-is-one-of-the-gre at-acts-of.

22. For a pertinent analysis of the contemporary use of dog whistles, see Ian Haney López, *Dog Whistle Politics: How Coded Racial Appeals Have Reinvented Racism and Wrecked the Middle Class* (New York: Oxford University Press, 2015).

23. Lizzie O'Leary, "Children Were Dirty, They Were Scared, and They Were Hungry," *The Atlantic*, June 25, 2019; and Caitlin Dickerson, "'There Is a Stench': Soiled Clothes and No Baths for Migrant Children at a Texas Center," *New York Times*, June 21, 2019, www.nytimes.com/2019/06/21/us/migrant-children-border -soap.html.

24. To read this letter and the many additional statements the AMA has made regarding immigrant detention centers, see American Medical Association, "Southern Border: Conditions at Immigrant Detention Centers, 2018–2020," www .ama-assn.org/delivering-care/population-care/southern-border-conditions-im migrant-detention-centers (accessed July 30, 2020).

25. Aura Bogado, "Doctor Giving Migrant Kids Psychotropic Drugs Lost Certification Years Ago," *Reveal: From the Center for Investigative Reporting*, June 25, 2018, www.revealnews.org/blog/exclusive-shiloh-doctor-lost-board-certification -to-treat-children-years-ago/.

26. Natalie Escobar, "Family Separation Isn't New," *The Atlantic*, August 14, 2018, www.theatlantic.com/family/archive/2018/08/us-immigration-policy-has-tr aumatized-children-for-nearly-100-years/567479/; and Jessica Pryce, "The Long History of Separating Families in the US and How the Trauma Lingers," *The Conversation*, June 26, 2018, https://theconversation.com/the-long-history-of-separa ting-families-in-the-us-and-how-the-trauma-lingers-98616.

27. Corey G. Johnson, "Female Inmates Sterilized in California Prisons without Approval," *Reveal: From the Center for Investigative Reporting*, July 7, 2013.

28. "Tennessee Judge Who Offered Inmates Reduced Sentences for Sterilization Rebuked," *CBS News*, November 22, 2017.

29. Project South, "Lack of Medical Care, Unsafe Work Practices, and Absence of Adequate Protection Against COVID-19 for Detained Immigrants and Employees Alike at the Irwin County Detention Center," September 14, 2020, https://pr ojectsouth.org/wp-content/uploads/2020/09/OIG-ICDC-Complaint-1.pdf; Tina Vasquez, "Exclusive: Georgia Doctor Who Forcibly Sterilized Detained Women Has Been Identified," *Prism*, September 15, 2020, www.prismreports.org/article /2020/9/15/exclusive-georgia-doctor-who-forcibly-sterilized-detained-women -has-been-identified; and Caitlin Dickerson, Seth Freed Wessler, and Miriam Jor-

dan, "Immigrants Say They Were Pressured into Unneeded Surgeries," *New York Times*, September 29, 2020.

30. Alondra Nelson, *Body and Soul: The Black Panther Party and the Fight against Medical Discrimination*, reprint (Minneapolis: University of Minnesota Press, 2013), 153–80.

31. Carey, *On the Margins of Citizenship*.

32. Roland Johnson, "Lost in a Desert World," Disabilitymuseum.org, 1994, www.disabilitymuseum.org/dhm/lib/detail.html?id=1681&page=all (accessed July 30, 2020); and Self Advocates Becoming Empowered, *Who Is in Control*, 1993, www.youtube.com/watch?v=QCVLzHQgLEM (accessed July 30, 2020).

33. Bogdan and Taylor, *Inside Out*; Edgerton, *Cloak of Competence*; and Ben-Moshe, *Decarcerating Disability*.

34. Ben-Moshe, *Decarcerating Disability*, 2.

35. Adelaida R. Del Castillo, "La Visión Chicana," in *Chicana Feminist Thought: The Basic Historical Writings*, ed. Alma M. García (New York: Routledge, 1997), 44–47, 46.

36. Del Castillo, "La Visión Chicana," 46; and Rosie C. Bermudez, "La Causa de Los Pobres: Alicia Escalante's Lived Experiences of Poverty and the Struggle for Economic Justice," in *Chicana Movidas: New Narratives of Activism and Feminism in the Movement Era*, ed. Dionne Espinoza, María E. Cotera, and Maylei Blackwell (Austin: University of Texas Press, 2018), 123–37.

37. Espino, "'Woman Sterilized As Gives Birth,'" 73.

38. Alma M. Garcia, ed., *Chicana Feminist Thought*, 1st edition (New York: Routledge, 1997), 107; Del Castillo, "Sterilization"; Espino, "'Woman Sterilized As Gives Birth,'" 65–81; and Gutiérrez, *Politics of Mexican-Origin Women's Reproduction*.

39. Espino, "'Woman Sterilized As Gives Birth,'" 77–78; and Gutiérrez, *Politics of Mexican-Origin Women's Reproduction*, 94–108.

40. For critiques of liberal notions of "choice" and "privacy," see Roberts, *Killing the Black Body*; Bridges, *Poverty of Privacy Rights*; Ross, "Reproductive Justice as Intersectional Feminist Activism," 286–314; Luna, "From Rights to Justice"; and Silliman et al., *Undivided Rights*.

41. Roberts as quoted in Loretta Ross et al., eds., *Radical Reproductive Justice: Foundations, Theory, Practice, Critique* (New York: Feminist Press, 2017), 10.

42. Ross et al., *Radical Reproductive Justice*, 14.

43. As quoted in Bogdan and Taylor, *Inside Out*, 146.

44. As quoted in Bogdan and Taylor, *Inside Out*, 90.

45. Roth, "'She Doesn't Deserve to Be Treated Like This'"; Arneta Rogers, "How Police Brutality Harms Mothers: Linking Police Violence to the Reproductive Justice Movement," *Hastings Race and Poverty Law Journal* 12, no. 2 (Summer 2015): 205–34; and Ben-Moshe, *Decarcerating Disability*.

46. Tyra Bosnic, "What Defunding Police Means for Mental Health Care," *Teen Vogue*, July 21, 2020.

47. Cecilia Nowell, "Protesters Say Tear Gas Caused Them to Get Their Period Multiple Times in a Month," *Teen Vogue*, July 2, 2020, www.teenvogue.com/story /protestors-say-tear-gas-caused-early-menstruation.

48. Ross, "Trust Black Women," 83.

Bibliography

Abel, Emily K. "'Only the Best Class of Immigration.'" *American Journal of Public Health* 94, no. 6 (June 1, 2004): 932–39. https://doi.org/10.2105/AJPH .94.6.932.

Abrams, Laura S., and Laura Curran. "Wayward Girls and Virtuous Women: Social Workers and Female Juvenile Delinquency in the Progressive Era." *Affilia* 15, no. 1 (February 1, 2000): 49–64. https://doi.org/10.1177/088610990 001500104.

Abu-Lughod, Lila. "The Romance of Resistance: Tracing Transformations of Power through Bedouin Women." *American Ethnologist* 17, no. 1 (1990): 41–55.

Administrative Files. 1949, 1943. F3640:2709, F3640:2772. Earl Warren Papers, California State Archives.

Administrative Files 1950. n.d. F3640: 2764. Earl Warren Papers, California State Archives.

Admin-Subject Files. Hospitals and Institutions. n.d. R350.005 10/20, 10/19. Social Welfare, California State Archives.

"Aliens Load Relief Roll." *Los Angeles Times*. March 4, 1934.

Almaguer, Tomás. *Racial Fault Lines: The Historical Origins of White Supremacy in California*. Berkeley: University of California Press, 1994.

Alvarez, Luis. *The Power of the Zoot: Youth Culture and Resistance during World War II*. Berkeley: University of California Press, 2009.

American Medical Association. "Southern Border: Conditions at Immigrant

Detention Centers, 2018–2020." www.ama-assn.org/delivering-care/popu
lation-care/southern-border- conditions-immigrant-detention-centers.
Accessed July 30, 2020.

Annamma, Subini Ancy. *The Pedagogy of Pathologization: Dis/Abled Girls of Color in the School-Prison Nexus*. New York: Routledge, 2017.

Balderrama, Francisco E. *In Defense of La Raza, the Los Angeles Mexican Consulate, and the Mexican Community, 1929 to 1936*. Tucson: University of Arizona Press, 1982.

Balderrama, Francisco E., and Raymond Rodríguez. *Decade of Betrayal: Mexican Repatriation in the 1930s*. Revised edition. Albuquerque: University of New Mexico Press, 2006.

Banay, Ralph. "A Psychiatrist Looks at the Zoot Suit." *Probation* 22 (1944): 81–85.

Barber, Faith C. "A Study of the Program of a State Institution for the Feeble-minded and Epileptic." Master's thesis, Claremont Colleges, 1935.

Barclay, Jenifer L. "'The Greatest Degree of Perfection': Disability and the Construction of Race in American Slave Law." *South Carolina Review* 2, no. 46 (2014): 27–43.

———. "Mothering the 'Useless': Black Motherhood, Disability, and Slavery." *Women, Gender, and Families of Color* 2, no. 2 (Fall 2014): 115–40.

Baynton, Douglas C. *Defectives in the Land: Disability and Immigration in the Age of Eugenics*. Chicago: University of Chicago Press, 2016.

———. "Disability and the Justification of Inequality in American History." In *The Disability Studies Reader*, 4th ed., edited by Lennard J. Davis, 17–33. New York: Routledge, 2013.

Benjamin, Ruha. "Catching Our Breath: Critical Race STS and the Carceral Imagination." *Engaging Science, Technology, and Society* 2 (2016): 145–56.

Ben-Moshe, Liat. *Decarcerating Disability: Deinstitutionalization and Prison Abolition*. Minneapolis: University of Minnesota Press, 2020.

———. "Disabling Incarceration: Connecting Disability to Divergent Confinements in the USA." *Critical Sociology* 39, no. 3 (2011): 385–403.

Ben-Moshe, Liat, Allison C. Carey, and Chris Chapman. "Reconsidering Confinement: Interlocking Locations and Logics of Incarceration." In *Disability Incarcerated: Imprisonment and Disability in the United States and Canada*, edited by Liat Ben-Moshe, Chris Chapman, and Allison C. Carey. London: Palgrave Macmillan, 2014.

Bermudez, Rosie C. "La Causa de Los Pobres: Alicia Escalante's Lived Experiences of Poverty and the Struggle for Economic Justice." In *Chicana Movidas: New Narratives of Activism and Feminism in the Movement Era*, edited by Dionne Espinoza, María E. Cotera, and Maylei Blackwell, 123–37. Austin: University of Texas Press, 2018.

Black, Edwin. *War against the Weak: Eugenics and America's Campaign to Create a Master Race*. Dialog Press, 2012.

Bogado, Aura. "Doctor Giving Migrant Kids Psychotropic Drugs Lost Certification Years Ago." *Reveal: From the Center for Investigative Reporting.* June 25, 2018. www.revealnews.org/blog/exclusive-shiloh-doctor-lost-board-certification-to-treat-children-years-ago/.

Bogdan, Robert, and Steven J. Taylor. *Inside Out: Two First-Person Accounts of What It Means to Be Labeled "Mentally Retarded."* Toronto: University of Toronto Press, 1982.

Bosnic, Tyra. "What Defunding Police Means for Mental Health Care." *Teen Vogue.* July 21, 2020. www.teenvogue.com/story/what-defunding-police-means-for-mental-health-care/amp.

Boster, Dea H. *African American Slavery and Disability: Bodies, Property and Power in the Antebellum South, 1800–1860.* New York: Routledge, 2012.

"Boys Flee Spadra Colony." *Los Angeles Times.* October 15, 1930.

Brainard, Elizabeth Ballantyne. "Individual Summaries and Intake Interviews in Social Group Work Practice: A Study of the Participation of Five Members of a Club Group in a State Hospital for The Mentally Deficient." Master's, social work, University of Southern California, 1955.

Bridges, Khiara M. *The Poverty of Privacy Rights.* Stanford, CA: Stanford Law Books, 2017.

Brockley, Janice. "Rearing the Child Who Never Grew: Ideologies of Parenting and Intellectual Disability in American History." In *Mental Retardation in America*, edited by Steven Noll and James W. Trent, 130–64. New York: New York University Press, 2004.

Bunker, Edward. *Education of a Felon: A Memoir.* New York St. Martin's Griffin, 2000.

Burch, Susan. *Committed: Remembering Native Kinship in and Beyond Institutions.* Chapel Hill: University of North Carolina Press. 2021.

———. "'Dislocated Histories': The Canton Asylum for Insane Indians." *Women, Gender, and Families of Color* 2, no. 2 (Fall 2014): 141–62.

Bush, William S. *Who Gets a Childhood?: Race and Juvenile Justice in Twentieth-Century Texas.* Athens: University of Georgia Press, 2010.

Butler, Fred O. "California's Legal Approach and Progress in the Rehabilitation of the Defective and Psychopathic Delinquent." *Journal of Mental Deficiency* 53, no. 1 (July 1948): 76–79.

Carby, Hazel V. "Policing the Black Woman's Body in an Urban Context." *Critical Inquiry* 18, no. 4 (1992): 738–55.

Carey, Allison C. *On the Margins of Citizenship: Intellectual Disability and Civil Rights in Twentieth-Century America.* Philadelphia: Temple University Press, 2010.

Carey, Allison C., and Lucy Gu. "Walking the Line between the Past and the Future: Parents' Resistance and Commitment to Institutionalization." In *Disability Incarcerated: Imprisonment and Disability in the United States and*

Canada, edited by Liat Ben-Moshe, Chris Chapman, and Allison C. Carey, 101–20. London: Palgrave Macmillan, 2014.

Carpio, Genevieve. "Unexpected Allies: David C. Marcus and His Impact on the Advancement of Civil Rights in the Mexican-American Legal Landscape of Southern California." In *Beyond Alliances: The Jewish Role in Reshaping the Racial Landscape of Southern California*, edited by George Sanchez, 1–31. West Lafayette, IN: Purdue University Press, 2011.

Carter, Julian B. *The Heart of Whiteness: Normal Sexuality and Race in America, 1880–1940*. Durham, NC: Duke University Press Books, 2007.

Castañeda, Antonia. "The Political Economy of Nineteenth-Century Stereotypes of Californianas." In *Three Decades of Engendering History: Selected Works of Antonia I. Castañeda*, 37–63. Denton: University of North Texas Press, 2014.

Chapman, Paul D. *Schools as Sorters: Lewis M. Terman, Applied Psychology, and the Intelligence Testing Movement, 1890–1930*. New York: New York University Press, 1988.

Chavez, Nicole, and Melissa Alonso. "Police Took a 6-Year-Old Girl to a Mental Health Facility in Florida Because She Was 'out of Control' at School." *CNN*. February 16, 2020. www.cnn.com/2020/02/15/us/florida-girl-mental-health -baker-act/index.html.

Chávez-García, Miroslava. *Negotiating Conquest: Gender and Power in Califor-nia, 1770s to 1880s*. 3d edition. Tucson: University of Arizona Press, 2006.

———. *States of Delinquency: Race and Science in the Making of California's Juvenile Justice System*. 1st edition. Oakland: University of California Press, 2012.

———. "Youth, Evidence, and Agency: Mexican and Mexican American Youth at the Whittier State School, 1890–1920." *Aztlán: A Journal of Chicano Studies* 31, no. 2 (2006): 55–83.

Clark, Willis W. "A Statistical Study of 102 Truants." *Journal of Delinquency* 3, no. 5 (September 1918): 213–34.

Clark, Willis W., and J. Harold Williams. *A Guide to the Grading of Neighbor-hoods: Directions for Using the Whittier Scale for Grading Neighborhood Conditions, with the Standard Score Sheet of Comparative Data*. Whittier State School Department of Research Bulletin 8. Whittier, CA: Whittier State School Department of Printing Instruction, 1919.

Cohen, Cathy J. "Deviance as Resistance: A New Research Agenda for the Study of Black Politics." *Du Bois Review* 1, no. 1 (2004): 27–45.

Cohen, Jodi S. "How Often Do Schools Use Seclusion and Restraint? The Federal Government Isn't Properly Tracking the Data, According to a New Report." *ProPublica*. April 23, 2020. www.propublica.org/article/how-often-do-schoo ls-use-seclusion-and-restraint-the-federal-government-isnt-properly-tracking -the-data-according-to-a-new-report.

———. "A Teenager Didn't Do Her Online Schoolwork. So a Judge Sent Her to

Juvenile Detention." *ProPublica*. July 14, 2020. www.propublica.org/article
/a-teenager-didnt-do-her-online-schoolwork-so-a-judge-sent-her-to-juvenile
-detention.

"Colony Children Sought." *Los Angeles Times*. October 27, 1930.

Correspondence. November 1936. R350.005 10/20. Social Welfare. Admin-
Subject Files. Hospitals and Institutions. California State Archives.

Crafts, L. W., and E. A. Doll. "The Proportion of Mental Defectives among
Juvenile Delinquents (I)." *Journal of Delinquency* 2, no. 3 (May 1917):
119–43.

———. "The Proportion of Mental Defectives among Juvenile Delinquents (II)."
Journal of Delinquency 2, no. 4 (July 1917): 191–208.

Cross, Austin. "Take Two® | Audio: In the Eugenics Era, Mexican American
Women Were Prime Targets of Sterilization in California | 89.3 KPCC."
www.scpr.org/programs/take-two/2018/04/05/62481/in-the-eugenics-era
-mexican-american-women-were-pr/. April 5, 2018.

D'Antonio, Michael. *State Boys Rebellion*. New York: Simon & Schuster, 2005.

Davis, Angela. "Racism, Birth Control, and Reproductive Rights." In *Women,
Race & Class*, 202–21. New York: Vintage Books, 1983.

Davis, Mike. *City of Quartz: Excavating the Future in Los Angeles*. London:
Verso, 1990.

Davis, Peggy Cooper. *Neglected Stories*. New York: Hill and Wang, 1998.

Del Castillo, Adelaida R. "Sterilization: An Overview." In *Mexican Women in
the United States: Struggles Past and Present*, edited by Magdalena Mora
and Adelaida R. Del Castillo, 65–70. Los Angeles: UCLA Chicano Studies
Research Center Publications, 1980.

———. "La Visión Chicana." In *Chicana Feminist Thought: The Basic Historical
Writings*, edited by Alma M. García, 44–47. New York: Routledge, 1997.

Deverell, William. *Whitewashed Adobe: The Rise of Los Angeles and the Remaking of Its Mexican Past*. Oakland: University of California Press, 2005.

Diaz-Cordova, Stacy. Phone interview by Natalie Lira Regarding Stacy Diaz-
Cordova's Aunt Mary Franco. January 12, 2017.

Dickerson, Caitlin. "'There Is a Stench': Soiled Clothes and No Baths for Migrant
Children at a Texas Center." *New York Times*. June 21, 2019. www.nytimes.com
/2019/06/21/us/migrant-children-border-soap.html.

Dickerson, Caitlin, Seth Freed Wessler, and Miriam Jordan. "Immigrants Say
They Were Pressured into Unneeded Surgeries." *New York Times*. September
29, 2020. www.nytimes.com/2020/09/29/us/ice-hysterectomies-surgeries-ge
orgia.html.

Dickinson, Charles Alvah. "An Evening Recreational Program in a State Institution for the Feebleminded." Master's education, Claremont Colleges, 1934.

Dorr, Gregory Michael. *Segregation's Science: Eugenics and Society in Virginia*.
1st edition. Charlottesville: University of Virginia Press, 2008.

"Dr. Fenton to Join Faculty: Head of State Research in Juvenile Work." *Pomona Progress*. August 26, 1932.

Edgerton, Robert B. *The Cloak of Competence*. Berkeley: University of California Press, 1993.

———. "A Patient Elite: Ethnography in a Hospital for the Mentally Retarded." *Journal of Mental Deficiency* 68, no. 3 (November 1963): 372–84.

Edgerton, Robert B., George Tarjan, and Harvey F. Dingman. "Free Enterprise in a Captive Society." *Journal of Mental Deficiency* 66, no. 1 (July 1961): 35–41.

"Eight Escaped Youths Sought." *Los Angeles Times*. May 10, 1946.

Eighth Biennial Report of the State Board of Charities and Corrections of the State of California from July 1, 1916 to June 30, 1918. Sacramento: California State Printing Office, 1918.

Erevelles, Nirmala. *Disability and Difference in Global Contexts: Enabling a Transformative Body Politic*. 1st edition. New York: Palgrave Macmillan, 2011.

Erevelles, Nirmala, and Andrea Minear. "Unspeakable Offenses: Untangling Race and Disability in Discourses of Intersectionality." *Journal of Literary & Cultural Disability Studies* 4, no. 2 (2010): 127–45.

Escobar, Edward J. *Race, Police, and the Making of a Political Identity: Mexican Americans and the Los Angeles Police Department, 1900–1945*. 1st edition. Berkeley: University of California Press, 1999.

Escobar, Natalie. "Family Separation Isn't New." *The Atlantic*. August 14, 2018. www.theatlantic.com/family/archive/2018/08/us-immigration-policy-has-tra umatized-children-for-nearly-100-years/567479/.

Escobedo, Elizabeth R. *From Coveralls to Zoot Suits: The Lives of Mexican American Women on the World War II Home Front*. 1st edition. Chapel Hill: University of North Carolina Press, 2013.

Espino, Virginia. "'Woman Sterilized As Gives Birth': Forced Sterilization and Chicana Resistance in the 1970s." In *Las Obreras: Chicana Politics of Work and Family*, edited by Vicki L. Ruiz, 65–81. Los Angeles: Chicano Studies Research Center Publications, University of California, 2000.

Excerpt from Minutes of Meeting. August 9, 1927. R350.005 10/19. Social Welfare. Admin-Subject Files. Hospitals and Institutions. California State Archives.

Excerpt from Minutes of Meeting. September 11, 1929. R350.005. Social Welfare. Admin-Subject Files. Hospitals and Institutions. California State Archives.

Excerpts from Minutes of Meeting. December 10, 1930. R350.005 10/19. Social Welfare. Admin-Subject Files. Hospitals and Institutions. California State Archives.

Excerpts from Minutes of Meeting of State Department of Social Welfare. June 26, 1929. R350.005. Social Welfare. Admin-Subject Files. Hospitals and Institutions. California State Archives.

Fairchild, Amy L. *Science at the Borders: Immigrant Medical Inspection and the*

Shaping of the Modern Industrial Labor Force. 1st edition. Baltimore, MD: Johns Hopkins University Press, 2003.

"Family Separation under the Trump Administration—a Timeline." Southern Poverty Law Center. June 17, 2020. www.splcenter.org/news/2020/06/17/fami ly-separation-under-trump-administration-timeline.

Fenton, Norman. "Pacific Colony Plan." *Journal of Juvenile Research* 16 (October 1932): 298–303.

"Fifth Biennial Report of the Department of Institutions of the State of California: Two Years Ending June 30, 1930." Sacramento: California Department of Institutions, 1930.

Foner, Eric. *The Second Founding: How the Civil War and Reconstruction Remade the Constitution.* New York: W. W. Norton & Company, 2019.

"For Feeble-Minded: Expert Adviser to Pacific Colony Guest at Dinner Given by Friday Morning Club." *Los Angeles Times.* July 11, 1918.

"Fourth Biennial Report of the Department of Institutions of the State of California: Two Years Ending June 30, 1928." Sacramento: California Department of Institutions, 1928.

Frank, Margaret. "Factors Contributing to Indefinite Leave Failures of Five Adolescent Female Patients from Pacific Colony." Master's, social work, University of Southern California, 1953.

Frisch, Florence. "Factors in the Decision of Parents to Apply for Commitment of Mentally Defective Children to Pacific Colony." Master's of social work, University of Southern California, 1952.

Fuentes, Marisa J. *Dispossessed Lives: Enslaved Women, Violence, and the Archive.* Philadelphia: University of Pennsylvania Press, 2016.

Garcia, Alma M., ed. *Chicana Feminist Thought.* 1st edition. New York: Routledge, 1997.

García, Ana María. *La Operacíon.* Latin American Film Project, 1982.

Garcia v. State Dept. of Institutions. No. Civ. No. 12533. Second Appellate District December 18, 1939.

Gardner, Martha. *The Qualities of a Citizen: Women, Immigration, and Citizenship, 1870–1965.* Princeton, NJ: Princeton University Press, 2009.

Garland-Thomson, Rosemarie. "Integrating Disability, Transforming Feminist Theory." In *Feminist Disability Studies,* edited by Kim Q. Hall, 13–47. Bloomington: Indiana University Press, 2011.

Goddard, Henry H. *Feeble-Mindedness: Its Causes and Consequences.* New York: Macmillan Company, 1914.

Gonzalez, Gilbert G. *Chicano Education in the Era of Segregation.* Austin: University of North Texas Press, 2013.

Goodheart, Lawrence B. "Rethinking Mental Retardation: Education and Eugenics in Connecticut, 1818–1917." *Journal of the History of Medicine and Allied Science* 59, no. 1 (2004): 90–111.

Gould, Stephen Jay. *The Mismeasure of Man*. Revised and expanded edition. New York: W. W. Norton & Company, 1996.

"Governor's Office- Institutions- Hospitals- Sonoma State." 44 1943. F3640:2413. Earl Warren Papers, Administrative Files, California State Archives.

Green, Laurie B., John Mckiernan-González, and Martin Summers, eds. *Precarious Prescriptions: Contested Histories of Race and Health in North America*. Minneapolis: University of Minnesota Press, 2014.

Gullett, Gayle. *Becoming Citizens: The Emergence and Development of the California Women's Movement, 1880–1911*. Urbana: University of Illinois Press, 2000.

Gurr, Barbara. *Reproductive Justice: The Politics of Health Care for Native American Women*. 1st edition. New Brunswick, NJ: Rutgers University Press, 2014.

Gutiérrez, David G. *Walls and Mirrors: Mexican Americans, Mexican Immigrants, and the Politics of Ethnicity*. Berkeley: University of California Press, 1995.

Gutiérrez, Elena R. *Fertile Matters: The Politics of Mexican-Origin Women's Reproduction*. Austin: University of Texas Press, 2008.

Haley, Sarah. *No Mercy Here: Gender, Punishment, and the Making of Jim Crow Modernity*. Chapel Hill: University of North Carolina Press, 2016.

Hartman, Saidiya. "Venus in Two Acts." *Small Axe* 12, no. 2 (June 2008): 1–14.

——. *Wayward Lives, Beautiful Experiments: Intimate Histories of Social Upheaval*. 1st edition. New York: W. W. Norton & Company, 2019.

Hedva, Johanna. "Sick Woman Theory." *Mask Magazine*. www.maskmagazine .com/not-again/struggle/sick-woman-theory. Accessed April 12, 2016.

Hernández, Kelly Lytle. *City of Inmates: Conquest, Rebellion, and the Rise of Human Caging in Los Angeles, 1771–1965*. Chapel Hill: University of North Carolina Press, 2017.

"Hunt Four Missing Colony Inmates." *The Pomona Progress Bulletin*. October 6, 1942.

"Informe de Proteccion." May 1935. Secretaria de Relaciones Exteriores. Archivo Historico Genaro Estrada.

Jacobson, Matthew Frye. *Whiteness of a Different Color: European Immigrants and the Alchemy of Race*. Cambridge, MA: Harvard University Press, 1999.

Johnson, Corey G. "Female Inmates Sterilized in California Prisons without Approval." *Reveal: From the Center for Investigative Reporting*. July 7, 2013.

Johnson, Roland. "Lost in a Desert World." Disabilitymuseum.org. 1994. www .disabilitymuseum.org/dhm/lib/detail.html?id=1681&page=all. Accessed July 30, 2020.

Joinson, Carla. *Vanished in Hiawatha: The Story of the Canton Asylum for Insane Indians*. Lincoln: University of Nebraska Press, 2016.

Jones, Martha S. *Birthright Citizens: A History of Race and Rights in Antebellum America*. Cambridge, MA: Cambridge University Press, 2018.

Journal of Psycho-Asthenics 5, no. 35 (June 1929): 47–48.

"Juvenile Prisoners Escape; Three Boys Overpower Guards." *Los Angeles Times*. December 2, 1943.

Kafer, Alison. *Feminist, Queer, Crip*. 1st edition. Bloomington: Indiana University Press, 2013.

Kelley, Robin D. G. *Race Rebels: Culture, Politics, and the Black Working Class*. New York: Free Press, 1996.

Kennedy, Angie C. "Eugenics, 'Degenerate Girls,' and Social Workers during the Progressive Era." *Affilia* 23, no. 1 (February 1, 2008): 22–37.

Kevles, Daniel. *In the Name of Eugenics: Genetics and the Uses of Human Heredity*. Cambridge, MA: Harvard University Press, 1998.

Kim, Jina B. "Toward a Crip-of-Color Critique: Thinking with Minich's 'Enabling Whom?'" *Lateral: Journal of the Cultural Studies Association* 6, no. 1 (Spring 2017). https://csalateral.org/issue/6-1/forum-alt-humanities-critical-disabi lity-studies-crip-of-color-critique-kim/

Kline, Wendy. *Building a Better Race: Gender, Sexuality, and Eugenics from the Turn of the Century to the Baby Boom*. Oakland: University of California Press, 2005.

Kohler, Hugh. "Pacific State Hospital, 1921–1965." *The Pomona Valley Historian* 8, no. 1 (January 1972): 1–29.

Kraut, Alan M. *Silent Travelers: Germs, Genes, and the Immigrant Menace*. Baltimore, MD: Johns Hopkins University Press, 1995.

Ladd-Taylor, Molly. *Mother-Work: Women, Child Welfare, and the State, 1890–1930*. Champaign: University of Illinois Press, 1995.

———. "The 'Sociological Advantages' of Sterilization: Fiscal Policies and Feebleminded Women in Interwar Minnesota." In *Mental Retardation in America: A Historical Reader*, edited by Steven Noll and James W. Trent, 281–99. New York: New York University Press, 2004.

Lambert, Diana. "Lawsuit Challenges Use of Restrain, Seclusion in California Special Education School." *EdSource*. May 20, 2019. https://edsource.org/20 19/lawsuit-challenges-use-of-restraint-seclusion-in-california-special-educ ation-school/612690.

Lamp, Sharon, and W. Carol Cleigh. "A Heritage of Ableist Rhetoric in American Feminism from the Eugenics Period." In *Feminist Disability Studies*, edited by Kim Q. Hall, 175–89. Bloomington: Indiana University Press, 2011.

Laughlin, Harry Hamilton. *Eugenical Sterilization in the United States*. Chicago: Municipal Court of Chicago, 1922.

"League Center Approves of Three Bills out of Eleven." *San Francisco Chronicle*. June 23, 1916.

Leahy, Todd E. *They Called It Madness: The Canton Asylum for Insane Indians 1899–1934*. Baltimore, MD: America Star Books, 2009.

Letter. January 26, 1931. R350.005 10/19. Social Welfare. Admin-Subject Files. Hospitals and Institutions. California State Archives.

Lira, Natalie, and Alexandra Minna Stern. "Mexican Americans and Eugenic Sterilization: Resisting Reproductive Justice in California, 1920–1950." *Aztlán: A Journal of Chicano Studies* 39, no. 2 (Fall 2014): 9–34.

Lombardo, Paul A. *Three Generations, No Imbeciles: Eugenics, the Supreme Court, and Buck v. Bell*. 1st edition. Baltimore, MD: Johns Hopkins University Press, 2010.

López, Ian Haney. *Dog Whistle Politics: How Coded Racial Appeals Have Reinvented Racism and Wrecked the Middle Class*. New York: Oxford University Press, 2015.

Luna, Zakiya T. "From Rights to Justice: Women of Color Changing the Face of US Reproductive Rights Organizing." *Societies without Borders: Human Rights and the Social Sciences* 4 (2009): 343–65.

Markel, Howard, and Alexandra Minna Stern. "Which Face? Whose Nation? Immigration, Public Health, and the Construction of Disease at America's Ports and Borders, 1891–1928." *American Behavioral Scientist* 42, no. 9 (July 1999): 1314–31.

Martinez, Jr., Ramiro, and Abel Valenzuela Jr., eds. *Immigration and Crime: Race, Ethnicity, and Violence*. 1st edition. New York: New York University Press, 2006.

Mazón, Mauricio. *The Zoot-Suit Riots: The Psychology of Symbolic Annihilation*. Austin: University of Texas Press, 2010.

Mckiernan-González, John. *Fevered Measures: Public Health and Race at the Texas-Mexico Border, 1848–1942*. 1st edition. Durham, NC: Duke University Press Books, 2012.

Memorandum. June 21, 1949. F3640:2772. Earl Warren Papers. Administrative Files, Department of Mental Hygiene, California State Archives.

Menchaca, Martha. *Recovering History, Constructing Race: The Indian, Black and White Roots of Mexican Americans*. Austin: University of Texas Press, 2002.

Meredith, William F. "Factors Contributing to Indefinite Leave Failures of Nine Adolescent Male Patients from Pacific Colony." Master's, social work, University of Southern California, 1953.

Metzl, Jonathan. *The Protest Psychosis: How Schizophrenia Became a Black Disease*. Boston: Beacon Press, 2011.

Minich, Julie Avril. *Accessible Citizenships: Disability, Nation, and the Cultural Politics of Greater Mexico*. Philadelphia: Temple University Press, 2013.

———. "Enabling Whom? Critical Disability Studies Now." *Lateral: Journal of the*

Cultural Studies Association 5, no. 1 (Spring 2016). http://csalateral.org/issue /5-1/forum-alt-humanities-critical-disability-studies-now-minich/.

———. "Thinking with Jina B. Kim and Sami Schalk." *Lateral: Journal of the Cultural Studies Association* 6, no. 1 (Spring 2017). https://csalateral.org/is sue/6-1/forum-alt-humanities-critical-disability-studies-response-minich/.

Minton, Henry L. *Lewis M. Terman: Pioneer in Psychological Testing*. New York: New York University Press, 1988.

Molina, Natalia. *Fit to Be Citizens?: Public Health and Race in Los Angeles, 1879–1939*. Berkeley: University of California Press, 2006.

———. *How Race Is Made in America: Immigration, Citizenship, and the Historical Power of Racial Scripts*. Berkeley: University of California Press, 2014.

———. "Medicalizing the Mexican: Immigration, Race, and Disability in the Early-Twentieth-Century United States." *Radical History Review*, no. 94 (December 21, 2006): 22–37.

Mora, Magdalena, and Adelaida R. Del Castillo. *Mexican Women in the United States: Struggles Past and Present*. Occasional Paper No. 2. Los Angeles: Chicano Studies Research Center Publications, University of California, 1980.

Muhammad, Khalil Gibran. *The Condemnation of Blackness: Race, Crime, and the Making of Modern Urban America*. 2nd edition. Cambridge, MA: Harvard University Press, 2019.

Murillo, Lina-Maria. "Birth Control on the Border: Race, Gender, Religion and Class in the Making of the Birth Control Movement, El Paso, Texas, 1936–1973." PhD dissertation, history, University of Texas–El Paso, 2016.

Murphy, Stephen T. *Voices of Pineland: Eugenics, Social Reform, and the Legacy of Feeblemindedness in Maine*. Charlotte, NC: Information Age Publishing, 2011.

Nelles, Fred C. "Juvenile Delinquency Measures Adopted by the California Legislature of 1921." *Journal of Delinquency* 6, no. 3 (May 1921): 402–409.

Nelson, Alondra. *Body and Soul: The Black Panther Party and the Fight against Medical Discrimination*. Minneapolis: University of Minnesota Press, 2013.

"New Era Seen in Mental Ills." *Los Angeles Times*. July 13, 1932.

Ngai, Mae M. *Impossible Subjects: Illegal Aliens and the Making of Modern America*. Updated edition with a New Foreword. Princeton, NJ: Princeton University Press, 2005.

Nielsen, Kim E. *A Disability History of the United States*. Boston: Beacon Press, 2012.

"Nine of Delinquents Escaping from Pacific Colony Caught." *Los Angeles Times*. December 11, 1942.

Noll, Steven. *Feeble-Minded in Our Midst: Institutions for the Mentally Retarded in the South, 1900–1940*. Chapel Hill: University of North Carolina Press, 1995.

Novak, Nicole L., Natalie Lira, Kate E. O'Connor, Siobán D. Harlow, Sharon L.R. Kardia, and Alexandra Minna Stern. "Disproportionate Sterilization of Latinos under California's Eugenic Sterilization Program, 1920–1945." *American Journal of Public Health* 108, no. 5 (May 2018): 611–13.

Nowell, Cecilia. "Protesters Say Tear Gas Caused Them to Get Their Period Multiple Times in a Month." *Teen Vogue*. July 2, 2020. www.teenvogue.com/story/protestors-say-tear-gas-caused-early-menstruation.

O'Leary, Lizzie. "Children Were Dirty, They Were Scared, and They Were Hungry." *The Atlantic*. June 25, 2019. www.theatlantic.com/family/archive/2019/06/child-detention-centers-immigration-attorney-interview/592540/.

Odem, Mary E. *Delinquent Daughters: Protecting and Policing Adolescent Female Sexuality in the United States, 1885–1920*. 2nd edition. Chapel Hill: University of North Carolina Press, 1995.

Ordahl, George. "Mental Defectives and the Juvenile Court." *Journal of Delinquency* 2, no. 1 (January 1917): 1–13.

Ordahl, Louise E., and George Ordahl. "Delinquent and Dependent Girls." *Journal of Delinquency* 3, no. 2 (March 1918): 41–73.

Ordover, Nancy. *American Eugenics: Race, Queer Anatomy, and the Science of Nationalism*. 1st edition. Minneapolis: University of Minnesota Press, 2003.

Orozco, Cynthia E. *No Mexicans, Women, or Dogs Allowed: The Rise of the Mexican American Civil Rights Movement*. Austin: University of Texas Press, 2.

Ostrow, Al. "People in the Dark: A Series of Ten Articles on California's Hospital System." *San Francisco News*. 1946.

Owens, Deirdre Cooper. *Medical Bondage: Race, Gender, and the Origins of American Gynecology*. Athens: University of Georgia Press, 2018.

"Pacific Colony Battle Is Won." *Los Angeles Times*. May 10, 1923.

"Pacific Colony Is Not in Shape for Patients." *San Bernardino Sun*. May 3, 1921.

"Pacific Colony to Start Soon." *Los Angeles Times*. July 6, 1919, sec. V.

"Pacific Colony Youths Escape: Two Guards Overpowered as 21 Make Getaway from State Institution." *Los Angeles Times*. December 10, 1942.

"Pacific to Establish Moron Colony." *Los Angeles Times*. June 5, 1918.

Pagan, Eduardo Obregon. *Murder at the Sleepy Lagoon: Zoot Suits, Race, and Riot in Wartime L.A.* 1st edition. Chapel Hill: University of North Carolina Press, 2003.

Palace, Arthur Lawrence. "A Comparative Description of Anglo-White and Mexican-White Boys Committed to Pacific Colony." Master's thesis, University of Southern California, 1950.

Parsons, Anne E. *From Asylum to Prison: Deinstitutionalization and the Rise of Mass Incarceration after 1945*. Chapel Hill: University of North Carolina Press, 2018.

Patient Card Files, 1930s–1960s. Department of Developmental Services, Lanterman Development Center, California State Archives.

Patient Synopsis, 1927–1947. C01882. Department of Developmental Services, Lanterman Development Center, California State Archives.

Paul, Diane B. *Controlling Human Heredity*. Amherst: New York Humanity Books, 1995.

Pérez, Emma. *The Decolonial Imaginary: Writing Chicanas into History*. Bloomington: Indiana University Press, 1999.

———. *Forgetting the Alamo, Or, Blood Memory: A Novel*. 1st edition. Austin: University of Texas Press, 2009.

Perry, Harry Maynard. "A Study of Origin, Background, Intelligence, Race, and Other Factors Contributing to the Behavior of Boys Committed to Los Angeles Welfare Centers 1930–1934." Master's, science in education, University of Southern California, 1938.

Platt, Anthony M. *The Child Savers: The Invention of Delinquency*. New Brunswick, NJ: Rutgers University Press, 2009.

Popenoe, Paul. "Attitude of Patient's Relatives toward the Operation." *Journal of Social Hygiene* 14, no. 5 (1928): 271–79.

Popenoe, Paul, and E. S. Gosney. *Twenty-Eight Years of Sterilization in California*. Pasadena, CA: Human Betterment Foundation, 1938.

Pratt, Margaret P. Letter dated October 3, 1929. R350.005. Social Welfare. Admin-Subject Files. Hospitals and Institutions. California State Archives.

"Prepared to Build Largest School for Feebleminded." *Madera Weekly Tribune*. December 5, 1918.

"The Present Status of Juvenile Delinquency in California." *Journal of Delinquency* 5, no. 5 (September 1920): 183–91.

Proceedings of the Third California State Conference Charities and Corrections. Sacramento: California Preston School of Industry, 1904.

Project South. "Lack of Medical Care, Unsafe Work Practices, and Absence of Adequate Protection against COVID-19 for Detained Immigrants and Employees Alike at the Irwin County Detention Center." Complaint, September 14, 2020. https://projectsouth.org/wp-content/uploads/2020/09/OIG-IC DC-Complaint-1.pdf.

Pryce, Jessica. "The Long History of Separating Families in the US and How the Trauma Lingers." *The Conversation*. June 26, 2018. https://theconversation .com/the-long-history-of-separating-families-in-the-us-and-how-the-trauma -lingers-98616.

Puar, Jasbir K. *The Right to Maim: Debility, Capacity, Disability*. Durham, NC: Duke University Press, 2017.

Rafter, Nicole H. "Claims-Making and Socio-Cultural Context in the First U.S. Eugenics Campaign." *Social Problems* 39, no. 1 (February 1992): 17–34.

———. *Creating Born Criminals*. Urbana: University of Illinois Press, 1998.

Ramírez, Catherine S. *The Woman in the Zoot Suit: Gender, Nationalism, and the Cultural Politics of Memory*. 1st edition. Durham, NC: Duke University Press Books, 2009.

Rankin, John E. "Zoot Suiter Termites." Congressional Record, 78th Congress, 1st Session, June 15, 1943.

Rapley, Mark. *The Social Construction of Intellectual Disability*. 1st edition. New York: Cambridge University Press, 2004.

Raz, Mical. *What's Wrong with the Poor?: Psychiatry, Race, and the War on Poverty*. Chapel Hill: University of North Carolina Press, 2013.

Rembis, Michael. *Defining Deviance: Sex, Science, and Delinquent Girls, 1890–1960*. Urbana: University of Illinois Press, 2013.

"Report Escape of Five Boys from Cal. Reform School." *Los Angeles Herald*. July 2, 1921.

"Report of the 1915 Legislature: Committee on Mental Deficiency and the Proposed Institution for the Care of Feebleminded and Epileptic Persons." Whittier State School, Department of Printing, Whittier, CA, 1917.

"Report to Governors Council Psychology Department Pacific Colony." May 1947. Boxed Records, Box 1. Department of Developmental Services, Lanterman Development Center, California State Archives.

Roberts, Dorothy. *Killing the Black Body: Race, Reproduction, and the Meaning of Liberty*. New York: Vintage, 1998.

———. *Shattered Bonds: The Color of Child Welfare*. New York: Hachette Book Group, 2002.

"Rolph Aides Dedication." *Los Angeles Times*. March 31, 1931, 8.

Rogers, Arneta. "How Police Brutality Harms Mothers: Linking Police Violence to the Reproductive Justice Movement." *Hastings Race and Poverty Law Journal* 12, no. 2 (Summer 2015): 205–34.

Rose, Sarah F. *No Right to Be Idle: The Invention of Disability, 1840s–1930s*. Chapel Hill: University of North Carolina Press, 2017.

Ross, Loretta. "Conceptualizing Reproductive Justice Theory." In *Radical Reproductive Justice: Foundations, Theory, Practice, Critique*, edited by Loretta Ross, Lynn Roberts, Ericka Derkas, Whitney Peoples, and Pamela Bridgewater, 170–232. New York: Feminist Press, 2017.

———. "Reproductive Justice as Intersectional Feminist Activism." *Souls: A Critical Journal of Black Politics, Culture, and Society* 19, no. 3 (2017): 286–314.

———. "Trust Black Women: Reproductive Justice and Eugenics." In *Radical Reproductive Justice: Foundations, Theory, Practice, Critique*, edited by Loretta Ross, Lynn Roberts, Erika Derkas, Whitney Peoples, and Pamela Bridgewater Toure, 58–85. New York: Feminist Press, 2017.

Ross, Loretta, and Rickie Solinger. *Reproductive Justice: An Introduction*. Oakland: University of California Press, 2017.

Ross, Loretta, Lynn Roberts, Ericka Derkas, Whitney Peoples, and Pamela Bridgewater, eds. *Radical Reproductive Justice: Foundations, Theory, Practice, Critique*. New York: Feminist Press, 2017.

Roth, Rachel. "'She Doesn't Deserve to Be Treated Like This': Prisons as Sites of

Reproductive Injustice." In *Radical Reproductive Justice: Foundation, Theory, Practice, Critique*, edited by Loretta Ross, Lynn Roberts, Ericka Derkas, Whitney Peoples, and Pamela Bridgewater, 285–301. New York: Feminist Press, 2017.

Rothman, David. *The Discovery of the Asylum: Social Order and Disorder in the New Republic*. London: Routledge, 2002.

Rouble, Jewel Minna. "Social and Industrial Adjustment of the Feebleminded on Parole." Master's thesis, University of California, 1942.

Ruiz, Vicki L. *From out of the Shadows: Mexican Women in Twentieth-Century America*. 10th edition. New York: Oxford University Press, 2008.

———, ed. *Las Obreras: Chicana Politics of Work and Family*. Los Angeles: UCLA Chicano Studies Research Center Publications, 2000.

Sabagh, G., and Robert B. Edgerton. "Sterilized Mental Defectives Look at Eugenic Sterilization." *Eugenics Quarterly* 9, no. 4 (December 4, 1962): 213–22.

Sabagh, G., G. Tarjan, and S. W. Wright. "Social Class and Ethnic Status of Patients Admitted to a State Hospital for the Retarded." *Pacific Sociology Review* 2 (1959): 76–80.

Sanchez, George. *Becoming Mexican American: Ethnicity, Culture, and Identity in Chicano Los Angeles, 1900–1945*. Reprint. Oxford University Press, 1995.

———. "'Go after the Women': Americanization and the Mexican Immigrant Woman, 1915–1929." *Stanford Center for Chicano Research* 6. Stanford University, 1984.

Schalk, Sami. "Critical Disability Studies as Methodology." *Lateral: Journal of the Cultural Studies Association* 6, no. 1 (Spring 2017). http://csalateral .org/issue/6-1/forum-alt-humanities-critical-disability-studies-methodology -schalk/.

Schlossman, Steven, and Stephanie Wallach. "The Crime of Precocious Sexuality: Female Juvenile Delinquency in the Progressive Era." *Harvard Educational Review* 48, no. 1 (February 1978): 65–94.

Schoen, Johanna. "Between Choice and Coercion: Women and the Politics of Sterilization in North Carolina, 1929–1975." *Journal of Women's History* 13, no. 1 (Spring 2001): 132–56.

Scott, James C. *Weapons of the Weak: Everyday Forms of Peasant Resistance*. New Haven, CT: Yale University Press, 1987.

Schweik, Susan. "Disability and the Normal Body of the (Native) Citizen." *Social Research* 78, no. 2 (Summer 2011): 417–42.

———. *The Ugly Laws: Disability in Public*. New York: New York University Press, 2010.

"Second Biennial Report of the Department of Institutions in the State of California: Two Years Ending June 30, 1924." Sacramento: California Department of Institutions, 1924.

"Seek to Keep Moron Colony." *Los Angeles Times*. March 23, 1923, sec. I.

Self Advocates Becoming Empowered. *Who Is in Control*. 1993. www.youtube
.com/watch?v=QCVLzHQgLEM. Accessed July 30, 2020.

Shah, Nayan. *Contagious Divides: Epidemics and Race in San Francisco's
Chinatown*. Berkeley: University of California Press, 2001.

"Short History of Mental Institution of the State of California under the
Administration of Governor Earl Warren." September 1948. F3640:2695.
Earl Warren Papers, Administrative Files, Department of Mental Hygiene,
California State Archives.

Shropshire, Lee, William M. Morris, and Edward L. Foote. "Suppression
of Menstruation: A Hygienic Measure in the Care of Mentally Retarded
Patients." *Journal of the American Medical Association* 200, no. 5 (May 1,
1967): 414–15.

Sickle, Florence Perrigo Van. "The Function of the Mental Hygiene Clinic at
Juvenile Hall in Los Angeles, California." Master's, social work, University of
Southern California, 1944.

Sides, Josh. *L.A. City Limits: African American Los Angeles from the Great
Depression to the Present*. Oakland: University of California Press, 2003.

Siebers, Tobin Anthony. *Disability Theory*. Ann Arbor: University of Michigan
Press, 2008.

Silliman, Jael, Marlene Gerber Fried, Loretta Ross, and Elena Gutierrez.
Undivided Rights: Women of Color Organizing for Reproductive Justice.
Cambridge, MA: South End Press, 2004.

Sion, Alvin P. "Mentally Deficient Mexican-American Delinquent Boys Who
Made Good after Institutional Care: An Analysis of Six Cases." Master's, social
work, University of Southern California, 1951.

Smith, Andrea. *Conquest: Sexual Violence and American Indian Genocide*.
Cambridge, MA: South End Press, 2005.

Solinger, Rickie. "The First Welfare Case: Money, Sex, Marriage, and White
Supremacy in Selma, 1966, A Reproductive Justice Analysis." *Journal of
Women's History* 22, no. 3 (Fall 2010): 13–38.

———. *Pregnancy and Power: A Short History of Reproductive Politics in America*. New York: New York University Press, 2007.

———. *Wake up Little Susie: Since Pregnancy and Race before Roe v. Wade*.
London: Routledge, 1992.

Somerville, Siobhan B. *Queering the Color Line: Race and the Invention of
Homosexuality in American Culture*. 1st edition. Durham, NC: Duke University Press Books, 2000.

"Statistical Report of the Department of Institutions of the State of California:
Year Ending June 30, 1936." Sacramento: California Department of Institutions, 1936.

"Statistical Report of the Department of Institutions of the State of California:

Year Ending June 30, 1940." Sacramento: California Department of Institutions, 1940.

"Statistical Report of the Department of Institutions of the State of California: Year Ending June 30, 1941." Sacramento: California Department of Institutions, 1941.

"Statistical Report of the Department of Institutions of the State of California: Year Ending June 30, 1942." Sacramento, CA: California Department of Institutions, 1942.

"Statistical Report of the Department of Institutions of the State of California: Year Ending June 30, 1943." Sacramento: California Department of Institutions, 1943.

"Statistical Report of the Department of Institutions of the State of California: Year Ending June 30, 1944." Sacramento: California Department of Institutions, 1944.

"Statistical Report of the Department of Institutions of the State of California: Year Ending June 30, 1945." Sacramento: California Department of Institutions, 1945.

"Statistical Report of the Department of Institutions of the State of California: Year Ending June 30, 1946."Sacramento: California Department of Institutions, 1946.

"Statistical Report of the Department of Institutions of the State of California: Year Ending June 30, 1947." Sacramento: California Department of Institutions, 1947.

"Statistical Report of the Department of Institutions of the State of California: Year Ending June 30, 1948." Sacramento: California Department of Institutions, 1948.

"Statistical Report of the Department of Institutions of the State of California: Year Ending June 30, 1949." Sacramento: California Department of Institutions, 1949.

Sterilization Records. Department of Institutions, Department of Mental Hygiene, California State Archives.

Stern, Alexandra Minna. *Eugenic Nation: Faults and Frontiers of Better Breeding in Modern America*. Berkeley: University of California Press, 2005.

Stepan, Nancy Leys. *The Hour of Eugenics: Race, Gender, and Nation in Latin America*. Ithaca, NY: Cornell University Press, 1996.

"A Survey of the Mental Institutions of the State of California." December 27, 1949. F3640:2709. Earl Warren Papers, Administrative Files, Department of Mental Hygiene, California State Archives.

Surveys in Mental Deviation in Prisons, Public Schools, and Orphanages in California. California State Printing Office, 1918.

Tajima-Peña, Rene. *No Más Bebés*. Moon Canyon Films, 2015.

Tenth Biennial Report of the State Board of Charities and Corrections of the State of California from July 1, 1920, to June 30, 1922. Sacramento: California State Printing Office, 1923.

"Tennessee Judge Who Offered Inmates Reduced Sentences for Sterilization Rebuked." *CBS News.* November 22, 2017.

Terman, Lewis M. "Feeble-Minded Children in the Public Schools of California." *School and Society* 5, no. 111 (February 10, 1917): 161–65.

———. "Introductory Statement." *Journal of Delinquency* 1, no. 1 (March 1916): 54.

———. *The Measurement of Intelligence: An Explanation of and Complete Guide for the Use of the Stanford Revision and Extension of the Binet-Simon Intelligence Scale.* Cambridge, MA: Riverside Press, 1916.

———. "Research on the Diagnosis of Pre-Delinquent Tendencies." *Journal of Delinquency* 9, no. 4 (July 1925): 124–30.

Terman, Lewis M., Virgil Dickson, and Lowry Howard. "Backward and Feeble-Minded Children in the Public Schools of 'X' County, California." In *Surveys in Mental Deviation in Prisons, Public Schools, and Orphanages in California.* Sacramento, CA: State Board of Charities and Corrections, 1918.

"Third Biennial Report of the Department of Institutions of the State of California: Two Years Ending June 30, 1926." Sacramento: California Department of Institutions, 1926.

"Three Young Colony Fugitives Hunted." *The Pomona Progress Bulletin.* November 10, 1941.

"To Establish Moron Colony." *Los Angeles Times.* June 5, 1918, sec. I.

Trent, James W. *Inventing the Feeble Mind: A History of Mental Retardation in the United States.* Oakland: University of California Press, 1995.

Tucker, Lorna. *Amá.* Raindog Films, 2018.

U.S. Census Bureau. 1910.

U.S. Census Bureau. 1930.

Vasquez, Tina. "Exclusive: Georgia Doctor Who Forcibly Sterilized Detained Women Has Been Identified." *Prism*, September 15, 2020. www.prismreports.org/article/2020/9/15/exclusive-georgia-doctor-who-forcibly-sterilized-detained-women-has-been-identified.

Waggaman, Mary T. "Labor Colonies for the Feeble-Minded." *Monthly Labor Review* 11, no. 3 (September 1920): 12–19.

Wardell, Winifred Ruth. "Care of the Feeble-Minded in California Illustrated by Care Given Three Generations in a Single Family." Master's thesis, University of California–Berkeley, 1944.

Wellerstein, Alex. "States of Eugenics: Institutions and Practices of Compulsory Sterilization in California." In *Reframing Rights: Bioconstitutionalizm in the Genetic Age*, edited by Sheila Jasanoff, 29–58. Cambridge, MA: MIT Press, 2011.

White, Deborah Gray. *Ar'n't I a Woman?: Female Slaves in the Plantation South.* Revised edition. New York: W. W. Norton & Company, 1999.

Williams, J. Harold. "Delinquency and Mental Deficiency." *Journal of Delinquency* 1, no. 2 (May 1916): 101.

———. "Delinquent Boys of Superior Intelligence." *Journal of Delinquency* 1, no. 1 (March 1916): 33–52.

———. *A Guide to the Grading of Homes: Directions for Using the Whittier Scale for Grading Home Conditions, with the Standard Score Sheet of Comparative Data.* Whittier State School Department of Research Bulletin 7. Whittier, CA: Whittier State School Department of Printing Instruction, 1918.

Wise, Justin. "HHS Secretary: We're Doing 'Great Acts of American Generosity' for Migrant Children." *The Hill.* July 7, 2018. https://thehill.com/latino/3964 42-hhs-secretary-what-were-doing-for-migrant-children-is-one-of-the-great -acts-of.

Yellow Bird, Pemina. "Wild Indians: Native Perspectives on the Hiawatha Asylum for Insane Indians." National Empowerment Center. https://power2u .org/wild-indians-native-perspectives-on-the-hiawatha-asylum-for-insane-in dians-by-pemima-yellow-bird/. Accessed June 15, 2020.

"Youth Hangs Self in Jail." *Los Angeles Times.* April 19, 1941.

Zaborskis, Mary. "Queering Black Girlhood at the Virginia Industrial School." *Signs: Journal of Women in Culture and Society* 45, no. 2 (2020) 373–94.

Zavella, Patricia. *Women's Work and Chicano Families: Cannery Workers of the Santa Clara Valley.* Ithaca, NY: Cornell University Press, 1987.

Zipf, Karin Lorene. *Bad Girls at Samarcand: Sexuality and Sterilization in a Southern Juvenile Reformatory.* Baton Rouge: Louisiana State University Press, 2016.

Zuberi, Tufuku, and Eduardo Bonilla-Silva. *White Logic, White Methods: Racism and Methodology.* New York: Rowman & Littlefield Publishers, 2008.

Index

ableism
    definition of, xiv
    and disability, 10, 13–14, 190
    and eugenics, 36, 80, 167, 184
    and feeblemindedness, 23, 28
    and institutionalization, 179, 183–84
    and intelligence, 41, 47–48
    and race, 32–33, 83, 99, 122, 142, 178, 181, 191
    and reproductive oppression, 185, 191
    and sexual delinquency, 88, 98–99
    and sterilization, 179, 183–84, 190
abortion, 11, 143, 180
adoption, 82, 94, 145
African Americans, 39–40, 48, 116, 120, 127
    See also Black people
Aguilar, Rafaela (Pacific Colony patient), 162–63
Allison, Chas. L., 91
Alvarez, Monica (Pacific Colony patient), 96–97
Alvarez, Rosa (Pacific Colony patient), 153
American Academy of Child Psychiatry, 142
American Association on Intellectual and Developmental Disability. *See* AMOAIIFP
American Association on Mental Deficiency, 142
American Medical Association, 186–87

American Psychiatric Association, 142
American Psychological Association, 208n57
Applegate, Carl E., 162
Association of Medical Officers of American Institutions of Idiotic and Feeble-Minded Persons (AMOAIIFP), 34–38, 63–64, 67, 206n28
Avila, Joe (Pacific Colony patient), 163, 165, 169
Azar, Alex, 186

Balderrama, Francisco E., 174
Banay, Ralph S., 83
Barber, Faith, 68
Baynton, Douglas, 10, 18
Benjamin, Ruha, 183–84
Ben-Moshe, Liat, 189
Berkeley, CA, 38
Betty (Pacific Colony patient), 27, 204n1
Binet, Alfred, 42, 208n59
Black Panthers, 188
Black people
    in California, 40, 48
    and claims of mental inferiority, 32–33, 39, 178
    and criminality, 114, 116, 120–23, 127, 206n34, 223n33
    and feeblemindedness, 48, 209n79
    and institutionalization, 185–86, 212n124

Black people *(continued)*
  at Pacific Colony, 16, 27, 142, 196(t)
  women, 11, 27, 76, 94, 172, 185, 216n24
  See also African Americans
Blaisell, James A., 138
Bonilla-Silva, Eduardo, 124, 224n53
Bosnic, Tyra, 192
Brainard, Elizabeth, 101–3
Brennan, Mary Ellen, 185–86
Bright, William, 163
Bryant, Carrie Parsons, 29–30, 36
Buck, Carrie, 95
Buckley, Elizabeth, 179
Buck v. Bell, 49, 95, 207n41, 209n83
Bunker, Edward (Pacific Colony patient),
  156–57
Butler, Fred O., 85, 89–91, 99
Byers, Joseph P., 64

California
  Americanization programs in, 79–80
  demographics of, 17, 48, 78
  history of, 39–40, 77
  history of sterilization in, 3–4, 27, 86–88,
    232n89
  institutionalization in, 37–39, 75, 82–83,
    130–31
  institutions in (*See individual institutions*)
  reform schools in (*See individual schools*)
  sterilization laws in, 69, 170, 177–80, 183,
    207n41, 233–34n114
California Bureau of Juvenile Research
  (CBJR), 61–62, 115–16, 122–29, 133, 137,
  142, 222n13
California Department of Health, 90
California Department of Institutions, 20–21,
  53–54, 89–90, 94, 97, 112, 131, 133, 135,
  168, 170–72, 175, 178
California Department of Public Health, 20
California Department of Social Welfare, 5,
  89–90
California Division of Juvenile Justice. *See*
  California Youth Authority
California Home for the Care and Training of
  Feeble-Minded Children, 37
California Prisoners' Union, 188
California Public Health Department, 4–5
California State Archives, 221n1
California State Board of Charities and Cor-
  rections, 37–38, 47, 53
California State Legislature, 5, 9, 28–30,
  37–38, 49, 50, 55–56, 64, 124, 132, 158, 181,
  211n111

California Superior Court, 26, 59–60
California Youth Authority, 130, 140, 226n98
Campos, Frank (Pacific Colony patient), 136
capitalism, 14, 16–17, 29, 31, 33–34, 125
Carey, Allison C., 31, 34, 166
Carlotta (Pacific Colony patient), 27, 204n1
Chavez, Luis (Pacific Colony patient), 135
Chávez-García, Miroslava, 59–60, 156
Chicago, IL, 64
Chicago Municipal Court, 19
Chicano Studies, 114, 221n2
  See also feminism
Chicano Welfare Rights Organization, 189
Chinese people, 40, 61, 196(t), 212n124
citizenship status, xiii, 4, 7, 17–19, 31–35, 57,
  61, 77, 79, 93, 174–75
Claremont Colleges, 138
Clark, Willis W., 122, 224n43
Clark University, 41
classism, xiv, 3, 23, 28, 30, 33, 41, 51, 80, 183–
  85, 201n24
  See also middle-class norms
Club Woman, 50
colonialism/imperialism, 31–32, 63, 77
Committee Opposing Psychiatric Abuse of
  Prisoners, 188
confinement. *See* institutionalization
Connecticut, 34
Connecticut Training School for the Feeble-
  minded, 63
consent forms (Pacific Colony), 2, 21–22,
  96–97, 111, 147, 167, 170–71, 179
Contreras, Juan (Pacific Colony patient), 136
Cordova, Valentina (Pacific Colony patient),
  72–76, 82, 107, 214n1
Coronado, Fred (Pacific Colony patient), 129
Cortez, Freddy (Pacific Colony patient), 135
Cortez, George (Pacific Colony patient), 173
COVID-19 pandemic, 186, 191
Crafts, Leland W., 119–21, 131, 223n37
criminalization
  biologization of, 116–18, 188, 222n21
  and feeblemindedness, 8–9, 112–13, 119–20,
    129, 131, 138
  as hereditary trait, 115, 117, 122
  and immigrants, 120–21
  and intelligence, 117, 122–24, 133, 135, 137
  and Mexican-origin people, 110–11, 114, 221n2
  and poverty, 6, 9, 29–30, 34–35, 37–38,
    48–49, 57, 77, 80, 120, 127
  and race, 24, 110–24, 130, 132, 134, 137, 141–
    43, 185, 188, 223n33
  See also incarceration; juvenile delinquency

Critical Disability Studies, 2, 11, 13–14, 21, 204n5
Cuba, 213n131

Davenport, Charles, 36, 39, 115
deinstitutionalization, 188–89
Del Castillo, Adelaida R., 184
Díaz, José, 110, 221n2
Dickinson, Alvah, 213n138
(dis)ability, 13–14, 28–29, 99, 204n5
disability, concept of, 10
Disability Justice, 191
    See also Critical Disability Studies
disease, 17–20, 48–49, 80, 95, 101, 106, 127, 134–35, 228n6
Doll, Edgar A., 119–21, 131, 223n25, 223n37
Dugdale, Richard Louis, 35
Duran, Antonio (Pacific Colony patient), 133–34

Ed (patient), 191
Edgerton, Robert, 103–4, 151, 171, 230n40
education. See intelligence; reform schools
electroencephalography, 139(f), 140
Elena (Pacific Colony patient), 74
"emotional disturbance," 152–54, 227n104
Encinas, Antonio (Pacific Colony patient), 161
epilepsy, 50, 89, 160–61, 198n5
Erevelles, Nirmala, 14, 148
Escalante, Alicia, 189
Escobar, Edward, 132
Escobedo, Elizabeth R., xiii
Espino, Virginia, 184
Estrada, Blanche (Pacific Colony patient), 160–61
eugenics
    and ableism, 36, 80, 167, 184
    and feeblemindedness, 6, 39, 57, 75–76, 184
    and intelligence, 41, 43, 46, 51, 126, 181
    and juvenile delinquency, 115, 117, 126, 131
    and race, 15, 18–19, 121, 131–32
    and reproductive oppression, 13, 69
    rise of, 35–37
    and sexuality, 80, 86–87
    and sterilization, 3–4, 37, 69, 85, 88, 90, 95, 99–100, 170, 177, 184–90, 207n41
    and women, 51, 89
Eugenics Quarterly, 1–2
Eugenics Records Office (ERO), 115

feeblemindedness
    and ableism, 23, 28
    and Black people, 48, 209n79
    and criminalization, 9, 112–13, 119, 131
    and eugenics, 6, 39, 57, 75–76, 184
    and gender, 3, 9, 12, 14–15, 23, 45, 48, 75–76, 148, 183
    institutionalization of, 4, 15–16, 29, 34–37, 58–59, 63–64, 84, 88, 130, 135, 155, 159
    and intelligence, 3, 7–9, 25, 27, 29–30, 43–45, 57, 84, 223n28
    and juvenile delinquency, 112, 114–20, 122, 124, 127, 129, 130–33, 150
    and Mexican-origin people, 3, 5, 7, 9–10, 14, 16, 60, 76, 83, 129, 134, 149, 158
    and poverty, 9, 21, 150, 181, 184
    and psychology, 5–6, 8, 29–30, 48
    and race, 3, 6–10, 16, 18, 23, 28, 48–50, 121–22, 223n37
    and sexual delinquency, 86–89, 94, 97, 217n44
feminism, 2, 11, 23, 228n6
    Chicana, 75, 77, 189, 190
Fenton, Norman, 61–63, 65–68, 138, 207n46
Fernald, Grace M., 47–48
Fernald State School, 154, 166
Filipino people, 54, 121n124, 196(t)
Flint, Marie C., 50
Florence Crittenton Home, 82, 167, 216n29
Florida, 185
Franco, Mary (Pacific Colony patient), 155–56
Frank, Margaret, 147
Fred (Pacific Colony patient), 158
Friday Morning Club, 50
Frisch, Florence, 59
Fry, Florine (Pacific Colony patient), 162
Fuentes, Trinidad (Pacific Colony patient), 162

Galton, Francis, 35–36
Garcia, Andrea (Pacific Colony patient), 22, 177–80, 233–34n114
Garcia, Sara Rosas, 177–79, 233–34n114
Garcia v. State Department of Institutions, 177–80, 190
Gardner, Martha, 77
Garis, Roy, 132
Garland-Thomson, Rosemarie, 99
gender
    and disability, 7, 11, 13, 75
    and eugenics, 5
    and feeblemindedness, 3, 9, 12, 14–15, 23, 45, 48, 75–76, 148, 183
    and institutionalization, 2, 4–5, 51, 93, 148, 179
    naturalization of hierarchies, 6, 9, 12, 76

gender *(continued)*
and Pacific Colony, 50, 67, 105
and reproductive oppression, 2, 12, 51, 54, 67, 114
and sexual delinquency, 71, 75–76, 80, 85, 88, 91, 92–93, 99, 113–14
General Laws of California, Act 3690, Section 16, 44
Georgia Detention Watch, 187
Georgia Latino Alliance for Human Rights, 187
Germany, 136
Goddard, Henry H., 39, 43, 57
Gomez, Frank (Pacific Colony patient), 164
Gomez, Gabriella (Pacific Colony patient), 94, 218n66
gonorrhea, 94, 97
Goodheart, Lawrence B., 213n131
Gosney, E. S., 86–90, 170
Grant, Madison, 18
Great Depression, 17, 20, 53, 56, 63, 74, 78, 144
Green, Corinthian (Pacific Colony patient), 161
Griswold v. Connecticut, 180
Gu, Lucy, 166
Guerrero, Antonio (Pacific Colony patient), 130
Gutiérrez, Elena R., xiii, 78, 184

Haley, Sarah, 23, 76
Hall, Granville Stanley, 41, 81, 208n57
Hartman, Saidiya, 23
Hatch, Charles, 166
Haynes, Cora L., 50
Healy, William, 225n63
Hedva, Johanna, 148–49, 228n6
Heffner, Dora Shaw, 168
Hernandez, John, 52, 159
Hernandez, Miguel (Pacific Colony patient), 175–76
heteronormativity, 8, 10, 86, 104
heterosexuality, 102–4
Hewitt, Ann Cooper, 166
Hiawatha Asylum, 32
Hilquemup, Juan (Pacific Colony patient), 89
Holmes, Oliver Wendell, Jr., 209n83
homosexuality, 101–5, 153
See also queerness
Hoyte, Elizabeth, 165, 173
hyperfertility, 3, 76, 78–79, 86–88, 99, 112
hysterectomy, 155, 188

Illinois, 34, 60

immigration, 16–20, 33–35, 77, 79–80, 121, 132, 186–87, 206n34
See also citizenship status
Immigration Act of 1924, 18–20
Immigration and Customs Enforcement (ICE), 187
Immigration Problem, The, 121
immorality, 6, 29–30, 34–35, 48, 80, 82, 84–85, 181, 216n24
See also juvenile delinquency; sexual delinquency
incarceration, 40, 114–15, 140, 143, 186–88, 192, 223n33
See also criminalization
Indiana, 37, 41
Indian Health Services, 185
institutionalization
and ableism, 179, 183–84
of Black people, 185–86, 212n124
in California, 37–39, 75, 82–83, 130–31
early history of, 31–33
of the feebleminded, 4, 15–16, 29, 34–37, 58–59, 63–64, 84, 88, 130, 135, 155, 159
and gender, 2, 4–5, 51, 93, 148, 179
in Los Angeles, 112, 127, 144, 161, 163–65, 177
of Mexican-origin men, 93, 129, 137, 141–42, 226–27n100
of Mexican-origin women, 2–3, 167
of Mexican-origin youth, 3–5, 17, 53, 59–61, 120, 141–42, 178
as pipeline to low-wage work, 63, 68, 107, 135–37
and poverty, 15, 57–58, 58(t), 153, 155
and race, 16, 21, 61–62, 143, 179, 183, 196(t)
and reproductive constraint, 5–6, 9, 26, 30, 36, 51, 53, 76, 165, 178–79, 182–83, 185
resistance to, 149, 177–80, 188–89, 210n95
role of families in, 166–72
See also deinstitutionalization; *individual institutions*
intellectual disability, 13, 31, 34, 142, 189
intelligence
and criminality, 117, 122–24, 133, 135, 137
as diagnostic tool, 42
and eugenics, 41, 181
and feeblemindedness, 3, 7, 9, 25, 27, 29–30, 43, 45, 57, 84
hierarchical, 42–44, 46
and juvenile delinquency, 118–20, 126, 128, 141
and race, 32, 39, 41–42, 45–46, 120–24, 130, 134, 140–41

and sexual deviance, 83–84
testing of, 7–8, 41–47, 109, 111, 122–23, 126, 128–29, 183, 208n59, 221n1, 225n63
See also intellectual disability; IQ (Intelligence Quotient) tests; Stanford-Binet intelligence test
International Congress of Charities, Correction and Philanthropy, 64
IQ (Intelligence Quotient) tests
creation of, 208n59
and criminality, 117, 118, 127–28, 133, 141–42
and diagnostic practices, xiv, 7–8, 44–45, 94, 126, 133, 140–41, 158
and feeblemindedness, 8, 43–45, 57, 223n28
and juvenile delinquency, 11, 109, 117–19, 126–27, 129, 158
and sexual delinquency, 85, 94
and social hierarchy, 42, 44–47
Terman on, 41–42
See also Stanford-Binet intelligence test
Irish people, 48
Irwin County Detention Center, 187–88
Italian people, 48, 196(t)

Japanese people, 40, 196(t), 212n124
Jefferson, Thomas, 32
Jenks, Jeremiah, 121
Jensen, Earl E., 78–79
Jesus (Pacific Colony patient), 153–54, 162
Jewish people, 40
Jim Crow, 213n131
John (Pacific Colony patient), 164–65
Johnson, J. C., 150
Johnson, Roland, 188
Johnson–Reed Act. *See* Immigration Act of 1924
Journal of Delinquency, 84, 116–20, 122, 124, 131
Joyce, Thomas, 90–91, 111–12
juvenile delinquency
and eugenics, 115, 117, 126, 131
and feeblemindedness, 112, 114–20, 122, 124, 127, 129, 130–33, 150
and intelligence, 118–20, 126, 128, 141
and IQ tests, 11, 109, 117–19, 126–27, 129, 158
and reproductive constraint, 124
and sterilization, 131–37
See also criminalization

Kennedy, John F., 142
Kerlin, Isaac, 34–35
Kline, Wendy, 166, 217n44

Knight, George H., 63–64
knowledge production, 13, 127, 137–38
at Pacific Colony, 137–43, 139(f)
Kratt, Frank (Pacific Colony patient), 162

labor
free, 15, 33, 137, 150
at institutions, 52–53, 62–63, 65–69, 146–47, 150–51
low-wage, 14–15, 40, 66, 68, 76, 86, 88, 106–7, 135–37
resistance to forced, 151–52
LaChappa, Florida (Pacific Colony patient), 89
Ladd-Taylor, Molly, 15
Lago, Teresa (Pacific Colony patient), 144–48, 170
Lanterman Development Center, xiii–xiv, 21, 221n1
See also Pacific Colony
Latinx people, 5, 16
Lauck, W. Jett, 121
Laughlin, Harry Hamilton, 19, 115
Leiva, Edward (Whittier State School resident), 163
Leon, Alfredo (Pacific Colony patient), 129
Leon, Jose (Pacific Colony patient), 133–34
Logan, Mrs., 91
Lombroso, Cesare, 116
Lopez, Adriana (Pacific Colony patient), 172
Lopez, Miguel (Pacific Colony patient), 132–33
Lopez, Willy (Pacific Colony patient), 136
Los Angeles, CA
demographics of, 73–74
institutionalization in, 112, 127, 144, 161, 163–65, 177
Mexican-origin people in, 17, 40, 78–79, 132, 174
and Pacific Colony, 51–52
schools in, 25, 27
sterilization in, 91
Los Angeles Bureau of Indigent Relief, 91
Los Angeles Chamber of Commerce, 39, 41
Los Angeles City Schools, 179
Los Angeles County Health Department, 78
Los Angeles County–USC Medical Center, 189
Los Angeles Department of Public Welfare, 89
Los Angeles Health Department, 91
Los Angeles Herald, 159
Los Angeles Juvenile Hall, 109, 111, 128–29, 221n1

Los Angeles Mexican Consulate, 174, 176–77, 233n105, 233n111–12
Los Angeles Police Department, 110, 179, 221n2
Los Angeles State Normal School, 47, 208n58
Los Angeles Times, 78, 159–60, 162
Los Angeles Welfare Department, 189
Los Angeles Youth Authority, 156

Madrigal v. Quilligan, 180, 190
Maldonado, Louis (Pacific Colony patient), 52, 159
Malm, Mildred, 109–11, 128, 221n1
Marcus, David C., 177–78, 233n112, 233–34n114
Margarita (Pacific Colony patient), 25–27, 204n1
"marked for management," 77, 215n6
See also institutionalization
Martha (patient at Pacific Colony), 59, 68, 157–58, 230n40
Martinez, Raul (Pacific Colony patient), 109–12, 114, 128–29, 221n1
Martinez, William (Pacific Colony patient), 161
Mary (Pacific Colony patient), 107
Massachusetts, 154, 166
McGrath, Alice Greenfield, 216–17n33
Mckiernan-González, John, 19
medications
    amdol (amytal), 157
    barbiturates, 140, 157
    mestranol (Enovid), 100
    norethynodrel, 100
    sodium amytal, 140
men. *See* gender; Mexican-origin men
Mendez v. Westminster, 233n112
Mendoza, Francisco (Pacific Colony patient), 134
Mendoza, Marco (Pacific Colony patient), 173
menorrhagia, 59, 157, 230n40
menstruation, 100, 182
mental deficiency, definition of, xiv
    See also feeblemindedness
"mental retardation," 184
Mercedes (Pacific Colony patient), 204n1
methodology, of book, 2–3, 13, 21–23
    See also Critical Disability Studies; Reproductive Justice
Mexican American Political Association, 188
Mexican Americans. *See* Mexican-origin men; Mexican-origin women; Mexican-origin youth
Mexican Fact-Finding Commission in California, 78

Mexican-origin men
    criminalization of, 110–14, 116, 122, 130–34, 138, 141, 221n2, 226–27n100
    and feeblemindedness, 129, 134
    institutionalization of, 93, 129, 137, 141–42, 226–27n100
    and low-wage work, 17, 136
    at Pacific Colony, 113–14, 129, 132, 135–38
    sterilization of, 93, 113, 132–36, 143
    See also Mexican-origin women; Mexican-origin youth
Mexican-origin women
    and disability, 11, 108
    and feeblemindedness, 76, 83
    hyperfertility of, 78, 88
    institutionalization of, 2–3, 167
    and low-wage work, 17, 76, 79
    at Pacific Colony, 76, 80, 88, 91–100, 114
    resistance of, 147, 156, 165, 180, 190
    and sexual delinquency, 71, 75–78, 82–83, 86, 218–19n66
    sterilization of, 2, 24, 88, 91–100, 180, 290
    See also Mexican-origin men; Mexican-origin youth
Mexican-origin youth
    criminalization of, 109–12, 122–23, 137, 160–61, 221n2
    and feeblemindedness, 3, 5, 7, 9–10, 14, 16, 60, 149, 158
    institutionalization of, 3–5, 17, 53, 59–61, 120, 141–42, 178
    and intelligence, 121–22, 141
    at Pacific Colony, 6, 16, 21, 23, 137–38, 148–49, 154, 163, 172, 186
    resistance of, 148, 151–52, 154, 160–61, 179
    and sexual delinquency, 24
    sterilization of, 3–5, 70–71
    See also Mexican-origin men; Mexican-origin women
Mexican Revolution, 17, 40
Mexico
    and California, 39, 77
    and citizenship, 174
    deportation to, 20–21
    immigrants from, xiii, 17–20, 25–26, 186, 215n20
    U.S. border, 17, 19
middle-class norms, 4, 8, 10, 28, 81–82, 126–27, 158
Minear, Andrea, 148
Minnesota, 60
miscegenation, 132
Molina, Natalia, 19
Morales, David (Pacific Colony patient), 135

Moreno, Benny (Whittier State School resident), 163
Moreno, Inez (Pacific Colony patient), 95
motherhood, 48, 86, 94–95, 97–98, 107, 217n44
Muhammad, Khalil Gibran, 223n33

National Association for the Advancement of Colored People (NAACP), 188
National Committee on Provision for the Feeble-Minded, 64
National Conference of Charities and Corrections, 35
National Organization for Women, 188
Native American people, 16, 27, 31–32, 39, 48, 89
nativism, 17, 33, 77, 79
Nelles, Fred C., 115, 222n13
New Immigration, The, 121
Ngai, Mae, 19
Nielsen, Kim E., 213n131
North Carolina, 60, 90, 185, 230n40
Nowell, Cecilia, 192

Oakland County, MI, 185
Odem, Mary, 216n24
Ohio, 34, 138
Oliver, John, 176
Olson, Harry, 19
Ordahl, George, 84–86
Ordahl, Louise, 84–85
Ortiz, Jose (Pacific Colony patient), 161
Ostrow, Al, 56, 159

pachuca/os, 83, 111, 221n2
Pacific Colony
   abuse at, 56, 155–58
   archives at, 21–23, 204n1
   buildings of, 26(f), 27, 53–57, 73(f), 89, 110(f), 114
   custodial class at, 63–67, 100, 106
   demographics of patients, xiii–xiv, 2, 5, 16–17, 23, 27, 53, 60–62, 70–71, 93, 113(t), 114, 194–96(t), 212n124
   early population of, 57–61
   economic status of residents, 57–58, 58(t)
   education at, 63, 66, 68–69
   escapes from, 52, 140, 154–66, 160(t), 179, 210n95
   forced labor at, 52–53, 62–63, 65–69, 146–47, 150–51
   founding of, 9, 28–29, 33, 36, 38–41, 50–57, 84, 86, 115, 211n111
   infants at, 105–7

institutional workers at, 53, 66–67, 152
knowledge production at, 137–43, 139(f)
love and relationships at, 101–5
overcrowding at, 55–57, 158–59, 165
resistance at, 24, 100, 107–8, 146–49, 150–54, 173
vocational class at, 66–68
vocational training at, 135–37, 150–51, 155
See also consent forms; Pacific Colony Bill (1917); Pacific Colony Plan; sterilization request forms
Pacific Colony Bill (1917), 30, 38, 43, 49–50, 52–53, 64, 67, 69, 124, 132
Pacific Colony Plan, 62–71
Pacific State Hospital, 100, 183
   See also Pacific Colony
Palace, Arthur Lawrence, 93, 140–41, 226–27n100
parens patriae, 128, 129
Parker, Clarence, 52, 159
patients (at Pacific Colony). See individual patients
Patty (patient), 191
Pauline (Pacific Colony patient), 27
Pennsylvania Training School for Feeble-Minded Children, 34
People v. Zamora, 83, 110, 114, 221n2
Perez, Bernard, 173
Pérez, Emma, 23
Perez, George (Pacific Colony patient), 129
Perry, Harry M., 127–28
Philadelphia, PA, 34
Philippines, 213n131
Philips, Byron A., 223n37
Platt, Anthony, 114, 222n7, 222n21
pneumoencephalography, 140
Pomona, CA, 4, 27, 51, 53
Poor Laws, 31
Popenoe, Paul, 86–88, 170
population control measures. See eugenics; reproductive constraint; segregation (racial); sterilization
Portuguese people, 45, 48, 196(t), 209n79
poverty
   and crime, 6, 9, 29–30, 34–35, 37–38, 48–49, 57, 77, 80, 120, 127
   and disability, 31, 60
   and eugenics, 15, 87
   and feeblemindedness, 9, 21, 150, 181, 184
   and institutionalization, 15, 57–58, 58(t), 153, 155
   and intelligence, 8, 29, 32
   and sexual delinquency, 81, 87, 94, 97, 153
   See also welfare

pregnancy, 94–95, 143–46, 167, 216n29, 230n40
Progressive Era, 80–82, 114, 120, 131, 216n23, 223n33
Project South, 187
Protestant Welfare Association of Los Angeles County, 210n97
psychiatry, 6, 12, 27, 83, 128–29, 137–38, 147, 154–55, 158, 187
psychology
    and criminalization, 109–11, 117, 119–21
    and eugenics, 13, 36, 39, 208n57
    and feeblemindedness, 5–6, 8, 29–30, 48
    and intelligence, xiv, 7, 27, 41–45, 84, 126, 208n59, 225n63
    at Pacific Colony, 3, 54, 57, 66, 73, 85, 138, 146, 153, 181, 222n13
    and race, 61, 227n104
    and sexual delinquency, 81, 83, 85
Psychopathic Association, 50, 53
psychosis, 146
Puerto Rico, xiv, 196(t), 213n131

queerness, 104–5, 228n6
    See also homosexuality
Quintanilla, Rodrigo (Pacific Colony patient), 133

race
    and ableism, 32–33, 83, 99, 122, 142, 178, 181, 191
    in California, 17, 39–40
    and criminalization, 24, 110–24, 130, 132, 134, 137, 141–43, 185, 188, 223n33
    and eugenics, 15, 18–19, 121, 131–32
    and feeblemindedness, 3, 6–10, 16, 18, 23, 28, 48–50, 121–22, 223n37
    and immigration, 17–18, 77
    and institutionalization, 16, 21, 61–62, 143, 179, 183, 196(t)
    and intelligence, 32, 39, 41–42, 45–46, 120–24, 130, 134, 140–41, 185–86
    and labor, 33, 35, 76
    and sexual delinquency, 24, 80, 83–84, 92, 216n24
    See also Jim Crow; segregation (racial); slavery; "white logic"; white supremacy
"race suicide," 19, 77, 121
Ralph (Pacific Colony patient), 161, 163–65
Ramirez, Albino (Pacific Colony patient), 162
Ramírez, Catherine, 83, 216–17n33
Ramirez, George (Pacific Colony patient), 168–69

Ramirez, Laura (Pacific Colony patient), 97–98
Ramirez, Manuela (Pacific Colony patient), 165
Rankin, John E., 111
rape. See sexual violence
Rapley, Mark, 8, 199n11–12
Rappleye, Willard C., 52
Ray, Isaac, 116
Reconstruction, 35
reform schools, 60, 74, 115, 121, 130, 159, 216–17n33, 222n9
    juvenile, 59, 84, 132, 155–56, 207n46
    state, 82, 122–23, 226n90
    See also individual schools
Rembis, Michael, 95
reproduction, politics of, 2, 11–12
reproductive capacity, 2, 6, 10–11, 13, 30, 46, 147, 164, 172–74, 185, 215n5
reproductive constraint
    and institutionalization, 5–6, 9, 26, 30, 36, 51, 53, 76, 165, 178–79, 182–83, 185
    and juvenile delinquency, 124
    and sexual delinquency, 84, 90, 92, 94, 97
    state-mandated, 16, 36
    and sterilization, 2, 92, 107
    See also sterilization
Reproductive Justice, 11–14, 16, 21, 143, 180, 182, 190–92, 234n2
reproductive oppression, 2, 10–13, 23, 143, 179, 182, 184–85, 188, 190–91
resistance
    "emotional disturbance" as, 152–54
    escape from institutions, 154–66, 179
    to forced labor, 151–52
    to institutionalization, 149, 177–80, 188–89
    at institutions, 146–49, 210n95
    legal actions, 177–80, 183, 189–90, 233–34n114
    at Pacific Colony, 24, 100, 107–8, 146–47, 148, 149, 152–54, 173
    property damage as, 152–53
    punishment for, 154, 161, 164
    to racial discrimination, 40
    riots as, 150
    to sterilization, 147, 170, 173–80
Rivera, Joe (Pacific Colony patient), 52, 159
Roberts, Dorothy, 15, 33, 172, 191
Roberts, Kenneth, 17–18
Roberts, Peter, 121
Roe v. Wade, 180
Rolph, James, 53–54, 62
Ronaldo (Pacific Colony patient), 151–53
Rosa (Pacific Colony patient), 27, 204n1

Ross, Loretta, 12, 192
Ruiz, Vicki, 94, 167, 216n29
Rush, Benjamin, 116

Salvation Army, 82
Sam (Pacific Colony patient), 169
San Bernardino, CA, 208n58
Sanchez, Erica (Pacific Colony patient), 164
Sanchez, Felix (Pacific Colony patient), 138, 140, 160
Sanchez, George, 79, 215n20
Sanchez, Rafaela (Pacific Colony patient), 94–95
San Diego County, CA, 89
San Dimas, CA, 161
San Fernando Valley, CA, 164
San Francisco, CA, 37
San Francisco News, 56, 158–59
San Jose, CA, 84
San Quentin State Prison, 96
Saturday Evening Post, 17
Schalk, Sami, 13–14, 204n5
School for Feeble-Minded Girls and Boys, 39
Schweik, Susan, 33
sedatives, 157
segregation (racial), 6, 18–19, 31–32, 40, 76
seizures, 100
sexual agency, 215n5
sexual delinquency
  and class, 81–85, 216n23–24
  and feeblemindedness, 86–89, 94, 97, 217n44
  and intelligence, 83–85
  Progressive reformers and, 80–82, 216n23
  and race, 24, 80, 83–84, 92, 216n24
  and sterilization, 85, 87, 92–95, 97–98, 100, 218n62, 218–19n66
  See also hyperfertility
sexuality. *See* homosexuality; queerness; sexual promiscuity; sexual violence
sexual promiscuity, 8, 74, 86–87, 96–97, 146, 217n44, 218n62
sexual violence, 82, 95–96, 104, 216n24
sex work, 48–49, 86, 98, 216n24, 218n62
Sherman Institute, 27
"Sick Woman Theory," 148–49, 228n6
Siebers, Tobin, 60
Sirch, Margaret, 89–91
Sivella, Rebecca (Pacific Colony patient), 162
slavery, 32–33, 178, 216n24
Sleepy Lagoon Defense Committee, 216–17n33
Social Darwinism, 116
Sofia (Pacific Colony patient), 25–27

Solinger, Rickie, 94, 215n5
Sonoma State Home for the Feebleminded
  abuse at, 154, 230n38
  architecture of, 55
  feeblemindedness at, 217n44
  patients at, 74, 82, 130, 149, 163, 166, 168
  psychologists at, 84–86
  sterilization at, 4, 37–38, 60, 85, 88–89, 99
Sosa, Gerardo (Pacific Colony patient), 172
South Georgia Immigrant Support Network, 187
Spadra, CA, 53, 160
Spanish people, xiv, 48, 196(t), 209n79
Spencer, Herbert, 116
Springs Harbor, NY, 115
Stanford-Binet intelligence test, 7, 41–43, 225n63
  See also IQ (Intelligence Quotient) tests
Stanford University, 42, 115
State Joint Committee on Defectives in California, 29, 36, 38
sterilization
  and ableism, 179, 183–84, 190
  as condition of discharge, 27, 63, 69–70, 135, 146, 170, 185, 232n89
  and eugenics, 3–4, 37, 69, 85, 88, 90, 95, 99–100, 170, 177, 184–90, 207n41
  history in California, 3–4, 27, 86–88, 232n89
  justifications for, 198n5
  and juvenile delinquency, 131–37
  of Mexican-origin men, 93, 113, 132–36, 143
  of Mexican-origin women, 2, 24, 88, 91–100, 180, 290
  of Mexican-origin youth, 3–5, 70–71
  resistance to, 147, 170, 173–80, 183, 189, 190, 233–34n114
  role of families in, 6, 24, 111, 147, 164–67, 170, 170–80, 190
  and sexual delinquency, 85, 87, 92–95, 97–98, 100, 218n62, 218–19n66
  See also consent forms (Pacific Colony); reproductive constraint; sterilization laws; sterilization request forms (Pacific Colony)
sterilization laws, 37, 69, 170, 177–79, 183, 207n41, 233–34n114
sterilization request forms (Pacific Colony), xiii, 2, 5, 21, 70–71, 91–99, 111, 132–35, 153, 165, 179, 194(t), 214n1, 232n89
Stoddard, Theodore L., 18
St. Vincent's (Catholic reform school), 74, 214n1
Suarez, Saul (Pacific Colony patient), 134

suicide, 163
syphilis, 94

Talcott, Agnes, 91
Tarjan, George, 142, 175
Teen Vogue, 192
Tellez, Alberto, 176
Tellez, Maria (Pacific Colony patient), 176
Tennessee, 187
Terman, Lewis M., 7, 30, 38–50, 57, 115–17,
   119, 121–23, 127, 205n8, 208n56, 208n58,
   225n63
Teros, Sam B. (Pacific Colony patient), 162
Treaty of Guadalupe Hidalgo, 121
Trump, Donald, 186
tuberculosis, 20, 25, 101, 122, 134, 208n56
Twenty-Eight Years of Sterilization in Cali-
   fornia, 86–88

Union Pacific Railroad, 162
United Farmworkers Organizing Committee,
   188
University of California, Berkeley, 52
University of California, Los Angeles (UCLA),
   188
University of Southern California (USC),
   101
urbanization, 34, 80
U.S. Border Patrol, 18
U.S. Constitution, 178, 180
   Fourteenth Amendment, 35, 77, 177,
      233–34n114
U.S. Health and Human Services, 186
U.S. House of Representatives, 187
U.S. Supreme Court, 37, 49, 95, 180, 207n41

Valley, Ida Lawson, 179
Vanderbilt University, 132
Vasquez, George (Pacific Colony patient),
   163
Vasquez, Juanita, 163
Ventura School for Girls, 82, 83, 216–17n33
Verde, Elena (Pacific Colony patient), 151–54
Villareal, Lino (Pacific Colony patient), 161
Vineland, NJ, 39, 223n25

Vineland Training School for Feeble-Minded
   Girls and Boys, 39, 223n25
Visalia, CA, 160
vocational fitness, 7, 48
vocational training, 56, 63, 106, 150–51, 155

Walnut, CA, 51–52, 210n97
Wardell, Winifred, 58–60
Warren, Earl, 56, 158, 175, 230n38
welfare, 28, 74, 78, 89, 124, 127–28, 144, 184–
   85, 187, 189, 215n16
Welfare and Institutional Code of the State of
   California, 233–34n114
White, Deborah Gray, 33
White, Judge, 178
"white logic," 124, 224n53
white supremacy, 12, 31–32, 34, 39, 124, 183,
   201n24, 224n53
   See also race
Whittier State School, 84, 115, 119, 121–22,
   125–26, 134–35, 138, 156, 163, 207n46,
   222n9, 222n13
Williams, J. Harold, 39, 47–48, 115–16, 118–19,
   121–22, 124, 131, 222n13
Williams, Willard (Pacific Colony patient), 52,
   159
women. *See* gender; Mexican-origin women
Women of Color, 11, 77, 86, 184–85, 190, 215n5
Women's City Club, 50
Women's Legislative Council of California
   (WLCC), 50
World's Columbian Exposition (1893), 64
World War I, 41
World War II, 56, 111, 114

xenophobia, 77

Young, Raymond E., 175
youth. *See* juvenile delinquency; Mexican-
   origin youth

Zavella, Rosie (Pacific Colony patient), 100–3,
   106, 108, 162
Zoot Suit Riots, 114, 221n2
Zuberi, Tukufu, 124, 224n53

Founded in 1893,
UNIVERSITY OF CALIFORNIA PRESS
publishes bold, progressive books and journals
on topics in the arts, humanities, social sciences,
and natural sciences—with a focus on social
justice issues—that inspire thought and action
among readers worldwide.

The UC PRESS FOUNDATION
raises funds to uphold the press's vital role
as an independent, nonprofit publisher, and
receives philanthropic support from a wide
range of individuals and institutions—and from
committed readers like you. To learn more, visit
ucpress.edu/supportus.

Printed in the USA
CPSIA information can be obtained
at www.ICGtesting.com
LVHW050955030224
770856LV00010B/483